The Religious World of Kīrti Śrī

The Religious World of Kīrti Śrī

Buddhism, Art, and Politics in Late Medieval Sri Lanka

John Clifford Holt

New York Oxford
OXFORD UNIVERSITY PRESS
1996

For

Clifford Hjalmer Holt

Oxford University Press

Oxford New York
Athens Auckland Bangkok
Calcutta Cape Town Dar es Salaam Delhi
Florence Hong Kong Istanbul Karachi
Kuala Lumpur Madras Madrid Melbourne
Mexico City Nairobi Paris Singapore
Taipei Tokyo Toronto

and associated companies in
Berlin Ibadan

Published by Oxford University Press, Inc.
198 Madison Avenue, New York, New York 10016

Library of Congress Cataloging-in-Publication Data
Holt, John, 1948–
The religious world of Kirti Sri : Buddhism, art, and politics in late medieval Sri Lanka / John Clifford Holt.
p. cm.
Includes bibliographical references and index.
ISBN 0–19–509705–X; ISBN 0–19–510757–8 (pbk.)
1. Buddhism—Sri Lanka—History. 2. Kīrti Śrī Rājasinha, King of Ceylon, d. 1780 or 1782—Religion. I. Title.
BQ372.H65 1996
294.3'91'09549309033—dc20 95–13942

1 3 5 7 9 8 6 4 2

Printed in the United States of America
on acid-free paper

Preface

The Religious World of Kīrti Śrī has been written primarily for undergraduate and graduate students of religion, particularly those who have found Buddhism to be a fascinating subject. My colleagues in the disciplines of the history of religions, social history, and art history, as well as those in the fields of Buddhist studies, South Asian studies, and Sri Lankan studies, may also find some novel interest in this book.

Unlike many previous and more conventional approaches that Western religion scholars have taken in the study of Buddhism, this book is not concerned primarily with philosophical ideas or philological issues germane to a specific school or authoritative text of South or East Asian Buddhism, though some interesting philosophical notions from literary and artistic sources will be considered throughout this book. Nor is this book solely a social history of the political dynamics that affect cultural transformations within the context of Buddhism's oldest continuing historical tradition, though social history and cultural renaissance are the fundamental venues and significant consequences of the events that will be considered. Rather, this work is primarily an interdisciplinary examination of what it meant for various people, lay and monastic, to be Buddhists during the advent of European colonialism and before indigenous Sinhalese reactions to Western intellectual and political hegemony began to foster the contours of what has become a "modern" Buddhist (yet sometimes reactionary) religious perspective. It is an exploration of "classical" Buddhist world views, especially the one revived and represented by a harried and insecure king, Kīrti Śrī Rājasinha, during the middle of the eighteenth century in Kandy, an up-country kingdom in what is now known as the island country of Sri Lanka, located off the southern tip of India.

In this study I have sometimes used the term *classical* with much trepidation, and only after considering a number of other terms that, in the end, produced their own sets of grave heuristic difficulties. By deploying the category of "classical," I am attempting to draw attention to several features of Sinhala society and thought that were prevalent in the late medieval Buddhist kingdom of Kandy. In particular, my aim is to highlight the fact that, socially, Kandyan society was feudal and hierarchical; that wealth and social prestige were closely correlated; that Kandy had a completely preindustrial and largely subsistence economy with few opportunities for trade; that education was limited to those with leisure (either upper-class or monastic incumbents); that political power was legitimated by appeals to divine authority; and that this power and its legitimation were articulated publicly through mythic models of an idealized past, which, in turn, were dramatized by conscious orchestrations of rituals and symbols. In the first chapter of this book, it becomes evident that this classical world was under a concerted siege by colonial powers whose presence and assertions tried to undermine the ontology of ideological certainty upon which the classical Buddhist culture had been traditionally based. In Sri Lankan history, Kīrti Śrī's eighteenth-century reign marks the last time that indigenous structures of society, religion, and culture were successfully revived. The renaissance of art, literature, and monastic institutions that he fostered marked the beginning of the end of the classical era. Some three decades following his reign, the British disestablished Kīrti Śrī's dynasty and indigenous social, political, and religious institutions never fully recovered, at least not in a coordinated way. When Buddhism was reasserted in the late nineteenth and twentieth centuries, during British colonialism in Ceylon, it was politically populist and Protestant in character, a religion of the oppressed.

In further terms of religion, in this case Sinhala Theravada Buddhism, "classical" here also refers to the unquestioned authority invested in sacred texts, myths, rituals, and symbols to articulate normatively the essentials of an orthodox world view. That is, "classical" refers specifically to those institutions that had been established as the "second order" foundation of the religion—those conceptual and social structures, instituted by the Buddhist community following the demise of Gotama the Buddha in ancient India, which, from an indigenous perspective, had continued unbroken throughout history by virtue of material and moral support from a long line of patronizing Buddhist kings.[1] In the history of Buddhism in Sri Lanka and in Southeast Asian countries such as Burma and Thailand, the king's fundamental responsibility was to ensure the health and strength of these foundations. The era with which this book is concerned included a final royal attempt in Sri Lanka to kindle a renaissance of these foundations. Kirti 4ri revived the Buddhist *sangha* (monastic community) through institutional reforms, supported the proclamation of the *dharma* [*dhamma* in Pali] (teachings or truths of the Buddha) by promoting the public preaching and learned study of Pali Buddhist texts, and glorified the Buddha (the founder of the tradition) by lavishly refurbishing the art of Kandyan Buddhist temples.

Thus, the focus of this work is concerned with the underlying question of what it meant, during this time of revival, for various individuals to be Buddhists in the classic sense. By describing the context as classic, I do not wish to convey that religious meaning was static, an ancient fossil given but a final rebirth. A plethora of contemporary issues specifically conditioned King Kīrti Śrī's late medieval answer, his brilliant attempt to take refuge in the Buddha, *dharma*, and *sangha*. Kīrti Śrī was, of course, very much a product of his own milieu, and his initiatives in the field of religion (aimed at reviving Buddhism) were, in part, motivated by the compelling and complicated social and political circumstances he inherited and then contrived to cope with effectively during his long eighteenth-century reign (1751–1782 C.E.). The expediency demanded by the pressures of these social and political exigencies stimulated what apparently became one of his most vital concerns: to demonstrate to the people within his realm of power that he was genuinely a Buddhist and, in particular, a quintessential Theravāda Buddhist king.

Chapter 1 explains why Kīrti Śrī was so concerned about articulating his religious identity as a Buddhist. Chapters 2–4, which form the heart of the book, explain how Kīrti Śrī articulated his understanding of Buddhist religious thought and identity through the expression of his religious works, especially the temple wall paintings that have become such a remarkable icon and legacy of his reign; my aim is to show clearly the substance and patterns of "classical" Buddhism in its late medieval Sinhalese cultural guise. Chapters 5 and 6 cover two issues that transcend the specific historical context of the book. Chapter 5 is concerned with the necessity for students of religion to focus on materials other than literary texts, especially if they hope to gain a more thorough understanding of what it has meant to be religious in cultures for which the written word is less definitive. Chapter 6 reveals how an understanding of the dynamics of Kīrti Śrī's predicament in the eighteenth century might help put into perspective some of the vexing issues that contribute to the current conflict between the Sinhalese and Tamils in contemporary Sri Lanka.

Citations throughout the text to the following epic chronicles, popular literature, and doctrinal discourses are as follows.

Cūlavaṃsa (13th–18th century) from Wilhelm Geiger, trans. and ed. (1953), *Cūlavaṃsa: Being the More Recent Part of the Mahāvaṃsa*, 2 vols. (Colombo: Ceylon Government Information Department).

Mahāvaṃsa (5th cent. C.E.) from Wilhelm Geiger, trans. and ed. (1964), *The Mahāvaṃsa or The Great Chronical of Ceylon* (London: Luzac and Co. for Pali Text Society).

Dīpavaṃsa (4th century C.E.) from Hermann Oldenberg, trans. and ed. (1982), *The Dīpavaṃsa: An Ancient Buddhist Historical Record* (reprint) (New Delhi: Asian Educational Services).

The *jātakas* from E. B. Cowell (1895–1913), *The Jātaka; or, Stories of the Buddha's Former Births*, 6 vols. (London: Luzac and Co. for Pali Text Society), and from John Garrett Jones (1979), *Tales and Teachings of the Buddha: The Jātaka Stories in Relation to the Pali Canon* (London: George Allen and Unwin).

The *Dīgha Nikāya* from I. B. Horner, trans. and ed. (1954–1959), *The Middle Length Sayings* (*Majjhima Nikāya*), 3 vols. *Sacred Books of the Buddhists*, vols. 29–31 (London: Luzac and Co. for Pali Text Society) and from T. W. Rhys Davids and C. A. Folsy, trans. and eds. (1899– 1921), *Dialogues of the Buddha* (*Dīgha Nikāya*), 3 vols. *Sacred Books of the Buddhists*, vols. 2–4 (London: Luzac and Co. for Pali Text Society).

In preparing this work for publication, I have benefited greatly from comments and suggestions made about early drafts of the first three chapters by P. B. Meegaskumbura, K. M. de Silva, and Jon Walters. Samuel Holt prepared the map and I made the photographs in the plates.

Research for this study was assisted by a grant from the Joint Committee on South Asia of the Social Science Research Council and the American Council of Learned Societies, with funds provided by the National Endowment of the Humanities and by the Ford Foundation. Bowdoin College provided a subsidy so that sixteen photos could appear in color.

Brunswick, Maine J.C.H.
July 1995

Contents

1 Kīrti Śrī's Predicament, 3

2 Discourses of a Buddhist King, 15

3 A Visual Liturgy, 41

4 Royalty Reborn, 73

5 Implications for Theory and Method, 91

6 Postscript: Ethnic Identity and Ethnic Alienation, 97

Appendix: The Religious Works of Kīrti Śrī at Gangārāma and Ridī Viharā, 109

Notes, 115

Bibliography, 135

Index, 141

Details of the Liturgy: Plates follow page 72

The Religious World of Kīrti Śrī

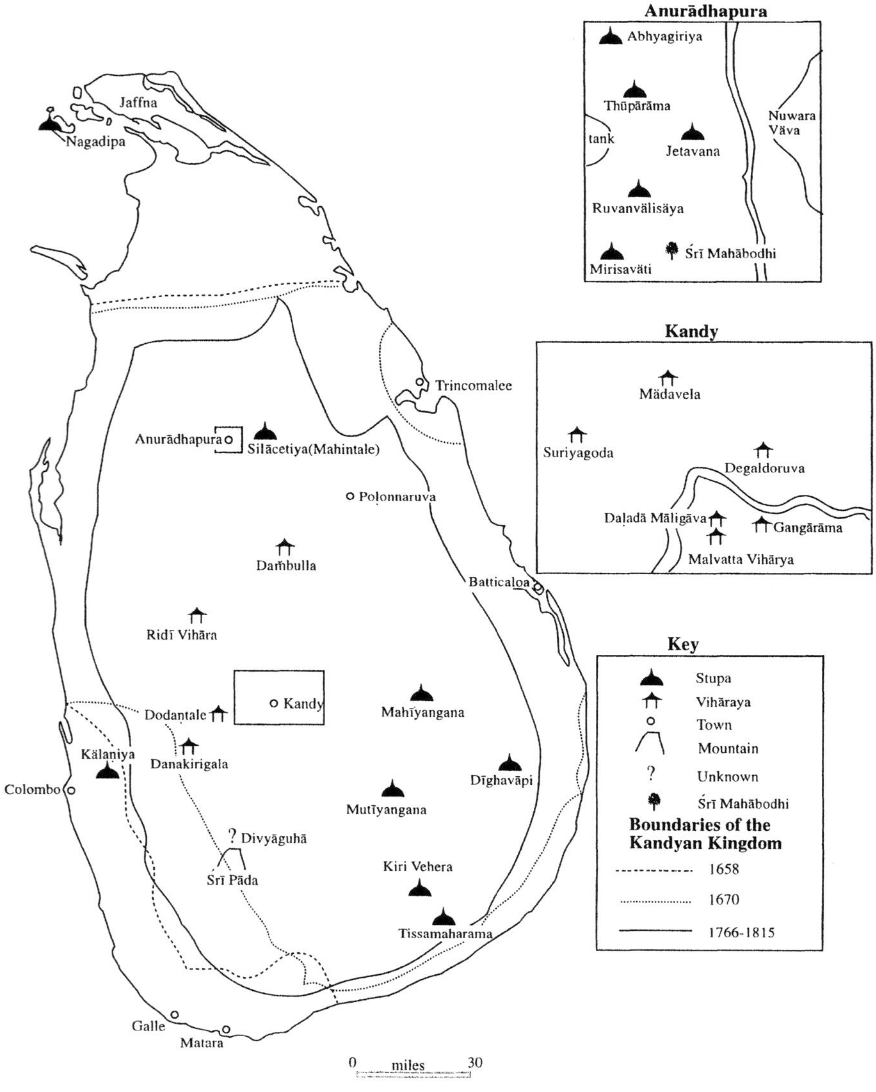
Anurādhapura
Abhyagiriya
Thūpārāma
tank
Jetavana
Nuwara
Väva
Ruvanvälisäya
Mirisaväti
Śrī Mahābodhi
Kandy
Mädavela
Suriyagoda
Degaldoruva
Daḷadā Māligāva
Gangārāma
Malvatta Vihārya
Key
Stupa
Vihāraya
Town
Mountain
?
Unknown
Śrī Mahābodhi
Boundaries of the
Kandyan Kingdom
1658
1670
1766-1815
Jaffna
Nagadipa
Trincomalee
Anurādhapura
Silācetiya(Mahintale)
Polonnaruva
Daṁbulla
Batticaloa
Ridī Vihāra
Kandy
Dodantale
Mahīyangana
Kälaniya
Danakirigala
Colombo
Dīghavāpi
Mutīyangana
? Divyāguhā
Srī Pāda
Kiri Vehera
Tissamaharama
Galle
Matara
0 miles 30

Sri Lanka

1

Kīrti Śrī's Predicament

This book is primarily about how Kīrti Śrī Rājasinha expressed a classical understanding of Buddhism and appealed to various paradigmatic discourses of kingship through the religious works he sponsored. As I detail his enterprising program of reform, reestablishment, and renewal in chapters 2–4, the specific parameters of his classical Buddhist perspective will become quite apparent. Initially, it would be helpful to know why he expended such great effort and wealth to revive what had become essentially an institutionally moribund religious tradition.

In short, the answer lies in two related factors. First, Kīrti Śrī faced very serious outside threats to his reign by an imposing European Christian colonial power, the Dutch East India Company. Because the overwhelming majority of his countrymen were Buddhists by birth, his public proclamations in support of Buddhism were therefore expedient, a religio-political rallying cry in the face of a grave external danger to tradition. Second, from the inside, he faced a serious challenge to his authority by an elitist section of the aristocratic Sinhalese nobles of his court, a faction of this medieval society whose families also dominated the Buddhist religious establishment of his time. For various reasons that will be explored, some in this privileged group were cynical regarding the king's public proclamations in support of Buddhism, called into question his fitness to rule a nation primarily composed of traditionally Buddhist people, and unsuccessfully attempted to assassinate him.

Therefore, Kīrti Śrī's religious statements, literally and symbolically, had to be taken as genuine, convincing to the masses of Sinhalese Buddhists who were his subjects. He walked a tightrope between two powerful political forces and needed a broadly based supportive constituency to be successful in continuing his reign.

The External Threat

In the middle of the eighteenth century, Dutch colonial power, then anchored in Batavia (a city in Java, Indonesia), several thousand miles to the east, had also become firmly ensconced in the coastal regions of Sri Lanka. In collusion with an earlier Sinhalese Buddhist king of Kandy, Rājasinha II (1635–1687 C.E.), and a century before the period on which this work focuses, the Dutch had succeeded in wresting economic and political control over most of the island's low-country regions from the Portuguese, who had been the first European colonists to come to Sri Lanka, early in the sixteenth century, and had, despite considerable resistance by the Sinhalese, succeeded in establishing themselves as landlords of the littorals by the sea.[1] Though the Portuguese sought to garner a share of Asia's material riches by monopolizing trade, they were also driven by a counter-Reformation, missionary zeal to convert, either by persuasive proselytizing or by brute military force, the local South Asian inhabitants to Christianity. The later entrepreneurs from Holland (with whom I am more specifically concerned in this context) not only were supported by expert European military detachments and hordes of well-trained South Asian mercenaries but also brought with them bands of crusading Protestant Christian missionary zealots. However, the Dutch were much more preoccupied with controlling and profiting from any trade, chiefly for export, but including whatever goods might flow into and out of the largely landlocked Kandyan kingdom (see map). As the driving Dutch motives were preponderantly economic in nature, political (or, more accurately, military) authority, whether formally or legally constituted or not, was a necessary condition—from their point of view—for conducting business successfully from their strategic low-country port bases. So secure did they feel in exercising their power in Sri Lanka that one of the Dutch governors noted in 1762 (during Kīrti Śrī's reign), that, within all of the Dutch colonial dominions, there was "not place [other than Sri Lanka] where the Dutch have so much land as sole ministers" (Reimers, 1946: 9) and that Sri Lanka should become a "capital station" for Dutch interests in South and Southeast Asia.

For most of their history on the island, Dutch strategy was consistent: (1) to maintain tight political and social discipline over the coastal areas that they had captured from the Portuguese; (2) to accomplish this discipline not only through established military hegemony but also through the conversion of low-country inhabitants to the Protestant Christianity of the Dutch Reformed Church; and (3) to keep the power of the Kandyan kingdom at bay, in a perpetual state of economic and political atrophy. Largely, they succeeded in preventing the Kandyans from interfering with their trading pursuits and in pauperizing the Kandyans by means of their shrewd and often unfair trade practices. In addition to the cultivation and collection of their own goods for trade in the low-country regions that they controlled, all goods entering or leaving the Kandyan kingdom were heavily taxed in the form of a severe transportation surcharge if the goods were headed for or received from foreign destinations. The Dutch policy regarding political economy, which was designed to confine Kandyan political power and to weaken the Kandyans economically, served their principal aim and ultimate pursuit of exploiting opportunities in trade, chiefly the cultivation and export of cinnamon (some of which took place within the Kandyan kingdom per se) and other spices for sale in Asian or distant European markets, as well as the capture and sale of elephants to markets in India, a supremely profitable activity that the kings of Kandy looked upon with a deep degree of envy.[2] In this part of the Asian world in the eighteenth century, the Dutch had succeeded in becoming international middlemen par excellence.

Throughout their century-and-a-half occupation of coastal Sri Lanka, the Dutch, in spite of their obvious military superiority, continually feared, and on several occasions took military action to stifle, the ability of the Kandyan Buddhist kingship to incite rebellion among the low-country Sinhalese living in their midst. The official memoirs of eighteenth-century Dutch governors indicate that the Dutch often attempted to intimidate the low-country Sinhalese by expressing their own perceptions of social, economic, and spiritual superiority.[3] For the Dutch, at least according to their colonial governors, spiritual and material well-being were intrinsically related.[4] They sought to make clear to the indigenous inhabitants that it was completely in their own best interests to adopt a new way of life. At the same time that they were intimidating or enticing low-country Sinhalese with the Protestant ethic and spirit of capitalism, they contrived a coy political dance with the kings of Kandy, through imaginative and clever legal fictions, in order to preserve peace with the Kandyan highlanders for the purpose of ensuring continued economic exploitation. Despite their public posturing with low-country and Kandyan Sinhalese, the Dutch remained wary, as did the Sinhalese on their part, of the alien in their midst.

While the Dutch were spirited Calvinists, they were even more spirited as capitalists. They were anxious, in particular, about Kīrti Śrī's potential to forge his own profitable trade directly with South Indian ports, which would thereby short-circuit their monopolies. For example, in 1762, Governor Schreuder revealed in his departing memoir to his successor, Governor Van Eck, how the Dutch perceived the significance of South Indian contacts with the Kandyans:

> How harmful their intrusions and frequent comings and goings to and from Kandy of Nayakkars, Moors, Chetties and other such folk have been and still are to the [Dutch East India] Company; for in addition to eating up as it were our inhabitants and raising the price of our commodities they corrupt the Kandyans by their conversations. (Reimers, 1946: 24)

In that connection, the Dutch came to resent especially the king's cultivated ties not only with South Indian Nāyakkars but also with Muslims in Sri Lanka, not primarily because of centuries-old European xenophobic inclinations toward the presence of an expanding Islamic influence, but because the Muslim community constituted a conduit for trade and communication with South India (a linkage of great importance) and hence an economic threat to the vitality of their own interests. Again, it is notable that the same Dutch governor said that the Moors were "a people so cunning in trade that they cannot exist without it [smuggling]," and that "the Moors in particular will not give up smuggling although it is done at the risk of life and goods" (Reimers, 1946: 17–18). Such Dutch disdain was clearly derived from the contemplation of economic rivalry.

While the Dutch were successful in terms of their economic goals, their religious predicants who sought to convert low-country Sinhalese and Tamils met with only lackluster results. Indeed, the legacy of the Dutch Reformed Church in Sri Lanka today is more of an architectural than a social one, in striking contrast to the staying power of the Roman

Catholicism introduced by the Portuguese.[5] As Reformed Christian Calvinists, the Dutch insisted upon proselytizing their Protestant faith, sometimes with a fair measure of vigor, among the low-country Sinhalese and Tamils, many of whom had previously converted to the Roman Catholicism of the colonial Portuguese predecessors. But the intensity of these attempts was sporadic and inconsistent. At times, Dutch governors complained about the lack of enthusiasm displayed and of results obtained by church predicants who often seemed to see their mission as being aimed chiefly at maintaining the faith among representatives of the European community.[6] At other times in the low country, the pressure to convert Sinhalese became severe since conversion to Christianity was regarded by the Dutch administrators as a way to short-circuit Sinhalese loyalty to the Kandyan Buddhist king. Thus, religious conversion was one of the strategies tried to isolate low-country Sinhalese from their highland Buddhist king.[7]

As for some of the loyal South Asian, Sri Lankan Catholics of these times who resisted conversion to Protestantism, the enmities experienced in the battles of the Reformation a century or two earlier on the European continent were re-created for them in situ by many of the policies and practices put into effect by the Dutch Protestants in Sri Lanka. Ironically, many Sinhalese Catholic Christians in coastal areas were forced to flee oppression on numerous occasions to highland regions of the Kandyan kingdom where usually a Buddhist king might afford them protection from the fanaticism of rival Christians. Nevertheless, Kīrti Śrī's intermittent policy of providing Sinhalese Catholics a refuge from Dutch oppression, a policy first put in place by many of his royal Sinhalese predecessors, became one of the irritations that created a degree of alienation from an increasingly militant section of his own Buddhist community early in his reign, as it had for Kīrti Śrī's immediate predecessor, the first Nāyakkar, king, Śrī Vijaya Rājasinha.[8] On the whole, the Kandyan kings, especially the earlier Sinhalese kings, were far more tolerant in their religious dispositions toward religions other than their own than either the Portuguese or the Dutch colonial administrations.[9]

Here, then, it can be observed that although religion is frequently a powerful constituent of ethnic identity and a principal means of exclusion or definition, there are moments when its definitive importance can be transcended in the interest of wider appeals. At times in late medieval Sri Lanka, religion did not bar ethnic inclusion; yet at other times, it did—that is, religion is a variable, and not a constant factor, in what can constitute ethnicity. Chapter 6 will discuss this matter again, in relation to the current ethnic conflict on the island between the Sinhalese majority and the Tamil minority.

In the coastal regions, under the Dutch the Protestant ethic and the spirit of capitalism were presented not simply with great confidence and conviction but as a unified package, as a serious and complete challenge to the Sinhalese Buddhist and Sinhalese Catholic ways of comprehending the meaning of existence in the pursuit of living a religiously virtuous and economically prosperous life. To the low-country Sinhalese, the Dutch colonial administration also represented an alternative structure of power that demanded total practical submission. For instance, in order to legally own land within the Dutch domain of power, to be legally married, and to obtain a formal education, low-country Sinhalese were required to renounce their ties to the Buddha *śāsana* (tradition) and their allegiance to the king in Kandy, by becoming members of the Dutch Reformed Church. Under the Dutch, religious affiliation determined the legal statuses that in any material and social way were advantageous for local inhabitants to hold. Among the low-country Sinhalese, consequently, there emerged a community of "government Christians," some perhaps sincere in their religious preference, but many choosing to be dubbed Christian as a matter of legal convenience for economic advantage. Out of this social environment there eventually evolved, in especially accelerated fashion later under nineteenth-century British colonial rule, a privileged class of Western-educated Sinhalese and Tamil entrepreneurs, professionals, and government servants who came to rival, in economic power and social prestige, the traditional class of aristocratic Kandyans of the highlands who, nonetheless, for their part, continued to envisage themselves as the inheritors and sustainers of the ages-old Sinhala Buddhist tradition.

In eighteenth-century Sri Lanka, then, there were two political economies at work, two competing systems of social values, and more than two religious orientations in the two increasingly distinct regions of the country. Sri Lanka, in general, and Sinhalese society, in particular, were severely bifurcated by concerted pressures exerted by a European, Christian-legitimated political economy on the one hand and a traditional Sinhala Buddhist way of life struggling to survive on the other.

For the Kandyans, the Dutch represented a genuine political and economic threat that could potentially dislodge their own tenuous holds on power in the highlands, an alien presence to be tolerated and constrained as much as possible because it could not be realistically controlled or totally eliminated. Though the Dutch often postured, particularly in trade negotiations, that they were "His Majesty's humble servants"—a legal fiction that was rarely persuasive in fact—the kings of Kandy were well aware of the inherent dangers presented to their own sovereignty by the economically savvy Dutch. Kandyan kings had suffered repeated aggressive military invasions earlier by the Portuguese and suspected that eventually they could expect the same from the Dutch. Indeed, their fears were not misplaced, for after Kīrti Śrī had attempted to provide a modicum of support or encouragement for a low-country Sinhalese rebellion, based around Matara, over the "stringent agrarian policy" (Mirando, 1985: 58) of the Dutch in the early 1760s, the Dutch forcefully marched with an army of eight thousand men, mostly mercenaries, into the interior highlands and entered Kandy. In the process, they thoroughly looted and destroyed the royal palace, the Daḷadā Māḷigāva (Temple of the Tooth-relic), and other substantial dwellings of the nobility within the city.[10] In so doing, they temporarily forced Kīrti Śrī to abandon his capital and to retreat strategically to higher ground in the virtually impenetrable mountainous forests southeast of Kandy. Though Kīrti Śrī eventually recovered, it seems he was so chastened by these events—having been forced to sue for peace in 1766 on terms very favorable to the Dutch[11]—that he never conspicuously provoked the Dutch again and sought to minimize contact with his European adversaries as much as possible during the remaining years of his reign.

During Kīrti Śrī's reign, the British also made serious overtures to the king regarding a possible alliance against the Dutch, overtures that ultimately were rejected. The arrival of the first embassy, in 1762, led by the British emissary John Pybus, took place just before the Dutch sacking of Kandy. The second embassy, in 1782, just before Kīrti Śrī's untimely death, is more interesting since its leader, Hugh Boyd, describes something of the attitudes he found among the Kandyan Sinhalese toward the Dutch:

> The implacable hatred they bore the Dutch deterred the Cingalese from any communication with them; and though the court did not refuse to receive their ambassadors, they were treated with cold distrust, and watched with jealous vigilance. . . . [The king] instructed them to hold in eternal abhorrence a race of people, whom, as they appeared to them, no ties of honour could bind, and against whose treachery no prudence

could guard. . . . [The Dutch were regarded as possessing] a glutinous rapacity, generated by the rapid acquisition of riches. Campbell, 1800: 2:99)

King Kīrti Śrī, therefore, faced a serious external threat to his kingdom by an ever-present, surrounding, aggressive, and alien European Christian power that had effectively bifurcated political authority on the island, dominated its economic activity, and presented a religious challenge to Buddhist tradition. In part, we can understand Kīrti Śrī's attempt to reestablish and rehabilitate Theravāda Buddhism as a means of redefining himself and the people of his kingdom against this formidable adversary.

The Internal Threat

In the face of these severe economic and religio-political circumstances, Kīrti Śrī Rājasinha required as much loyalty as he could muster from the Sinhalese Buddhist countrymen in order to manage even an uncertain balance of power with the Dutch. The most salutary threat to his reign was not that he faced such a dangerous external foreign threat at his doorstep; rather, his greatest problem was internal: he could not unequivocally assume that unconditioned loyalty would be forthcoming from his people. For, by lineage and culture, Kīrti Śrī was not born Sinhalese, nor was his family background Buddhist. As the second in a line of four regents of the South Indian–derived Nāyakkar dynasty that succeeded the last of the ethnically Sinhalese kings in 1739, Kīrti Śrī's linguistic heritage was Tamil, and his given religious tradition was Hindu Saivism. On the other hand, the overwhelming majority of the population of his kingdom, as I have noted, spoke Sinhalese and were Buddhist in religious orientation. The background details of this situation reveal the sobriety of his condition as an "alien" king among the Sinhalese.

The last of the ethnically Sinhalese kings, Narendra Sinha (1707–1739), had died without a legitimate heir to the throne, though he had had a son through a Sinhalese concubine, who was supported as his successor by some of the nobility. Like his father and grandfather before him, Narendra Sinha had formally married a princess of the appropriate caste from Madurai (in what is now Tamilnadu) in South India, who became his *maheśi* (chief queen)—a practice of Sinhalese kings that had been inaugurated during the eleventh through thirteenth centuries in the Polonnaruva period. One year after his marriage to this South

Indian princess,[12] Narendra Sinha faced an internal revolt that foreshadowed the pattern of defiance encountered later by Kīrti Śrī. Even before his coronation, Narendra Sinha's succession had been threatened by a court faction that wished to place his Sinhalese half brother on the throne. Though he survived this attempted coup, his situation was exacerbated not only by his apparent neglect of the state of Buddhist affairs (the last formally recognized Buddhist monk [through the *upasampadā* ordination rite] died in 1729), but by the increasing dominance in matters of economics and finance that had been exercised by his South Indian Nāyakkar in-laws, who had arrived en masse in Kandy after his marriage to the Madurai princess; their influence at court and their expanding economic activities had become the basis of deep resentment among the Sinhalese nobility. In 1732, Narendra Sinha faced yet another rebellion among the Kandyan Sinhalese aristocrats because he had entrusted the most important royal stores to his foreign Nāyakkar kinsmen.[13] It is not surprising, therefore, that a faction of the Sinhalese nobility favored Narendra Sinha's own son by a Sinhalese high-caste concubine when his Nāyakkar brother-in-law was selected to be his successor and was crowned Śrī Vijaya Rājasinha in 1739. This first of the Nāyakkar kings died after only eight years of tenuous rule. Kīrti Śrī Rājasinha was the brother of Śrī Vijaya Rājasinha's chief queen and the son of the very influential behind-the-scenes kingmaker of the court, Narenappā Nāyakkar, and was only sixteen years old when he was selected. Until he was fully crowned four years later, the affairs of the kingdom were handled largely by his regent father—a development that further rankled the Kandyan Sinhalese aristocrats.

The Dutch, it should be noted, were anxious to exploit the growing internal rift in the Kandyan court; for, as we have seen, they despised the increasing Nāyakkar presence and control because the Nāyakkars represented an economic threat. The Dutch governor, Loten, wrote in his official 1752 memoir that the removal of the Nāyakkars in favor of the Sinhalese son of Narendra Sinha would be most welcome: "Should that at anytime happen, the Company would be in a favourable position of seeing removed once more from the Court and the hillcountry the so pernicious Coast Nayakkars, Malabars and Moorish scum, who practice, in every imaginable way, all manner of illicit trade entirely to the prejudice of the Company" (Reimers, 1935: 3). Loten noted that "[the Nayakkars are] most subversive of the Company's interests . . . [and are] malicious with an inordinate desire for gain" (Reimers, 1935: 10–11).

While the Dutch and Kandyan Sinhalese nobles shared an economic grouse with the Nāyakkars, Kīrti Śrī's religious identity also became an issue of political concern. Eventually, in a mid-nineteenth-century Buddhist text, it became a rationalized explanation for the attempted undermining of his kingship by disaffected Sinhalese nobles and members of the Buddhist *sangha* (monastic community). For the Sinhalese, the greatest historic crises threatening their political sovereignty and religious preference have come from military invasions that originated in South Indian Tamil Śaivite Hindu dominions. Despite the fact that, for most of their shared history on the island, the Sinhalese and Tamils have lived together amicably, memories of these historical crises are easily aroused. Their Buddhist monastic chronicles effusively describe the glories of a magnificent Sinhalese civilization in Anuradhapura from the third century B.C.E. through the tenth century C.E., and their storied capital at Polonnaruva from the eleventh through the thirteenth centuries C.E., both of which were overrun ultimately by armies under the command of "Tamil usurpers and heretics," according to these sources. What followed historically and politically for the Sinhalese Buddhists from the time of Polonnaruva's fall was a defensive retreat or "drift to the Southwest" throughout the next two centuries until confrontations with the Portuguese at Kotte (just southeast of the modern capital city of Colombo) had begun in the sixteenth century.

Indeed, indigenous Sinhalese mistrust of Kīrti Śrī, because of his native Tamil identity and Hindu religious background, was spectacularly manifest in the unfolding of an intricate plot hatched by Theravāda Buddhist monks and Sinhalese nobility (in apparent collusion with the Dutch) to assassinate him in 1760. The details of the plot will be provided in chapter 2, but here I should indicate that an attempt was made to place a Siamese (Thai) ostensibly Theravāda Buddhist, prince on the Kandyan throne, in Kīrti Śrī's stead.

There is not doubt that the Dutch were a consistent external worry to Kīrti Śrī, especially when they began to collaborate with the disaffected Kandyan nobility. Even in 1765, five years after the attempted assassination and when he had just sacked Kandy, forcing Kīrti Śrī to abandon his capital, the Dutch governor, van Eck continued to express his hope that the Thai usurper could be relocated so as to replace Kīrti Śrī.[14] Despite the ongoing Dutch threat, it would appear that Kīrti Śrī's greatest concern, that which made his royal legitimacy even more tenuous, was the internal question of his fitness, as a Tamil Hindu, to rule the up-country Kandyan Sinhalese Buddhists.

During his long reign, what Kīrti Śrī sought to do, then, more than anything else, was to articulate a royal discourse that appealed to Buddhist religious sentiments, sentiments that could affirm his public identity as a pious Buddhist king intent on supporting the religious culture and society that, for virtually all of the known history of civilization in Sri Lanka, had been the province and guardian of Theravāda Buddhist tradition. In view of this predicament, which found Kīrti Śrī beset by such serious external foreign threats and internal problems, it might be argued that very few other figures within the entire history of Asian Buddhist cultures would have been more pressed by the existential importance and expedience posed by two key questions: What does it mean to be Buddhist? What is Buddhist religious identity? For Kīrti Śrī, everything seemed to be at stake in his answer to these questions.

How Kīrti Śrī answered these questions during the eighteenth century, in a manner that has endured as a legacy in many forms of institutional, ritualistic, and artistic expression, is fully explored in this book. Yet his response remains relevant in modern Sri Lanka, despite the fact that it is a late medieval, revived form of classical religion and, as such, is not completely synchronized (in fact, it is often at odds) with the emphases and orientations of twentieth-century, urban Buddhist modernism.

I agree with the assessment of the Sinhalese social historian Kitsiri Malalgoda: Kīrti Śrī's efforts to convince his Sinhalese countrymen of his commitment to a genuinely Buddhist world view and Buddhist sentiments succeeded in re-creating a Buddhism "in the eighteenth century . . . [that was] revived and reestablished in classical form, as it happened, for the last time in the history of Ceylon" (Malalgoda, 1976: 258).

2

Discourses of a Buddhist King

The Kandyan epic ballad *Mandārampura Puvata*,[1] and the Theravāda monastic chronicle *Cūlavaṃsa*, both venerable sources of Sinhala Buddhist tradition, present, almost as a matter of course, a smooth transition in the middle of the eighteenth century from Sinhala royalty to "foreign" Tamil Nāyakkar rule, a transition accomplished with seeming ease as the result of the Nāyakkars' conversion to Theravāda Buddhism from Śaivite Hinduism and their continued appeal to the prestige of matrilineal descent (from the *Kṣatriya*, the warrior caste) through the South Indian house of Madurai.[2]

> [King Narendrasinghe], as [he] had neither son nor daughter to succeed to the royal splendour, acting in accordance with the wishes of the monk [Saranankara] and ministers [decided on] the brother of the queen who is descended from the pure royal line of Madurā and who is supreme in virtue [and] taking that *Vaḍiga* prince's right hand, [the king] placed it on the hand of the monk Saranankara [telling him], "teach him the [Buddhist] doctrine and the arts and get him to protect well the *śāsana* and the kingdom in the future."[3]

After Narindasiha's death, the younger brother of the Maheśi of this king became king, adorned with the ornament of virtue. Known by

> the name of Sirivijayarajasiha, he was, after the attainment of his consecration as king, piously attached to the Triad of the jewels. He was diligent in hearkening to the sermon of the doctrine, unwearied, discerning, ever full of zeal, intent on intercourse with pious and good people. . . . He won over the people in Lanka in the best manner possible by the four heart-winning qualities. . . . The Maheśis of the King, too, gave up the false faith to which they had been long attached, and adopted in the best manner possible the true faith which confers immortality. They heard the incomparable, true doctrine of the Buddha, the highest Protector of the world and thus adored with constant devotion the Buddha and the other (sacred) objects. (*Cūlavaṃsa* 2:246)

However, the facts as they are known to history have given rise to differing interpretations regarding just how successful the Nāyakkars were initially in winning over the perceptions of Kandy's Sinhalese Buddhists. I noted in chapter 1, for instance, that there were factions in the Kandyan nobility that contrived to place ethnically Sinhalese scions on the throne in lieu of both Śrī Vijaya Rājasinha, the first Nāyakkar king, and his successor, Kīrti Śrī. But there is little question that Kīrti Śrī is now regarded in the public's memory as heroic,[4] as one of the great kings of Sri Lankan tradition, who fully realized the ideals of Buddhist kingship by unstintingly patronizing and protecting the Buddha's religion. Indeed, while Kīrti Śrī faced serious legitimation problems during his reign, posterity remembers him differently. Moreover, there is a powerful corroborating consensus for this view that is articulated by a number of Sri Lankan scholars from a variety of academic disciplines.

For example, K. N. O. Dharmadasa, an expert in Sinhala literature who has written extensively on the nature of Sinhala ethnic identity, states that "the first three Nāyakkar kings could continue in power without any major opposition to their rule because each strove hard to play faithfully the role of the traditional Buddhist monarch" (1976: 11). Similarly, Lorna Dewaraja, a historian whose study of the politics and social institutions of the Kandyan kingdom during the eighteenth century has become a standard work on these subjects, stresses that the Nāyakkars were accepted in Kandy because they were "lavish patrons of Buddhism" (1971: 78). Ananda Coomaraswamy, whose careful study of Kandyan art has become almost canonical for students of late medieval Sinhalese culture, regarded Kīrti Śrī as perhaps the greatest patron of Buddhism in the history of Sri Lanka, a ruler who succeeded in fully integrating his problematic kingship with the religious ideals of Sinhala

Buddhist tradition. In discussing Kīrti Śrī, Coomaraswamy (1979: 13) quotes the *Cūlavaṃsa*, chap. 99:

> The list of Kīrti Śrī's buildings, restorations, dedications could be indefinitely extended. . . . The whole of this book [*Mediaeval Sinhalese Art*], which deals with the Sinhalese art of his and his brother's times, is really a monument to his greatness. . . . Kīrti Śrī lived in perfect harmony with his two brothers. . . . [Together they] "sought to do good in divers ways . . . and *made themselves one with the religion and the people*." (Coomaraswamy's italics)

This appreciative view of the Nāyakkars and, in turn, of Kīrti Śrī is fully extended by H. L. Seneviratne, an anthropologist whose studies of public rituals in the Kandyan kingdom are considered definitive.[5] Seneviratne argues that the Nāyakkar's "alien" character has been overplayed by other scholars. He points out that not only did the Nāyakkar youths who became kings grow up in Kandy (so that they could hardly be considered foreigners), but that the religio-cultural reforms and revivals usually attributed to their enthusiasm were, in fact, well under way before they came to power in 1739 (and that they were merely sustaining a Buddhist revivalist movement convenient to their political ends).[6] He also asserts that the Tamil language and other "alien" cultural forms were actually regarded as prestigious in the circles of Kandyan Sinhala Buddhist nobles, as forms of culture to be emulated, not resented (Seneviratne, 1976: 56). Finally, he marshals further support for this view by quoting the noted Sri Lankan historian K. M. de Silva, who emphasized that the Nāyakkars "not only identified themselves with the Kandyan interest but also blended the Nāyakkar personality with the Kandyan background . . . with consummate skill" (Seneviratne, 1976: 57).

It is clear, therefore, that Nāyakkar efforts, and those of Kīrti Śrī in particular, to promote themselves as pious Buddhist kings ultimately proved very effective, at least according to the retrospective views of the Sinhalese public and the considered historical insight given by Sinhala Sri Lankan scholars. When Kīrti Śrī's success is understood within the backdrop of the actual historical circumstances he faced in overcoming fierce internal opposition, an opposition that nearly cost him his life, his accomplishments must be seen as all the more remarkable. In chapters 3–5, I shall illustrate how he managed such a political coup, noting, at the same time, the nature of the internal opposition he faced; also, through a study of the language deployed in Kīrti Śrī's royal inscriptions and through an analysis of the symbolism in royally sponsored ritual and art, I shall indicate what it meant to be a Buddhist in this time and place.

Elements of Theravāda Buddhist Kingship

Kīrti Śrī's ultimate success in being perceived as a pious Buddhist monarch was the result of his consummate ability to be identified with Sinhala Buddhist ideals of political power and religion. He accomplished this identification by artfully articulating various facets and forms of political discourse that are constituents of Kandyan Buddhist kingship and by evincing a classical Theravāda Buddhist religious world view per se, which was expressed vividly through the meritorious works of religious culture, especially temple wall paintings, that he sponsored with great zeal.[7] By appealing to a variety of familiar motifs, themes, and patterns that are constituents of royal symbolism, and by articulating principal conceptions at the heart of the Buddhist soteriology and historical memory, Kīrti Śrī can be rightfully regarded as an exemplary figure who wholly concretized the traditional paradigmatic political and religious structures of Theravāda Buddhist thought. In this chapter I shall concentrate on his political discourse, and in chapters 3–4, on his religious discourse, though the two, as will be seen, are related.

In a recent study of royal symbolism that focuses on the evolving late medieval development projects of Kandy's urban cultural geography, James Duncan (1990: 38) suggests that "one can identify two major discourses within the large discursive field pertaining to kingship, the Sakran and the Asokan. Both formed an integral part of the definition of Kandyan kingship. The complexity lay in the fact that there was a tension between these discourses." Duncan is referring to two of the fundamental orientations intrinsic to Sinhala Buddhist kingship that were inherited and then superbly exploited by Kīrti Śrī. Kīrti Śrī appealed not only to these particular discourses cited by Duncan, but also to other powerful discourses of central importance that contributed to the legitimacy scenarios of Buddhist political rule as well. These other discourses include the myth of the primordial king (Mahāsammata), that of the great Brahmanic lawgiver Manu, and the ideal religious quest of the *bodhisatta*-king.

For his part, Duncan (1990: 38) succinctly describes what he means by the "Aśokan" model: "The Asokan model was based on the Mauryan emperor Asoka who was looked upon as an ideal Buddhist king. According to this view a king should be mild-mannered, righteous, and unfailingly protective of Buddhism and responsible for the welfare of his people." The Aśokan discourse identified by Duncan refers to conceptions of kingship epitomized by Aśoka, the great Indian emperor of the third century B.C.E., who has been mythicized in the Theravāda Buddhist Pali literary traditions of Sri Lanka and Southeast Asia as a *cakkavatti* (turner of the wheel of *dhamma*) a *dhammarāja* (king of *dharma*), a so-called ruler who fostered order in the world by appealing to the norms of ethical righteousness embodied in *pañcasīla* (fivefold morality),[8] rather than by means of expedient military power (*daṇḍa*).[9] In the *Mahāvaṃsa*, the fifth-century C.E. Theravāda Buddhist monastic chronicle that recounts a mythicized history (or *heilsgeschichte*) of Buddhism in India and Sri Lanka, Aśoka is portrayed as having sacrificed most of his great wealth for the benefit of the *sangha* by building thousands of *vihāras* (monasteries) and by holding a plethora of great festivals in honor of the *dhamma* (the Buddha's teaching) and the *sangha* (monastic community).[10] He is also eulogized for making religious pilgrimages throughout northern India, to "those spots which the Conqueror himself had visited (*Mahāvaṃsa*, 41); for building commemorative *stūpas* (reliquaries) there; and for convening a great council of learned monks from throughout India to settle doctrinal disputes, thereby purifying and reestablishing a unified *sangha* (*Mahāvaṃsa*, 49–50). At one point in the *Mahāvaṃsa* narrative, Aśoka even offers his throne to a *sāmaṇera* (a Buddhist monastic novice who has not yet received the higher ordination of *upasampadā*), seemingly to symbolize at once the identity of his own newly won spiritual tutelage and the total sacrifice of his kingdom for the well-being of Buddhism (*Mahāvaṃsa*, 28–31). In the Aśokan discourse on Buddhist kingship, the political ethos derived from a reading of the *Mahāvaṃsa* is nicely summarized in a traditional Sinhalese saying: "the country exists for the sake of the religion." Or, to put the matter in yet another way, the state ultimately exists for the welfare of religious pursuits, corroborating the *Mahāvaṃsa*'s views that the island of Sri Lanka realizes its primary raison d'être by becoming the abode of *dhamma*.[11]

In my account of his religious works, it will be abundantly clear that Kīrti Śrī participated fully in this Aśokan discourse. (Indeed, the *Mahāvaṃsa*'s account of Aśoka's religious activities might have actually functioned as a preparatory outline for the later *Cūlavaṃsa* chapter that depicts the religious works of Kīrti Śrī.)

The second complementary discourse of Kandyan kingship, according to Duncan, is the Śakran model of divine rule that was derived from Hindu conceptions of cosmic power but was taken over by the Buddhists and adapted to fit in with Theravāda cosmology and soteriology. In this model, the king attempted to present himself symbolically in such a manner that he might be regarded as a this-worldly counterpart of Indra (known to Buddhist literature as Śakra), who, in the Vedas and other genres of earlier Hindu literature, is regarded as the ever-victorious and mighty thunderbolt-wielding warrior king of the gods. In Vedic literature, Indra is imagined as preserving the natural and social order of the universe, providing for its sustained prosperity by courageously leading his divine forces (*devas*) of heaven into ongoing battles against a class of lesser beings known as the *asuras*, demigods of disorder who obstruct the flow and establishment of *ṛta* (order).[12] In a parallel manner, Kandyan kings wished to be perceived as heroic protagonists in the human version of this cosmic drama, wherein they championed the causes of order and well-being for their own people in the face of inimitable threats (natural or political) from the outside. Moreover, Indra was associated with the power to produce rain (Duncan, 1990: 39), and this particular motif was also thoroughly rehearsed throughout the cultic history of Sinhala Buddhist kingship (during the Kandyan and earlier periods), by virtually all kings,[13] but especially during late medieval times, within the context of the annually celebrated cultural pageant known as the *äsaḷa perahära*,[14] which was reformed and reestablished by Kīrti Śrī. In addition to the themes of cosmic order and prosperity, the Śakran discourse on kingship also "stressed the building of palaces, cities and lakes that glorify the god-king. These landscapes were modeled upon textual descriptions of the cities of the gods in heaven on top of Mount Meru" (Duncan, 1990: 40). That is, the symbolism of the royal capital, expressed through architectural references (to palaces) and through the presence of a water tank (symbolizing the aboriginal cosmic waters from which creation periodically springs), reinforced the imagery of the Kandyan king as a this-worldly counterpart of heavenly rule, while his capital city functioned symbolically as an *axis mundi*, through which divinely sanctioned power could flow and ensure well-being throughout the kingdom if moral and ritual prescriptions were rightly observed by the king and his court.[15]

The genius of the Nāyakkar kings, at least the first three kings of this dynasty, was, perhaps their almost uncanny ability to appeal simultaneously to both of these royal legitimation discourses. The Nāyakkar appeal to the Hindu-derived Śakran discourse would seem to have risked alienation from Kandy's Sinhalese Buddhists, since their Tamil Śaivite Hindu background constituted a basic reason for suspicion regarding the propriety of their rule. However, what the Nāyakkars managed to accomplish, especially through the religious works of Kīrti Śrī, was a concomitant invocation of both the Śakran discourse and the Aśokan, an accomplishment that, for the most part, managed to assuage Kandyan Sinhalese Buddhist anxieties. To a certain extent, it can be argued that the incorporation of the Śakran discourse with the Aśokan is parallel to the way that Sinhala Buddhists subordinated Hindu gods and goddesses (Viṣṇu, Pattini, and Skanda) to the Buddha in their evolving, hierarchically structured cosmology.[16] It can still be observed today by noting the sequenced appearance of ritual participants from various temples associated with these deities in the annual processions of the *äsaḷa perähara* in Kandy.

Furthermore, Kīrti Śrī, as I will note, was not content with appeals to only the Aśokan and Śakran discourses. In fact, he also identified himself with at least three other discourses of royal legitimation that could generate a positive appeal among the Kandyan Sinhalese Buddhists. These three other discourses consist of the themes and symbols associated with (1) the early Buddhist myth of Mahāsammata, the primordial human king who (according to the *Aggañña Sutta* of the *Dīgha Nikāya* [3:79–94]), after private property had been introduced, was elected *in illo tempore* to maintain peace and order in society in return for a share of rice cultivated by his subjects;[17] (2) Manu, the mythic, Brahmanic royal progenitor who rules the world according to social prescriptions derived from an understanding of how *dharma* applies to caste, gender, and familial role; and (3) the ideal of the *bodhisatta*, a Buddha-in-the-making, whose religious quest is patterned after that of Gotama Buddha himself—royal identification with the *bodhisatta* ideal had been expressed by Sinhalese kings possibly as early as the third century C.E. in Anuradhapura.[18]

A review of the religious works of Kīrti Śrī's reign would indicate that he left almost no stone unturned in his quest to be identified as a quintessential Buddhist king. His symbolically expressed affinities with the first four of these five discourses will be noted; the appeal to the *bodhisatta* discourse will be detailed in the discussion of classical religious ideals in chapter 4.

Kīrti Śrī's Royal Discourses

There are essentially two ways of understanding the religious works of Kīrti Śrī. The first is to understand them as spontaneous acts of religious piety generated by a genuinely righteous Buddhist king who was guided by his deep spiritual knowledge of the Buddha's *dhamma* and his great veneration of the *sangha*.[19] No doubt, this is precisely how Kīrti Śrī wanted to be viewed by his subjects. Without capitulating to an unwarranted cynicism, the second way is to understand Kīrti Śrī's religious endeavors as politically expedient acts, as discourses in response to the various powerful constituencies that brought pressure to bear on his ability and right to rule. Though the various discourses of Buddhist kingship to which Kīrti Śrī appealed provided for a legitimizing religious foundation for royal rule, it should never be forgotten that kingship is primarily an exercise in political power and that all royal actions have, or can be construed as having, placating or inciting effects on various constituencies. Indeed, kingship is always reactionary or responsive in character; religion in royal hands is always marked by expediency.

In the context of Kandyan Nāyakkar rule, it must also be kept in mind that the various constituencies (the aristocracy, monks, and lay peasants) who observed or were affected by royal actions, ritual or otherwise, were by no means a totally united community with universally similar problems and identical aims. For the lay peasants, for instance, a morally righteous monarch who did not oppress them with unreasonable calls to war or impose on them the hardships or burdens of excessive taxation was an underlying and persistent concern. On the other end of the spectrum of constituencies, the Dutch were ever present on the horizon of the kingdom's boundaries, so Kīrti Śrī had to be concerned about how they would perceive his royal postures, too. Thus, a variegation of royal observers or subjects ensured that the reactions of a sensitive Nāyakkar kingship in Kandy would involve a multiplicity of discourses, and that specific royal actions would be intended for the benefit of specific audiences or subjects, some explicitly to assuage particular grievances (perceived or real), and others for more general consumption. In this manner, we can attempt to judge the practical or political significance of Kīrti Śrī's religious works by noting which group's concerns were being addressed by which actions.

The Sinhalese aristocracy during the Nāyakkar kingship had its own particular concerns and agenda. Many were preoccupied with their recent experience of being relatively economically and politically disenfranchised by the king's own enterprising Tamil Nāyakkar relations. The intensification of trade links by Nāyakkar entrepreneurs with South Indian sources had introduced a relatively new means of acquiring and maintaining wealth within Kandy's political economy. Alienated aristocratic Sinhalese—that is, those without these South Indian contacts and thus those who were unable to compete economically with the Tamil Nāyakkars in the capital—shared an economic complaint similar to that of the Dutch and, on occasion, colluded with the European foreigners in minor economic conspiracies against the king (Bell, 1904: 11).

Indeed, in 1749, just two years after his selection as king and still two years before his actual coronation, Kīrti Śrī faced a rebellion from the Sinhalese nobility that ostensibly seems to have been generated by the high-handedness of his father, Narenappā, who, together with a *mudaliyar* from Jaffna, increasingly monopolized the business of trade in the capital and initiated the practice of exacting substantial bribes in exchange for royal influence. Lorna Dewaraja (1971: 108) believes that the high-handedness of the king's father, who seemed to be usurping the power of his son in terms of directing the course of major economic transactions involving the court, and whose petition had become so powerful and secure that he could "attack the entrenched position of the native nobility in the court," was the primary irritant causing aristocratic alienation.[20] Similarly, H. L. Seneviratne (1976: 58–59) describes the tension that was building in Kīrti Śrī's court at this time:

> In the case of the aristocrats of Kandy who opposed Nāyakkar rule, however, the meaning of "alienness" seems fairly clear. The kinsmen of the Nāyakkars in Kandy were steadily growing in wealth and in influence with the king, at least in the eyes of the Sinhalese aristocracy competing for the king's favours. . . . By their engagement in non-traditional forms of economic activity such as trade, the Nāyakkar aristocrats were gaining an excess of wealth. The sources of Nāyakkar wealth were outside the traditional field of competition and therefore not open for control by the Kandyan aristocracy: they were outside the ground and rules of the game . . . ; the forces were "alien" in a sense that the Kandyan aristocrats did not dream of, for the new wealth of the Nāyakkar aristocrats was ultimately such trade and thereby the emerging rational capitalist enterprise of the West.

Many of these same alienated Sinhalese Buddhist aristocrats seem to have been in league with Buddhist *gaṇinnānses*, a unique class of unordained Buddhist "holy men" who were completely lacking in the observance of monastic discipline and who, being scions of these high-caste noble families, in fact served as surrogate landlords or managers of the extensive properties that had been endowed by previous Sinhalese kings for the purpose of sustaining the material support of the *vihārayas*. [*Vihāraya* is Sinhala for Pali *vihāra*.] Malalgoda (1976: 57–58) describes what seems to have been the spiritually decrepit character of these emergent and "noble monks":

> The *gaṇinnānses*, in general, professed to observe the ten precepts prescribed for the *sāmaṇeras*. Yet, particularly after the death of Vimaladharmasurya II in 1707, very little care seems to have been taken by the majority of them in the actual observance of these precepts. The traditional practices and regulations within the order came to be forgotten or openly neglected; and those very practices which had been expressly prohibited to monks became more and more widespread. Quite apart from the more basic precepts, even the outward formalities regarding names and modes of dress, for instance, were manifestly disregarded. The *gaṇinnānses* clothed themselves in white or saffron cloth instead of the orthodox robe prescribed for Buddhist monks. Some of them retained their lay names even after joining the order. More conspicuous, undoubtedly, was their departure from the precept of celibacy; some of them, though certainly not all, maintained wives and children in houses close to their temples out of incomes derived from temple lands. Moreover, their ignorance of the Buddhist texts led them further and further away from the Buddhistic great tradition towards what the great tradition considered "beastly sciences" (*tiraścīna vidyā*) of the little tradition. Indulgence in magic and sorcery, astrology and divination was widespread among them. In fact, during this period, the role of the *gaṇinnānses* tended to be more and more that of a priest or magician than that of a Buddhist monk in its ideal and doctrinal sense.

It is in relation to these two allied disgruntled factions that we can understand how and why Kīrti Śrī appealed so strongly to the orthopraxy of the Aśokan discourse and, in the process, then allied himself with the reforming impulse of the *silvattänas*, the new fraternity of orthodox-minded *sāmaṇeras* (novices), who were led by the scholarly monastic reformer, Saranaṃkara. These elements of the Aśokan discourse may even have been inspired by Saranaṃkara, or at least directed especially toward him and his group's consumption, as they correlated with his own desires to rehabilitate the sagging fortunes of the *sangha*.[21] They included: (1) reintroducing the *upasampadā* higher ordination; (2) issuing a *katikāvata* (a royally instituted program of disciplinary reform that functioned as an appendum to the *vinaya* rules of monastic discipline); (3) supporting the preservation, translation, and public chanting of *Buddhavācana* (literally, sayings of the Buddha) in the form of Pali *sutta*s; and (4) creating newly consecrated monastic *sīmā*s (purified monastery boundaries or sacred space) within *vihāraya*s, which, in turn, became the beneficiaries of massive material royal support.[22] It is clear that these activities sponsored by Kīrti Śrī, actions of a type so reminiscent of Aśoka, were also aimed at displacing the old syndrome of control by *gaṇinnānse*s and aristocrats over vast tracts of valuable income-producing land and, in the process, disestablishing their economic and social power bases. At the same time, Kīrti Śrī's conspicuously generous material support for rehabilitating the *vihāraya*s, and his drive for a newly reestablished and purified *sangha* that would be headed by Saranaṃkara, provided for a rationalization of the use of his own increasing royal wealth that would seem to have been beyond any reproach on Buddhist grounds. Moreover, monastic reform was carried out by an appeal to thoroughly orthodox norms, a revival completely Buddhistic in substance and scope, leaving no room for a critique of his kingship on specifically Buddhist grounds. In such a manner, Kīrti Śrī temporarily robbed his Sinhalese Buddhist aristocratic adversaries of one of their potentially most powerful weapons—a popular appeal on Buddhist grounds to displace his kingship. In a sense, Kīrti Śrī had become more Buddhistic than they were, especially with regard to how he managed and spent his royal wealth. His alliance with Saranaṃkara and the *silvattäna*s resulted not only in reform but also in the creation of an alternative cadre of "holy men" who would receive their legitimation from an Aśokan-inspired king. In return, Saranaṃkara and his *silvattäna*s could legitimate the kings. This was a mutually beneficial partnership, but apparently Saranaṃkara was soon to become dissatisfied.

It is important to remember that the alienation of the Sinhalese aristocracy and the *gaṇinnānse*s was primarily economic in nature. But, if they were to be successful in criticizing or resisting Kīrti Śrī, it would have to be rationalized on the grounds that he exercised his power and wealth in un-Buddhistic ways. Insofar as Kīrti Śrī demonstrably donated most of his inherited and acquired wealth in support of Buddhism and its institutions, not "merely [for] material development but [for] the increase of learning, righteousness, and social order as well" (Kemper,

1990: 155), his own acquisition of wealth, and by extension the acquisition of wealth by his converted relations, could not effectively be called into question. What was in fact later called into question, apparently by Saranaṃkara himself, was Kīrti Śrī's own alleged private religious orientation.

In addition to the economic factor, the reforming Buddhist *sangha* (the *silvattänas*) and the peasant laity, as I have previously noted, had other various concerns, to which Kīrti Śrī responded. For these monks, epitomized by Saranaṃkara, these included (as I have said) the virtual eclipse of *vinaya* (monastic discipline) within the depleted ranks of the *sangha* and hence a corresponding need for the royally issued *katikāvata*; the disappearance of *upasampadā* (the higher, full monastic ordination) and the necessity of obtaining monks from another Theravāda country for its reinstitution; and the need for education in Pali grammar and literature, which was necessary for monks to gain a first-hand knowledge of the Buddha's *dhamma*.[23] The *Cūlavaṃsa* goes on at great length regarding the extent to which Kīrti Śrī's actions directly addressed these specific concerns (2:255–299) within the articulation of his Aśokan discourse. In particular, I am interested in what Kīrti Śrī did to formally reestablish the *sangha* through the importation of *bhikkhus* from Thailand to conduct the *upasampadā* ordination ceremony. For, in considering the events connected to this effort, I will discuss the issues involved in the attempted assassination of Kīrti Śrī by members of the *sangha* and the Sinhalese aristocracy. While appeals to the Aśokan discourse appear to have assuaged many of the devout Buddhists in Kandy, there remained hostility and alienation among some others, including none other than Saranaṃkara himself. Thus, Kīrti Śrī's strategy of creating a wedge between the alienated Sinhalese aristocracy and his newly created religious elite did not immediately succeed.

The Sinhalese practice of securing *upasampadā* from other Theravāda Buddhist countries has a long history in Sri Lanka. The Theravāda lineage was first exported from Sri Lanka to Burma in the eleventh century C.E., and the ability to reimport that lineage is derived from the success that the religion thereby enjoyed not only in Pagan (Burma), but later in northern Thailand as well. Burmese monks arrived at the invitation of Vimaladharmasuriya I, the first fully consecrated king of Kandy, in the 1590s and again during the reign of Vimaladharmasuriya II a century later in 1697. In fact, during Śrī Vijaya Rājasinha's eight-year reign, just preceding Kīrti Śrī's reign, two attempts inspired by Saranaṃkara had failed to bring monks from Thailand in order to reestablish *upasampadā*. But finally a third mission succeeded in 1753 when eighteen *thera*s and seven Thai *sāmaṇera*s arrived in Kandy, were warmly received by Kīrti Śrī himself, and proceeded with the business of formally ordaining Sinhalese *sāmaṇera*s into the *sangha* and establishing new *sīmā*s (the purified monastic boundaries within which rites of monastic discipline, the preaching of *dhamma*, and the practice of meditation may be rightly performed).[24] This reestablishment of the *sangha* in Kandy was followed by the spread of *upasampadā* rites and the consecration of *sīmā*s throughout and even beyond the boundaries of the Kandyan kingdom, much to the discomfort of the observant Dutch.[25] Presiding over this proliferation was Saranaṃkara himself, who had been duly appointed by Kīrti Śrī as *sangharāja* (literally, king of the *sangha*), the first such appointment to that supreme ecclesiastical post since the eleventh- through thirteenth-century C.E. Polonnaruva era.

Seven years after his appointment as *sangharāja*, Saranaṃkara seems to have fallen into a conspiracy to do away with Kīrti Śrī, which involved Kīrti Śrī's second *adigar* (prime minister), called Samanakkoḍi, and Tibboṭuvāve, a cousin of Samanakkoḍi and the chief prelate of the Malvatta Vihāra (the king's former flower garden in Kandy, which, following its donation to the *sangha* by Kīrti Śrī, had become the venue for the first *sīmā* and *upasampadā* consecrations by the visiting Thai *bhikkhu*s).[26] According to Dewaraja's analysis (1971: 121–122) of the relevant sources:

> The conspirators had first discussed whether one Paṭṭiye Baṇḍāra [Narendra Sinha's son by a Kandyan aristocrat] should be placed on the throne instead of the "Tamil heretic," meaning the king. But this choice was not acceptable to all; perhaps as often happened jealousy among the Kandyan nobles prevented the selection of one of their own number. So the matter was referred to the monks who had recently come from Siam. Very likely it was from them that the suggestion came to invite a prince from their homeland. A letter was despatched to the king of Siam requesting him to send a prince to be enthroned in Kandy. The Siamese monarch was made to understand that the monks, nobles and people were disgusted with the heretic who sat on the throne. Kīrti Śrī Rājasinha was made to believe that the letter to Siam merely contained a request for some rare religious books. A Siamese prince did arrive in the guise of a bhikkhu together with several monks bringing holy books with them. The unsuspecting king accommodated the visitors to the Malvatta vihāra where they remained till the arrangements for the assassination had been finalized. The prince, later re-

vealed to be Krumpty Pippit, son of King Boromkot of Siam (1732–58) by a secondary wife, made common cause with the conspirators. From these preliminary arrangements it is clear that the plot had been brewing for a considerable time, perhaps for several years. [In fact, the letter was sent in 1759 and the plot unfolded unsuccessfully in 1760.] It seems therefore that ever since the sangha recovered from its amorphous state and became a wealthy recognized institution it turned into a fertile breeding place for treason and intrigue.

The plotters chose rather an elaborate and peculiar method by which to kill the king. He was invited to a religious festival in the Malvatta vihāra in the course of which he would sit and listen to a sermon. Under the throne a pit was dug fitted with sharp spikes, the throne being so arranged that on the king taking his seat the draperies would give way and he would fall impaled upon the spikes. However, a few days before the eventful night, Galagoda Disāva who had gained knowledge of the plot secretly informed the king. Feigning ignorance of the treachery the king attended the ceremony together with his loyal supporters. He declined to seat himself on the throne provided until the preaching was over, as if in deference to the words of the Buddha. Apparently wrapped in devout attention he patiently stood till the sacred ceremony was complete. He then advanced as if to sit on the throne and to the horror of the conspirators he lifted the rich coverings with his royal staff, calmly ordered the iron spikes withdrawn and the pit to be filled up. After this the throne and drapery were replaced and the king seated himself as if nothing had happened. On the king's departure, the traitors were brought before him and justice meted out.

Dewaraja continues her account:

It is rather baffling why the monks of the Malvatta vihāra stooped to this treacherous activity. The ostensible reason assigned for this in the Śāsanāvatīrna Varṇanāva [a mid-nineteenth-century work in verse and prose that described the eighteenth-century revival in the up-country] was the king's continuous addiction to Hindu habits like using sacred ashes on his person. The charge leveled against him was that he was merely a nominal Buddhist. The king was referred to by the plotters as a "Tamil heretic." . . . When one considers the indefatigable zeal displayed by the king in the recent past, for the welfare of the sangha in general, and the Malvatta vihāra in particular, it is almost incredible that the *sangharāja* should have displayed such ingratitude.

Malalgoda (1976: 66) describes how Kīrti Śrī indeed managed to turn such a difficult turn of events to his advantage:

> When the plot was exposed, Kīrti Śrī faced the situation with shrewd judgement. He immediately deported the Siamese prince, executed the officials involved and appointed his own favourites to the vacant offices. Any possible alienation of the mass of Buddhists against him was thus averted, and he continued his policy of making generous religious endowments. His reputation as the greatest patron of Buddhism during the Kandyan period was thus preserved completely intact.

What Malalgoda is saying is that through this event, which was followed subsequently by the Dutch invasion of Kandy, Kīrti Śrī succeeded in consolidating his power by maintaining his public profile as a righteous Buddhist king while, at the same time, demonstrating his inclusiveness. The latter is indicated by the fact that Kīrti Śrī subsequently transferred extensive tracts of lands held by one of the plot's other conspirators, one Moladande Nilame, to a Muslim entrepreneur, Gopala Mudali, who had played a leading role in uncovering the conspiracy on Kīrti Śrī's behalf (Bell, 1904: 99–101).

What is perhaps more important to note here is that the reason given in hindsight for the plot to assassinate Kīrti Śrī is also the very reason that it failed. That is, the charge that Kīrti Śrī was a "heretic" was simply unconvincing because the king's record showed public expressions of orthodoxy, while, at the same time, he was able to maintain his good relations with non-Buddhist constituents (for example, the Muslims), who continued their loyal support for him. Even Saranaṃkara, the chief architect of monastic reform, was powerless to change public perceptions of Kīrti Śrī, though Kīrti Śrī, in fact, may have remained a Śaivite Hindu privately. In this instance, public persona predominated over alleged private religious preference, and the persona was unmistakenly Aśokan in character. In fact, one must look for other reasons to fully account for the attempt to assassinate Kīrti Śrī.

The attempt to assassinate him was based primarily on economic motives and rationalized by appealing to sentiments generated by considerations of the king's alleged religious otherness. Insofar as religion is often a powerful constituent of ethnic identity, disdain for Kīrti Śrī's private Śaivite religiosity was articulated in hindsight as one of the primary motivations.[27] To the disaffected monks and nobility, a genuine Theravāda Buddhist in the form of a colluding Thai prince was deemed preferable, despite the fact that he would also seem to be somewhat of an ethnic outsider due to his racial and linguistic background.

As Dewaraja has noted, it is incredible that Saranaṃkara and the other colluding monks of the Malvatta Vihāraya could have objected to Kīrti Śrī publicly on religious grounds. It is possible that the plot to assassinate the king was instigated originally by the alienated section of the Kandyan aristocracy for chiefly economic reasons and then sold to Saranaṃkara and some of his reform-minded monks on grounds of Kīrti Śrī's private "heretical" religiosity. In any case, the marketing of this project failed to win universal appeal, for among other monks at the Malvatta Vihāraya, there were several who helped to expose the plot and in turn betrayed their own *sangharāja*. In all likelihood, their loyalty in this instance was probably due to Kīrti Śrī's by then well-demonstrated public commitment to Buddhism.

The most demonstrable expressions of Kīrti Śrī's public Buddhist profile and his appeal to the Aśokan discourse had been, as would be expected, ritual in character. One of the most graphic of these involved the performance of the *upasampadā* ordination rite, which is still observed today in Kandy in fundamentally the same manner as during Kīrti Śrī's time. A telling detail of this ordination rite that appeals dramatically to the Aśokan discourse refers to symbolic abdication of the kingdom to the *sangha*. On the day of *upasampadā*, after it has been determined that a *sāmaṇera* has qualified for the higher ordination, the *sāmaṇera*, together with family and friends, proceeds to the Dāḷadā Māḷigava from either the Malvatta or the Asgiriya Vihāraya, where he dons a Thai-styled royal crown, is treated to a performance of classical dance (as if he were king), and then mounts an elephant, the royal vehicle, for a procession back to the monastery for the *upasampadā* rite proper. This monk-as-king theme refers back ritually, of course, to Aśoka's own symbolic abdication, which is mythically described in the *Mahāvaṃsa*. Ironically, it also satirically capitulates to the plot's conspirators in regard to their desire for Thai kingship.

Among other ritual actions—these purportedly performed by Kīrti Śrī and appealing ostensibly to the complementary Śakran mode of discourse—none was more symbolically conspicuous, or better understood across the lines of his various constituencies, or as highly reflective of how elements of the various royal discourses could be fully integrated, than Kīrti Śrī's own performances of ritual circumambulation. According to the *Cūlavaṃsa* (2:255–256), this ancient Indic ceremonial expression was the first formal action undertaken by Kīrti Śrī following his public ascension to power:

> After attaining his consecration as king, the Lord of men who was devoted to the faith of the Triad of the jewels, Buddha and others, strove unweariedly after merit. The highly famed one had the whole town (of Siriwaddhana) [Kandy] cleansed and decorated with stuffs, triumphal arches and the like. Then he gathered together the whole of the inhabitants of Lanka completely in the fair glorious town and moving along with royal magnificence, the Great king whose merit was now having its effect, marched round the town, his right side turned towards it, thus making known that the realm of Lanka bereft of its king had again a king.

The roots of circumambulation in the lay Buddhist context are probably embedded in the practice of *pradakṣiṇā*—veneration expressed by physically taking an encircling path clockwise around *stūpa*s that symbolize the legacy or presence of the Buddha. In the abstract, it is a ritual means of identifying what is regarded as sacred or worthy and setting it off from the mundane. It is therefore primarily an action of worship or ritual sacralization. In the context of kingship, it is also an action symbolizing the seizure of control and the establishment of order. This secondary theme of royal order being established becomes important within the *Cūlavaṃṣā*'s further account of Kīrti Śrī's other ceremonial acts of circumambulation; the most dramatic expression of this is related to Kīrti Śrī's reorganization of and participation in the *äsaḷa perahära*:

> After a sacrificial festival for the lotus-hued patron god [Vishnu] and other deities such as was popularly recognized as bringing luck even in the days of former sovereigns of Lanka, he had for the purpose of a military display, the whole town without exception put in order like the city of the gods. He gathered together all the inhabitants of Lanka and in the town he had the people from the individual provinces separated and made them dwell in different places, provided with standards. Then he had symbols in the temples of the gods placed on the back of an elephant. He had the elephant surrounded by divers beaters of drum and the tambourine and by crowds of dancers, . . . by people wearing the Brahman dress, . . . by women and various groups of dignitaries, by people carrying divers shields, swords, spears and various symbols and banners; by people who had come from various regions and who understood the different tongues, by such as were practised in the various arts by divers artisans—with such and many other people he had the elephant surrounded, ordering them to go immediately in front or behind. Thereupon the king set forth, like the Prince of the gods, with great (and) royal splendour and marched round

the whole town, his right side turned towards it. Finally, they all arrived again and entered (the town) according to their rank. (*Cūlavaṃsa*, 2:259–260)

Several themes germane to the discourses of kingship that I have already identified are revealed in this passage. The first is obvious symbolism whereby the center or capital city also symbolizes a this-worldly city of the gods (and hence the king is represented as a this-worldly Indra). As in the *Cūlavaṃsa*'s description (noted above) of Kīrti Śrī's circumambulatory rite following his consecration, the city of Kandy serves as a trope for the whole of Lanka as well. By his symbolic action, Lanka is magically secured. A parallelism with the world of the gods is ritually established with this symbolic capturing of the capital city. Through the performance of a rite, horizontally and vertically synchronized relationships are established between the center (the capital) and the periphery (the rest of the country) and between the human world (King Kīrti Śrī and his capital of Kandy) and the divine world (Indra and his city of the gods). The establishment of the latter sought to reinforce the appearance of pivotal centralized political power in the face of potentially fractious internal pressures; it was also for external consumption (by the Dutch). The former pattern, clearly emphasizing the power dynamics of an *axis mundi*, also sought to reaffirm the existing Kandyan social order within the traditional frames of its accepted hierarchy. Herein, Kandyans also publicly affirmed their places within society and within the cosmos. It was, therefore, an exercise in social, political, and military discipline, a ritual statement of formal ordering. Since the king's ritual action was sociocosmic in character, it was universally addressed to generate awe, the primary aim of the Śakran discourse.[28]

Related generically to the practice of royal ritual circumabulation is pilgrimage, one of the most powerful and sustained forms of religious behavior throughout the history of religions, both Hindu and Buddhist, in South and Southeast Asia. Attending the annual *äsaḷa perahära* in Kandy constituted a pilgrimage of sorts for many of the king's constituencies. It consisted of a defining journey to the center, or *axis mundi*, where sacralized power was at once accessible for personal appropriation and publicly expressed through the royal orchestration of rituals. Kīrti Śrī's reforms regarding the performance of the *perahära*, wherein Buddhist symbols, especially the *daḷadā* (tooth-relic), were given primacy over Hindu symbols in the circumambulatory processions around the capital, further established Kandy as a pilgrimage destination for all pious Buddhists—a status it retains to this very day.

The *Cūlavaṃsa* (2:258) details Kīrti Śrī's extensive efforts to patronize many sacred places of pilgrimage in Lanka other than Kandy in a manner that is further reminiscent of Aśoka's own paradigm-setting acts of pilgrimage:

> Yearning for merit the Lord of men betook himself with his retinue to superb Anuradhapura. Here the King sacrificed to the Bodhi tree and the sacred cetiyas [reliquary *stūpas*] with elephants, and horses, with gold, silver and the like, and thus in divers ways laid up a store of pious works. Then too in royal splendour the highly famed Lord of men visited Mahiyangana-cetiya and the superb Nakha-cetiya and reverenced them by the celebration of a great festival and so laid up a store of merit. In order to honour with sacrifices the beautiful cetiyas and viharas erected by the Lord of men, Parakkama in superb Pulatthinagara, the highly famed King rich in faith, betook himself thither with a great retinue and sacrificed to them in the right way.

These sacred sites that were visited and feted were not of course selected at random. Anurādhapura and Poḷonnaruva were the historical venues for the fruition of classical Sinhala Buddhist culture and political power. In popular memory, their association still generated a nostalgia for a past that Kīrti Śrī now sought to fully identify himself with. The pilgrimage to Mahīyangana reached into an even deeper level of the collective Sinhala Buddhist mythic memory. While Anurādhapura and Poḷonnaruva represent the past achievements and mature fruition of a great Buddhist civilization, Mahīyangana is a trope for its very origins. According to the *Mahāvaṃsa* (3–5), Mahīyangana was the site of the Buddha's first mythic visit to Lanka—a myth of how the Buddha tamed the native *yakkhas* (demons) of the island and converted them by preaching the *dhamma*. It has become a place of sacred pilgrimage that symbolizes Buddhism's domestication of the island's indigenous cultures. Kīrti Śrī's pilgrimages to each of these places were clearly strategic appeals to the discourses of Sinhala Buddhist kingship, recalling Aśoka's own paradigm-setting pilgrimage activities to places in India that were associated with cardinal events in the Buddha's life. They also refer to the heritage of religious works of Lanka's past heroic Buddhist kings, a heritage that Kīrti Śrī now sought to publicly reinvigorate.

But perhaps even more telling, in this connection, is how the *Cūlavaṃsa* (2:292) describes Kīrti Śrī's actions in relation to Śrī Pāda (Sumanakūṭa, or Adam's Peak), likely the most famous pilgrimage site in all of Sri Lanka, which is also associated with a onetime, hallowed visit of the Buddha; there the Buddha is said to have left his mark in the form of a footprint on the peak of this spectacular mountain, an indelible mark that symbolizes his imprint on Sinhala civilization:

> The wicked king known by the name of Rājasīha in the town of Sītāvaka who had committed parricide and destroyed the Order of the Victor, as he could not distinguish between what it was right to do, had adopted a false faith, was devoted to the adherents of the false faith and ordered them to take for themselves the income accruing from the sacred footprint of the Enlightened One on Sumanakūṭa. From that time onwards the adherents of the false faith destroyed everything there. When the highly famed great king heard of these things he realised, reverently devoted to the Enlightened One, that this was unseemly. He commanded the adherents of the false faith from now on not to do so, and charged the sons of the Buddha to carry out in the right way the many sacrificial ceremonies which should be performed there.

The "wicked" king referred to here is Rājasinha I, who, while ruling at Sītāvaka from 1581 to 1593, as one of three simultaneously self-professing kings of Lanka, had converted to Śaivite Hinduism. Kīrti Śrī's clear public repudiation of Rājasinha and Hinduism makes his identification with Buddhist kingship nowhere more apparent than in this particular case. This theme of separating himself from Tamil Śaivite Hindu rule is also stressed in a royal declaration at the Mädavela Rājamahāvihāraya (Great Royal Monastery).

In a later discussion on the elements of the visual liturgy that are represented by Kandyan Buddhist temple wall paintings, I will explain how pictorial references to sacred places of pilgrimage became a standard feature in virtually all temples rehabilitated by Kīrti Śrī. In addition to those places mentioned in the *Cūlavaṃsa*'s account of Kīrti Śrī's religious works, other landmarks of Buddhist history were incorporated into the systematic artistic representation of *soḷosmasthāna* (sixteen sacred places), a symbolization that indicated a temporal localization of Buddhist tradition.

Finally, Kīrti Śrī's appeals to the discourses of Buddhist kingship can be observed in the manner in which he chose to describe himself within the context of the numerous official land grants (*sannasa*s) that he issued to monastic *vihāraya*s throughout the Kandyan kingdom during his reign. *Sannasa*s were usually inscribed on copper plates, but sometimes in stone, on occasions when temples were rededicated. In these inscriptions, not only do we gain insight into the considerable generosity reflected therein but also the language deployed in these royal declarations comprises the most direct evidence of how Kīrti Śrī wished to be perceived by the Sinhala Buddhist public.[29] These *sannasas* often appeal to three or four royal discourses simultaneously, but on the whole they emphasize the Mahāsammatan, Manu, and Śakran discourses, though references to the *bodhisatta* ideal (Metteyya) are not infrequent. It should be pointed out that in describing himself by appealing to these various tropes, Kīrti Śrī was not being especially inventive. Rather, he was at pains to express himself conventionally.

A *sannasa* from Mädapitiye (located near Hañguranketa, southeast of Kandy), which dates from 1758 and is attributed to Kīrti Śrī, emphasizes the fair-mindedness of the king in his decision to rededicate temple land to the *sangha*. In this case, Kīrti Śrī's action is considered as splendid as Śakra's and he is likened explicitly to the king of the gods. Furthermore, because his action is considered so meritorious, it will contribute to his attainment of nirvāṇa in the future; thus a clear reference is made to his status as a king on the path to realizing the spiritual summum bonum, or the *bodhisatta* ideal. Finally, the last segment stresses the moral righteousness of the king and warns those who would attempt to undo his meritorious action. The consequences of appropriating temple lands illegally—a difficulty that had arisen prior to Kīrti Śrī's reign—are also clearly addressed. They consist of cosmic damnation and so link the power of the king to the karmic returns of universal justice. The *sannasa* runs as follows:

> During the reign in Lanka of the divine lord King Senewirat, the chief of the three divisions of Lanka, His Majesty heard that Pahala Arattana and Diyabubulewatta, which had originally been dedicated to Arattana Vihāra in Diyatilaka, had become king's property, and as such a state of things is unjust, His Majesty had the same re-dedicated to the vihare; but later on, a similar thing, having taken place during the reign of the divine lord King Kīrti Śrī, the chief of the whole of Lanka, while His Majesty was going on with the improvement of the country and the propagation of religion, one day His Majesty having heard it, he re-dedicated the same to the vihare for the purpose of carrying on almsgiving, flower and oil offerings, as it was unjust to take the Buddha's property, and with a view of securing to himself the benefits resulting from such donations, temporally and spiritually, and to attain Nirvana.
>
> On Wednesday, the eleventh day of the waning moon, of the month Binara in the year of Saka 1680, these fields were declared Buddha's property . . . ; so in order that no future king, prince, nor

minister lay claim to these, this copper Sannas is written and granted. Thus on the command given from the throne of Kandy in all the splendour and glory of Śakra, the king of gods, this copper Sannas was written and granted.

So let there be no one who, actuated by covetousness, dispute this donation and take this property by force, for he will be born and tortured in one of the four great hells; let the future generation defend and protect this meritorious act and thereby attain bliss in heaven and Nirvāṇa. (Lawrie, 1898: 2:577)

A 1781 *sannasa* from Kīrti Śrī, issued just before his death, similarly affirms lands endowed for the performance of monastic rituals at Suriyagoda, the *sangharāja* Saranaṃkara's original *vihāraya*. It ends with an even more graphic reference to the Śakran discourse: "This copper Sannas was issued by the order of His Majesty, seated on the throne of Kandy like the celestial Indra, conqueror of the Asura gods" (Lawrie, 1898: 1:801–802). Another *sannasa* from Urulewatte, dated from the end of Kīrti Śrī's reign and possibly commissioned by Rājādhi Rājasinha, his brother, not only makes explicit appeals to the Mahāsammatan and Manu discourses, but summarizes the royal accomplishments that constitute the Aśokan discourse. Increasingly, the issuing of a *sannasa* became an opportunity to remind the local public of the great accomplishments of Kīrti Śrī's thoroughly Buddhistic kingship:

When His Majesty King Kīrti Śrī Rāja Sinha, the descendant of King Manu of the illustrious royal family of Mahā Sammata, was reigning in Kandy the prosperous city, he inquired as to the state of religion in Lanka, and he was told that there were no ordained Buddhist priests, but only novices ("sāmaṇeras"); on this His Majesty said, "While I am reigning it is a pity to see the religion going down"; accordingly he took to his mind to patronize the faith, assisted by the sub-king Rājādhi Rāja Sinha; he sent an embassy to Siam with presents worth one lakh of coins, and invited priests from Siam, such as Upatissa and others, who came, bringing with them bana books. Then thousands of respectable men were robed, taught pitakas ["baskets" of Scriptures]; hundreds of them were daily fed; and hundreds of offerings of necessaries were made yearly; hundreds of ruined vihares were repaired in different places, including the Relic Temple, offerings of gardens, fields, and flower gardens were made to Anurādhapura, Samantakūṭaya, Mahīyangana vehera, the Daḷadā Maḷigāwa, and other viharas. (Lawrie, 1898: 2:888)

This *sannasa* goes on to note how Rājādhi restored the ruined *vihāraya* that was located on the local rock edifice, and gives a caveat that is repeated in many other *sannasas*:[30]

> Thus it is laid down as a rule that if anyone were to take forcible possession of temple properties given by him or by any others, he shall be born and re-born a worm in a heap of cowdung for 60,000 years, and any one who takes a stick of firewood, a blade of grass, a fruit, or a flower out of temple lands shall be born a "pretaya" with a body fifty to six yodun long and belly in proportion, to pass his time with a chain of sighs, eyes full of tears, heart full of sorrow, without obtaining even refuse as food, and without being able to slake his thirst even if the current of the Ganges and Jumna were to pass through his throat, as such a current would evaporate by the heat of his body as the current of the ocean is evaporated by the heat of hell fire. On the contrary he who defends the temple rights or improves them will never be born in the four cardinal hells, but in celestial worlds, and enjoy bliss in heaven and earth. It is further said that out of the two, the donor enjoys bliss in heaven and to the defender attains Nirvana. So virtuous men may you act up to these and attain Nirvana. (Lawrie, 1898: 2:888)

While these formal royal declarations are quite typical in terms of the manner in which the kingship of Kīrti Śrī is formally framed in Aśokan, Śakran, Manu, and Mahāsammatan terms, the following 1755 *sannasa* from Mädavela is remarkable insofar as it clearly states the Sinhalese origins of the *vihāraya* and seems to repudiate publicly any attempt that might be made to identify Kīrti Śrī's political interests with those of the Tamils. The *sannasa* effectively retells the saga of Walagamba (Vaṭṭagāmani), in whose reign so many cave temples were allegedly dedicated, and during whose period the Buddhist canon was first put in writing:

> During the reign of King Walagam Bahu, who brought the three divisions [of Lanka] under his sole dominion and who belong to the Khestriya [*sic*] race, which counts King Manu among its members, which had its origin from the time the world was peopled by Brahmas, Tamils conquered and took possession of the kingdom of Kandy. Thereupon the king, accompanied by his queen-mother, fled to Balawita and took their abode in Walagandeniya. After they had lived there for a number of years earning their livelihood by hard work, the king, actuated

> by kingly pride, thought to himself thus: "It is now fourteen years since the Tamils took possession of the kingdom, and I am living a life of concealment in this forest. When shall I protect the country and my religion?" Saying this to himself, he proceeded to Kaṭupulu Nuwara, took back the sword which had been hidden there, erected a seat at Mulmediyawa, placed the chank of victory on it, and began his invocations in this manner: "If there be any latent power in me by which I can expel the Tamils from Lanka and bring my country and my religion to their former state, let this chank speak." Whereupon the chank spoke thrice. The king proceeded to Kaṭupulu Nuwara, taking with him the people who were brought to the spot by the sound of the chank, built palaces, put up fortifications and remained there. The inhabitants of the three divisions of Lanka, having heard that their king had regained his kingdom, repaired thither from all directions. The king seeing this large concourse of his subjects started, like Indra with his 64 ornaments on, for war with the Tamils and overtook and killed them, who were ready to fight. After the war the king came back for the second time to the place in which he had led a life of hardship and misery, intent upon commemorating his temporary abode at Walagandeniya by a religious ceremony. There he built palaces, took up his abode, planted three bo-trees, and erected Medawela Vihare. (Lawrie, 1898: 1:581–582)

The *sannasa* then goes on to describe how the *vihāraya* later fell into ruins until the time of Parākramabāhu of Kurunegala in the early 1300s, when a new monk came, *rājakāriya* (royal service) was established for the temple's future maintenance,[31] and artists were sent to fashion sculptures and paintings. The *sannasa* then states that it again fell into a ruinous state before repairs and new paintings were made by Kīrti Śrī at great royal expense. In the process, the *sannasa* ostensibly links Kīrti Śrī with the mythical exploits, especially the anti-Tamil stance, of the highly revered Walagamba.

It is interesting to note how Kīrti Śrī continued to be styled in Mahāsammatan fashion by his brother in a *sannasa* composed shortly after his death. Indeed, this is how the 1786 Degaldoruva *sannasa* begins:

> When his Great Majesty King Kīrti Śrī Rājasinha, who was descended from the original Royal Race called the Mahāsammata, and who belonged to the family of Sūriyawanse, and who was possessed of immense wealth and pure wisdom, whose fame reached from and throughout our land, was reigning with equity and justice in the city of Siriwardanapura, which is styled Senkadagala Nuwara, and hav-

> ing won the affection of his subjects, His majesty caused new temples, dagabas, and images to be made, and others to be repaired, and . . . he was by such deeds promulgating the Buddhist religion. (Lawrie, 1898: 1:139)

The 1786 Bambaragala sannasa by Rājādhi not only continues the discussion in an expanded eulogistic vein that seems to appeal to all of the model discourses of royal Buddhist rule that I have discussed, but also details the principal elements of the visual liturgy of temple paintings that I will examine in the next chapter:

> The most powerful and great monarch Kīrti Śrī Rāja Sinha, of the illustrious race of Mahā Sammata, the first king on earth, which (race) counts King Manu among its members, who was a mine of virtues, and who was a devoted follower of the enlightened one's religion, of exceeding purity, like unto curd congealed in a silver chank, and whose fame was like that of a candidate for Buddhahood; after his succession to the throne, as sole monarch of Lanka, he was working for the advancement of the faith of the omniscient one; . . . it was at this time that [the local *bhikkhu* points out there is a cave there and the king then organizes local people of piety to cut and clear the cave] . . . therein [were] built fifteen images of Dewas and a Makara Torana, and on the walls thereof, both inside and out, were painted Buddhist birth stories, fifty-eight arhat figures, sixteen scenes from Buddha's life, on the canopy were painted the scenes of the 24 annunciations and the first seven weeks of Buddha on his attaining omniscience. There were also paintings of the future Buddha Maitri's celestial palaces, his own likeness as a Dewa. (Lawrie, 1898: 1:337–338)

What seems so clear from each of the sources I have examined in this chapter is that Kīrti Śrī opportunistically and conventionally articulated the discourses of his kingship in unmistakably Buddhist terms. Indeed, he proved himself a master of the use of symbols, images, and tropes. What I shall note in chapters 3 and 4 is that nowhere is this propensity and genius more clearly illustrated than in the visual liturgies that Kīrti Śrī had painted creatively within the halls of worship at the many *vihārayas* he rehabilitated. This will include an analysis of the Buddhist religious world view expressed within these paintings and how Buddhist kingship forms an intrinsic part of it.

3

A Visual Liturgy

Many of the traditional public rites and festivals, monastic and lay, that are still performed in the villages, towns, and temples of the contemporary Sinhala Buddhist religious culture within the Kandyan region of up-country Sri Lanka may be regarded, in part, as a legacy of what must have been Kīrti Śrī's unwearied efforts to articulate not only the royal discourses I discussed in chapter 2, but also a classical Sinhalese Theravāda Buddhist religious perspective. In chapter 1 I noted how, in general, the social, economic, and political predicament produced compelling reasons for why Kīrti Śrī felt so moved to engage in royal postures reminiscent of the ideal patterns of Buddhist political rule. I noted in chapter 2 how Kīrti Śrī accomplished this by revitalizing, in so conspicuous a fashion, various genres of public rituals, monastic and lay (*upasampadā*, *äsaḷa perahära*, pilgrimages, and so on), and by issuing formal written documents (*sannasa*s and *katikāvata*s) so copiously. His efforts directed at the performance of rituals gave form to, or, rather, reformed, the public articulation of Buddhism, and this is reflected even in the present-day enactment in up-country Sri Lanka. In fact, one might go so far as to say that Kīrti Śrī laid the foundation for the manner in which Buddhism has become a type of civil religion in Kandy for up-country Sinhalese.[1] Kīrti Śrī's efforts, quite obviously, revitalized the institutional life of Buddhism in ways still felt today in this region and, at the same time, helped to centralize his grip on power throughout the other various regions of his kingdom. In this chapter and the next, I shall examine the content of Kīrti Śrī's purported public commitment through rituals and formal documents—that is, what Kīrti Śrī took to be the essentials of Theravāda Buddhist thought (cosmology, historicized myth, and soteriological philosophy). Through an identification and analysis of the religious meanings symbolized in the pictorial art that Kīrti Śrī had painted by his highly skilled craftsmen on the walls of the many temples he so generously restored throughout his reign, my aim is to ferret out the principles and substance of this classic Sinhala Buddhist weltanschaung—a world view subsequently challenged and, in part, transformed by the turn of social, economic, and political events of the nineteenth and twentieth centuries.[2] The success of Kīrti Śrī's enterprise, I shall note, depended on how he was able to express the fundamentals of a religious world view in a manner that was clearly accessible and intelligible to the masses of lay Buddhists, his most important constituency.

The central premise of this chapter is that the paintings that covered the walls and ceilings inside Sinhala Buddhist image houses in the late medieval Kandyan period constitute a visual liturgy: consciously created and coordinated sets of religious themes, paradigms, and images didactically intended to be internalized and cultivated by *religieux* for the purpose of making progress on the path to the ultimate realization of Buddhism's summum bonum—*nibbāṇa*. Moreover, these paintings function not only didactically as soteriological devices, but also heuristically, insofar as they localize or represent the truths of cosmos and history as these have been known in the Sinhala Buddhist Theravāda tradition.[3] To enter one of these sanctuaries for the purpose of meditating or making a simple offering of flowers to the Buddha was, and is, also to enter into the world view first articulated and then represented by the Buddha's portrayed life and teachings. Entering these temples can be a genuinely *situating* experience, where one identifies with past and continuing expressions of the Buddhist world view; one is literally surrounded on all sides, engulfed by symbols and images of what it means and what it has meant to be Buddhist. The paintings constitute tropes for various dimensions and levels of realizing the religious truths of existence made known by the Buddha and exemplified in tradition. In the temple paintings done under Kīrti Śrī's direction, these truths were as simple in representation as they were profound in meaning. As I will explain, with illustrations, their presentation during the reign of Kīrti Śrī soon became quite standardized, a development allowing us to identify which aspects of doctrine and myth that he and his advisers sought to emphasize. The result is thoroughly Buddhist, but also distinctively Kandyan.

The Kandyan School of Temple Wall Paintings

The paintings of the late medieval Kandyan school are often regarded by art historians to be, in general, representative of a "folk" or of a more developed "primitive" style,[4] because of their two-dimensional mode of presentation; their heavy reliance on line; the absence of perspective, scope, nuance, and shade; and their exclusive use of primary or bright, gay colors (cinnabar red, yellow, green, white, black, and, rarely, blue).[5] These paintings are stylistically simple, sometimes monumental works, but more often are framed in murals that are either linear, narrative sequences that flow into one another or separated registers of successive scenes. Coomaraswamy (1979: 168) has said that "the value of these paintings lies not merely in their beauty and charm as decoration, but in the fact that they are priceless historical documents that could not be reproduced under modern conditions." While we can agree that these paintings are priceless historical documents, their value to students of religion is not so much that they cannot be reproduced under modern conditions, but that they reveal historical perceptions of what was regarded as quintessentially true and religiously meaningful for Sinhalese Theravāda Buddhists in the eighteenth century. Siri Gunasinghe (1978: 3), seeking to downplay the stylistic limitations of Kandyan painting, which might lead to a naive dismissal of its profound historical and religious significance, says:

> What is most appealing in Kandyan painting is the symbolic content and not the manner of presentation. . . . Like all other art traditions which are socially significant in that they are an integral part of the mental and spiritual make-up of a society at any given time, Kandyan painting is symbolic of popular aspirations and provides images of conviction in regard to acceptable social and spiritual values.

Further, Gunasinghe and N. B. M. Seneviratne warn against the tendency of other scholars (such as Coomaraswamy) who seem to overstress the connections between the Kandyan school and its affinities to the history of Indian painting in general and to the more ancient classical style of Sinhalese painting in particular, connections that can generate an inclination to reduce its religious meaning to more general philosophical and universalistic themes that distract us from seeing the specific relevance of Kandyan art to its own native milieu in time and space. Gunasinghe (1978: 5) states: "We must look outside the classical tradition of Sinhalese painting, in the milieu of the non-elite peasant society, for the sources of inspiration for both its form and meaning. The basic content would then be found to be the simple soteriology sanctioned by Buddhism which also provides this art with all its spirit and symbolic overtones." Gunasinghe (1978:7) adds: "The mural paintings we are discussing here are the visual expressions of what, therefore, should be considered the simplest religious experience of a peasant community without pretensions to higher learning and deep philosophical thought." N. B. M. Seneviratne (1965: 3) is also of the opinion that too much emphasis on how Kandyan art has an intimate kinship with the canons of Indian and ancient Sinhala artistic expression can lead to an eclipsed understanding:

> It was Ananda Coomaraswamy's intention to show how what seemed to be a stereotyped art language was the product of a long process of crystallisation and therefore full of content and meaning. Yet it can be shown that the medieval art medium had really been responsible to a number of cultural changes and was thus in important essentials perfectly dynamic and expressive of each of these changes in its cultural climate; such a justification as Coomaraswamy attempted can seem to be not much more than interesting and relevant, hardly of special importance.
>
> Once related to the spirit of each age and its world view, which would of course have been the product of an interaction between economic and political trends, of changes in social structure, and affected by movements in religion and education, each painting is better seen as a statement about contemporary life and an experience of that life by an individual artist, something that can be understood and "entered into" by others living in another age provided the world within which it came into being can be sufficiently known.

Gunasinghe and Seneviratne are challenging Coomaraswamy because of the latter's emphasis on what he called the "idealism" (stylization) of Kandyan paintings, which he juxtaposed with a simultaneously developing Indian school of "impressionism" (naturalism).[6] To follow Coomaraswamy, then, would be to regard Kandyan painting as but an extreme expression of, or but a cultural footnote to, an early form of

Indian idealistic art and religion. Such an approach could diminish its uniqueness. Further, it can lead to a misleading interpretation. In Coomaraswamy's case, it led to a non-Buddhistic *upaniṣadic* or Hinduized version of theological monism. Here is the essential outline of Coomaraswamy's argument as he presented it in his *Medieval Sinhalese Art* (1979: 169–170):

> The most essential character of Kandyan painting, as of Kandyan design in general, is its *idealism*. This idealism belongs to all Indian art; but in Kandyan art it appears in almost an extreme form. . . . Observe, for example, the trees on Pl. I on XIV., 8; these are not portraits of particular trees, but abstractions, representing the artist's generalised conception of all such trees. When I say "the artist," I do not refer to any individual, but imply the whole body of artists who together worked out the language long ago; and I say language because traditions and conventions are to the artist what words and metre are to the poet, and these no one man made. The idealism of Kandyan art is part of its inheritance from India; but as we have already observed, Kandyan art does not represent Indian art at its greatest or even a very great period, but rather Indian art at the level of a great and beautiful scheme of peasant decoration. Kandyan art as we see it represents a tradition handed down from the earliest stratum of Indian art, modified and enriched by subsequent influences but in many ways primitive. . . .
>
> This is the secret of the constancy of art forms, that the ideal form they represent is eternal and immutable, a thought in the heart of Īśvara; that is why the trees at Barahat and the trees in a Kandyan vihara are expressed by the same formula. The impulse to the expression of emotion in art, is born of the sense of the unity of all life, the recognition of the many in the one. The representation of ideal forms, the reduction of various complex appearances to their simplest terms is an expression of the desire to see the one in the many.

The argument here between these scholars is an important one, but both sides would seem to be only half right. To accept Coomarasamy's position is to capitulate to an understanding of Kīrti Śrī's expressions of Buddhism in Kandyan wall paintings as but one more example of a perennial philosophy, this one being in a Śaiva Hindu dress; for, the "Īśvara" that Coomaraswamy refers to here is an epithet for Śiva, who, for Coomaraswamy, is but a manifestation of what he regards as the timeless, absolute, sacred reality of existence that is merely qualified by culture and society when it reveals its presence in time and space.[7] To follow his interpretation is to place an unwarranted and truly speculative umbrella of religious meaning over history and to superimpose what amounts to a theological interpretation of a Theravāda tradition whose soteriology is decidedly anthropocentric and nontheological in nature. Unfortunately and with all due respect to this great scholar to whom we are all deeply indebted, it is a misplaced philosophy of religion. Philosophically, Coomaraswamy was a propounder of a popular cross-cultural view of his own time: that all religious manifestations are in reality varying expressions of one true sacred, transhistorical godhead-being. But Theravāda Buddhism, as is well known, denies the importance of God or gods in the soteriological process and reserves no ultimate ontological status for divinity. Metaphysically, this is what sets it off so clearly from Hinduism, or from other theological religious traditions as well. Furthermore, Kandyan Buddhist temple wall paintings are not illustrations of an attempt "to see the one in the many." They are various illustrations of how Buddhists have, or can, overcome the problem of suffering in *saṃsāra*, and they celebrate the various ways in which that teaching of that doctrine has been articulated and championed in the Sinhala Buddhist tradition.

On the other hand, to side entirely with N. B. M. Seneviratne is to reduce Kandyan paintings to a mere reflection of social, economic, and political conditions that affect individual artists at a given time and place—an approach that could lead to the most idiosyncratic or relativistic of interpretations. It is to ignore the obvious languages of artistic convention and religion that, undeniably, have been inherited from the traditional past. It is also to engage in a different form of reductionism: to attribute religious expression solely to what is socially expedient. While I have attributed expediency to Kīrti Śrī's motivation for undertaking religious public works, I should also recognize how the Buddhistic visual liturgy he sponsored and reformulated was also a superb distillation of an authentic Sinhalese Theravāda Buddhist world view that has been genuinely embraced by Kandyan Buddhists. By this I mean to say that the primary symbolic significance and function of these temple wall paintings is religious, and not social, economic, and political. But by "religious" I do not mean the kind of religious Esperanto that Coomaraswamy propagated, but, rather, "religious" as it was apprehended within a Sinhalese Theravāda Buddhist framework in Sri Lanka by lay and monastic adherents.

A more realistic approach to the interpretation of Kandyan temple wall paintings is to understand that they are, on the whole, a revitalized form of a classical style appropriated to express paradigmatic themes of religious meaning deemed significant or wholly relevant for their contemporary milieu. They signal a late medieval attempt to express what Buddhism has meant in the past and what it can mean to its masses of adherents in the present. Our task is to understand these paintings in relation to their two true referents: the traditional conceptual and mythic elements of Sinhalese Theravāda Buddhist cosmology that constitute an accepted normative world view; and their significance within the context of Sri Lankan Sinhalese religious experience in the eighteenth-century world of Nāyakkar rule in Kandy. These paintings also signal a late medieval apprehension of the past in their own right. In this work I need to answer fundamental questions: What were/are the fundamental elements of this Buddhist world view? And how were they experienced or "read," and by whom?

In part, the answer to this last question has already been provided: These paintings, celebrating the soteriology and history of the Sinhala Buddhist *śāsana*, were often used as objects of meditation by monastic adherents. But on the whole, they were intended for and experienced by the masses of ordinary and illiterate agrarian and service-caste village Buddhists who made simple offerings to the Buddha at their village temples. While much as been made about how veneration of the Buddha is a merit-making occasion that results in the positive accumulation of karmic benefits and better rebirth, what I want to stress is that a visit to temples also amounted to a primary occasion in which knowledge about Buddhist teachings could be imparted. Since we know that literacy was not widespread in the late medieval Kandyan village context, visual and aural apprehension was no doubt the fundamental means of gaining insight into the Buddhist world view. The narrative genre, choice of themes, and culturally stylized characterization of subjects in these paintings all played to the experience of visual imagination. The accompanying recitation for relevant texts provided an aural stimulus or cue for the orchestration of this liturgy. Hence, these paintings were designed to existentially engage, or be "read" by, the observer. Senake Bandaranayake and Gamini Jayasinghe (1986: 116), commenting on the narrative style of the *jātaka* stories that usually occupy a central focus within the total constellation of paintings that comprises this visual liturgy, note how these paintings actively engaged the pious:

> They are located in such a way—often at eye-level—that they attract immediate attention. At the same time, unlike the centralized compositions or other types of painting which can be taken in at a glance, the registers require the active participation of the observer and detailed scrutiny in the interpretation of successive scenes and the unravelling of the narrative content. . . . It is in the narrative paintings rather than the iconic or monumental compositions, that we find a greater range of variation from temple to temple. . . . In the final assessment, the narrative paintings project a very different kind of variety, liveliness and artistic expression . . . and are often more interesting and absorbing than the repetitive formula painting that we frequently encounter in iconic representations . . . Clearly they are executed by the same group of painters, employing the same vocabulary of stylization.

Coomaraswamy (1979: 167) also stresses that these paintings require the active participation of the observer if their narrative meaning is to be grasped: "The 'continuous narration' should be specially noted. In this primitive method, the same figures are repeated frequently in continuous pictures, in fresh situations revealing the progress of the story; so that the result is a panorama, where, however, the observer and the picture itself must move." He notes further (1979: 168): "The primary object is to tell an edifying story in an attractive way. The work is thus rather epic in character, [and not] artistic in the modern sense."

Before addressing the contents of these specific "edifying" stories, as well as the religio-historical symbolism of iconic representation, I also need to indicate where the Kandyan school fits in the relevant history of Buddhist art in Sri Lanka. This will provide a better grasp of how definitive Kīrti Śrī's enterprise at specific temples became for subsequent generations not only in the Kandy cultural region, but also in the western and southern littorals of the island.

The evolution of temple wall paintings in the long history of Sinhala culture in Sri Lanka has been chronicled admirably by other scholars.[8] But due to the scarcity of material evidence between the appearance of the exquisite thirteenth-century examples of classical paintings that survived at the Tivanka image house in Poḷonnaruva and the time of Kīrti Śrī's reign,[9] it is possible to offer only the very tentative conclusion that the Kandyan school of painting that erupted spectacularly in the mid-eighteenth century reflected a continuation of an earlier narrative tradition of Buddhist temple wall paintings that "runs parallel to similar developments in South and Southeast Asia" (Bandaranayake and Jayasinghe, 1986: 112). I should note, of course, that *jātakas* have been the subject of sculptural illustrations in Buddhist *stūpa* complexes from as early as the second century B.C.E. in Sanchi and Barhut in central India, and that the tradition of illustrating them, and the life of the Buddha, in stone and bronze, was also brilliantly accomplished in the eighth century C.E. in Borobudur in Indonesia and in thirteenth-century Pagan in Burma; these constituted thematic precursors later exemplified in the surviving paintings at Poḷonnaruva. It also can be noted that the *Mahāvaṃsa* (203–207) reports that Duṭṭhagāmaṇī decorated the relic chamber of the Ruvanvälisäya *thūpa* (*stūpa*) at Anurādhapura with depictions of many episodes drawn from the life of the Buddha and from the *jātakas*, including some episodes that became consistent elements of the later Kandyan Buddhist visual liturgy. These included a sculpted golden image of the Buddha seated under a bejeweled *bodhi* tree and depicted attendant *lōkapala* deities (guardians of the four directions of the world); *sat sati* (the seven weeks of reflection following the Buddha's enlightenment experience); the setting in motion of the wheel of *dhamma* (the Buddha's first public sermon, in which he enunciates the "four noble truths" and the "noble eightfold path"); the *parinibbāṇa* (the Buddha's final attainment of meditation at death); and, very significantly, the *Vessantara Jātaka*.[10] But locating firm evidence of painting subjects and styles between the thirteenth and eighteenth centuries in Sri Lanka is extremely rare and therefore makes it very difficult to come to a firm conclusion as to whether or not the Sri Lankan art I will discuss here is simply a continuation of established convention or a relatively new artistic phenomenon.[11]

Immediately before the ascension of the Nāyakkars to power, Narendra Sinha, according to the *Cūlavaṃsa* (2:242–243), had painted on two walls of the courtyard surrounding the *Daḷadā Māḷigāva*, thirty-three *jātakas*, among which are those *jātakas*, including the *Jātaka Vessantara*, that will be discussed in the next chapter. These paintings, no longer extant,[12] seem to be the only forms of evidence—and it is evidence of the indirect type—that indicate a continuing tradition of narrative or *jātaka* painting in Sri Lanka between thirteenth-century Poḷonnaruva and eighteenth-century Kandy, save for a reference to paintings observed by a German traveler (Heydt) at Mulgirigala in the Southern Province in the 1730s (Bandaranayake and Jayasinghe, 1986: 110).

The scarcity of painting evidence is due to several factors, but one stands out among them: Kīrti Śrī, his brother and successor, Rājādhi, and Vikrama Rājasinha (the infamous last of the Nāyakkar kings) rehabilitated so many temples, not only in the Kandy region but also in the Southern and Western provinces, that their coterie of painters simply covered over most of what might possibly have survived from earlier eras. In the many temples that the royally sponsored painters did not manage to refurbish, especially in the southern and western littorals, repainting by other, far less talented artists took place in the mid-nineteenth to the early-twentieth centuries. These latter paintings, in turn, though not accomplished with the same degree of aesthetic sensibility and expertise, were nonetheless inspired by the earlier eighteenth-century Kandyan style. They thoroughly emulated the choice of themes and patterns first manifested in the works of the royally sponsored artists that had worked in the up-country under Kīrti Śrī's direction. Thus, the paintings I will discuss, those which can be dated from the eighteenth-century reign of Kīrti Śrī, were genuinely paradigmatic,[13] at least until the late nineteenth century when the influence of Victorian art and other Western influences, now seen in many of the temples of the southern and western littorals, finally mark an end to the so-called Kandyan school.[14]

Reconstructing the chronology of temple wall paintings accomplished during the reign of Kīrti Śrī is no easy task, either. While some help comes from the temple *sannasa*s issued by Kīrti Śrī and his brother, in the final analysis I can speak only in the most general terms and, accordingly, will refer only to early (Mädavela), middle (Gangārāma and Ridī Vihāra), and late (Degaldoruva and Daṁbulla) phases in my discussion, following a general outline suggested by Bandaranayake and Jayasinghe (1986: 114). According to them (112):

> The early chronology of the central style is clear, from its first, dated manifestations at Madavala between 1755 and 1760, to its most complete expression at Degaldoruva in the 1770s and 1780s. What is uncertain is the precise sequence of development between these two dates and the continuations of this style during the reigns of Rajadhi Rajasinha and Sri Vikrama Rajasingha (1798–1815), both great patrons of Buddhist art and architecture. We confront this problem at Dambulla, for instance, where the paintings are generally ascribed to the time of Kirti Sri Rajasinha but display a variety of styles that may represent an evolutionary or chronological sequence extend-

> ing, possibly, from a period before Kirti Sri to the closing years of the 18th century, as well as some 19th- or 20th-century overpainting and restoration.

Though it is difficult to be precise with regard to a chronology, it would appear that Kīrti Śrī relied on a closely knit coterie of accomplished painters, almost a royal guild. In this regard, Anuradha Seneviratna (1983: 80) has also observed:

> There are a great deal of similarities between the paintings of Degaldoruwa, Gangaramaya, Ridi Viharaya, Suriyagoda, Medawela and Dambulla. In some places the same picture is found exactly the same in two places. . . . In style, technique and colour, they have so much in common that one could conclude that it was the work of a few families of Sittara artists that carried out the work in all the *vihara*s built or renovated by Kirti Sri Rajasinha in the eighteenth century.

It may have been impossible for only a few individuals to have performed the massive task of paintings in all the many temples refurbished or originally constructed under Kīrti Śrī's direction. Moreover, there are examples of various provincial styles within the Kandyan school that reflect the work of a significant number of diverse artists. My selected illustrations will also highlight the obvious differences of style employed at the same temples that Seneviratna, and Bandaranayake and Jayasinghe, have referred to. While the same theme or *jātaka* may be depicted in these various temples, their representations in different temple wall paintings were, in fact, never identical; that is, despite the existence of a guild of royally supported artists, examples of individual creativity and interpretation are clearly seen through comparisons.

The Degaldoruva *Sannasa* provides some details regarding the identity of the *sittara*s responsible for creating the wall paintings at the same temples cited by these scholars, the very same temples whose paintings I will discuss. Bandaranayake and Jayasinghe (1986: 120) provide some amplification in commenting on this *sannasa* and affirm Seneviratna's view that the temple wall paintings with which I am concerned were largely the work of the same coterie of artists:

> The painters [of Degaldoruva] were: Nilagama Patabanda, the chief layman or principal master, said to be from the village of Balavatvala and probably connected with the still existing atelier responsible for the paintings at Dambulla; Devaragampola Silvätanna Unnanse, an unordained monk, still remembered as "the best painter of his day"

and also associated with the work of Ridī Vihāra; Kosvatta Hitaranayide, thought to have painted the Sutasoma Jātaka panel. These painters and the *paramparāvas*—the lines of hereditary and pupillary descent—to which they belonged, are connected with other fairly well-known temples—such as Gangārama in Kandy, the Ridī Vihāra and Dambulla.[15]

The paintings I have selected to illustrate the emergent visual liturgy that expresses a classical Theravāda Buddhist religious world view are located at five temples: Gangārāma, Degaldoruva, Ridī Vihāra, Mädavela, and Daṁbulla; these temples are regarded as *rājamahāvihārayas*, or great royal temples. (See the map for these temple locations in up-country Sri Lanka. See the plates, "Details from the Liturgy: Wall Paintings from the Time of Kīrti Śrī.") These paintings have been chosen not only because they were done by a single guild of painters apparently under the direct supervision of Kīrti Śrī, but for several other compelling reasons as well. First, qualitatively, these paintings are the most aesthetically appealing, and, in the case of Daṁbulla, the most spectacular examples of extant Sri Lankan temple wall paintings. Second, they are the best-preserved specimens that date from Kīrti Śrī's reign. Third, because of their early dates, they functioned paradigmatically in history as models for style and content in the subsequent proliferation of the Kandyan school throughout the Sinhalese cultural regions of the island in the nineteenth century. Finally, we know from the *Cūlavaṃsa* and from Kīrti Śrī's *sannasas* that these were the very temples in which Kīrti Śrī himself took such an active personal interest in refurbishing. (For example, see the appendix to this volume, "The Religious Works of Kīrti Śrī at Gangārāma and Ridī Vihāra," which includes the *Cūlavaṃsa*'s detailed descriptions of the extensive rehabilitations undertaken by Kīrti Śrī at these two venerable monastic complexes.)

Elements of a Visual Liturgy

By "visual liturgy" I mean the articulation of a consciously contrived and coordinated set of symbolic tropes designed to encapsulate and engender meaningful religious experiences and knowledge in an engaging and formal ritual (including meditation) setting. Within the context of late medieval Sinhala Buddhism, this means the way in which religious experience in the Theravāda context was generated and understood by means of actively engaging the viewer in a cognitive apprehension of symbolic representations on the inside walls of Buddhist sanctuaries. Within these temple buildings, the figure that continuously dominates, through a seemingly endless and invasive series of guises, is that of the Buddha himself, who, for the *bhikkhu*, represents the quintessential model of religiosity that should be emulated and therefore venerated, and who, for the pious laity, is more akin to a culture hero who represents an ideal that is perhaps beyond their immediate ability to realize, but who, nevertheless, is a symbol of their own ultimate religious aspirations.

The scholarly study of Buddhist iconography, particularly of icons of the historical Buddha per se, is one of the most frequently addressed dimensions of the field of Buddhist studies and the discipline of Asian art history.[16] Specifically, there is now no shortage of illuminating inquiries focused on the historical and cultural significance of sculpted Buddha images in Sri Lanka.[17] Moreover, a French art historian, Marie Gatellier, has published a fairly comprehensive study that focuses directly on the iconography of temple wall paintings that comprise the "Kandyan school,"[18] the origins of which are contained in the temples with which I am concerned. But none of these studies is fundamentally concerned with an exegesis of religious meaning, especially how it has been expressed and experienced in the temples refurbished and reconsecrated by Kīrti Śrī.

Ostensibly, almost every trope contained in these revitalized, painted expressions of a classical Sinhalese Theravāda religious world view refers to an episode that is included in the elaborated and extended life of the Buddha and his legacy, and that has been discussed in various genres of Buddhist literature, sometimes canonical but more often otherwise. In the temple wall paintings I shall now discuss, the primary literary references that serve as sources of artistic inspiration include episodes occurring in the Pali canonical *sutta*s of the *Dīgha* and *Khuddhaka Nikāya*s of the *Suttapiṭaka*, especially the *jātaka*s and the *Buddhavaṃsa*; and events reported in the *Mahāvagga* section of the *Vinayapiṭaka*'s *Khandhaka* division. In addition to these canonical sources, other moments systematically portrayed are drawn directly from the Sinhalese monastic chronicles—the *Dīpavaṃṣa*, the *Mahāvaṃsa*, and the *Cūlavaṃsa*. Chapter 1 of the *Mahāvaṃsa*, as I shall note, seems especially important in this regard. What is accomplished by this process of literary reference is a clear linkage between the life of the Buddha per se and the continued vital history of his *śāsana* in Theravāda Buddhist Sri Lanka, the latter of which is understood as having been sustained through pious, merit-making acts of patronage that were undertaken by a long line of righteous kings, with which, in turn, Kīrti Śrī avidly sought to be identified. The general effect of the constellated paintings that comprise this visual liturgy is telescopic in nature. That is, the essence of the Buddhist teachings and of their known history in Sri Lanka is summarily localized, and thus given a sense of immediacy of time and space; it becomes instantly accessible. In citing this initial instance of a telescoping effect, I also can see that, in sponsoring the production of painted panoramas, Kīrti Śrī effectively linked his own activities and persona with the extended life of the Buddha and its heritage in Sri Lanka. That is, the traditions of the Buddha so wonderfully illustrated within these cave and wall paintings came to be immediately associated with the work of Kīrti Śrī himself. In this process, Kīrti Śrī himself came within the focus of the telescope, as did other nobles who managed to have their likenesses portrayed at *vihārayas* such as Doḍantale, Daṁbulla, and Mädavela. (See, for example, plates 1 and 2, for the eighteenth-century painted and sculptured portrayals of Kīrti Śrī at Doḍantale and Daṁbulla, respectively.) In chapter 4, I shall discuss how Kīrti Śrī indirectly seemed to further enhance his own religio-political identity through the selection of particular *jātaka* stories for illustration, especially the *Vessantara*, which, I contend, was consistently chosen to typify this king's wish to be regarded by the masses of peasant Buddhists as a *bodhisatta*-king who sacrificed all of his wealth in pursuit of the ideal of selflessness.

The earliest extant temple wall paintings that date from the reign of Kīrti Śrī, and, indeed, the earliest paintings of the Kandyan school and hence of the post-Poḷonnaruva period of Sri Lankan history, are those found at Mädavela. I have already noted the significance of the *sannasa* issued by Kīrti Śrī in 1755, in which the recently coronated Nāyakkar king appealed so dramatically to an anti-Tamil, Mahāsammatan royal discourse. (N. B. M. Seneviratne refers to all later eighteenth- and nineteenth-century paintings of the Kandyan school as being no more than "competent imitations of the Medawela technique.") From all accounts, it would seem that the paintings at Mädavela represent his first attempt to constellate a formal visual liturgy. Because of its stunning success and elegant simplicity, the painted configuration that forms a "complex cosmological symbolism . . . expressed in a remarkable combination of economy and elaboration" (Bandaranayake and Jayasinghe, 1986: 117) would seem to have become paradigmatic of Kīrti Śrī's further efforts to build, rehabilitate, and refurbish Kandyan temples. As such, the Mädavela paintings will be treated here as a beginning basis for analyzing this visual liturgy, but I shall supplement the discussion to note stylistic differences through comparisons with other temple paintings and to indicate where significant additions were made to the liturgy. My description and analysis in this chapter will culminate with a consideration of the great masterpiece of visual liturgy that was painted on the ceiling of the Mahārāja Vihāraya (cave 2) at Daṁbulla.

Bandaranayake and Jayasinghe (1986: 117) have aptly described, in general terms, the image house at Mädavela:

> A small timbered building, elevated on stone pillars, with a characteristic, double-pitched Kandyan roof and a railed, wooden balcony or elevated verandha surrounding a central, walled chamber, it represents the simplest and purest expression of Kandyan art and architecture. The chamber measures just 3.6 metres by 1.5 metres.

Directly opposite the entrance to the image house, they note (117), is an "elaborate *makara toraṇa* of carved and painted wood, in the centre of which is placed a seated Buddha image,"[19] in the standard fashion of most Kandyan image houses.[20] Bandaranayake and Jayasinghe (116) assert that the principal figures (accompanying gods) portrayed in this detailed carving are "probably denoting the four guardian gods of Sri Lanka, Saman, Upulvan (Viṣṇu), Vibhīṣana and Kataragama (Skanda)." But in examining the icons (see the spectacular plate 47 in Bandaranayake and Jayasinghe [1986: 122–123]), one finds that there are, in fact, six principal figures located in a row directly above the Buddha; four more gods above that row of six; and two more, one on each side of the Buddha, making a total of twelve. Iconographically, the absence of the usual telling motifs (colors, multiple faces, stylized *makuṭa*s [crowns], and the presence of *vāhana*s) associated with the four guardian gods they mention makes any specific identifications nearly impossible.[21] It just may be the case that the twelve figures in question represent the twelve *baṇḍāra*-class deities of a late medieval popular Kandyan cult. This would seem all the more probable if, as Bandaranayake and Jayasinghe (1986: 116) assert, "The arrangement reproduces spatial patterns and a semiology of a royal court or assembly"; as Obeyesekere (1984: 50–70) has shown, the divine pantheon of popular Kandyan cosmology was a mirror image of the fundamental power and authority structures in the Kandyan kingdom. In this case, just as the Buddha figure has a position parallel to the king, so the twelve gods parallel the twelve *disava*s (gov-

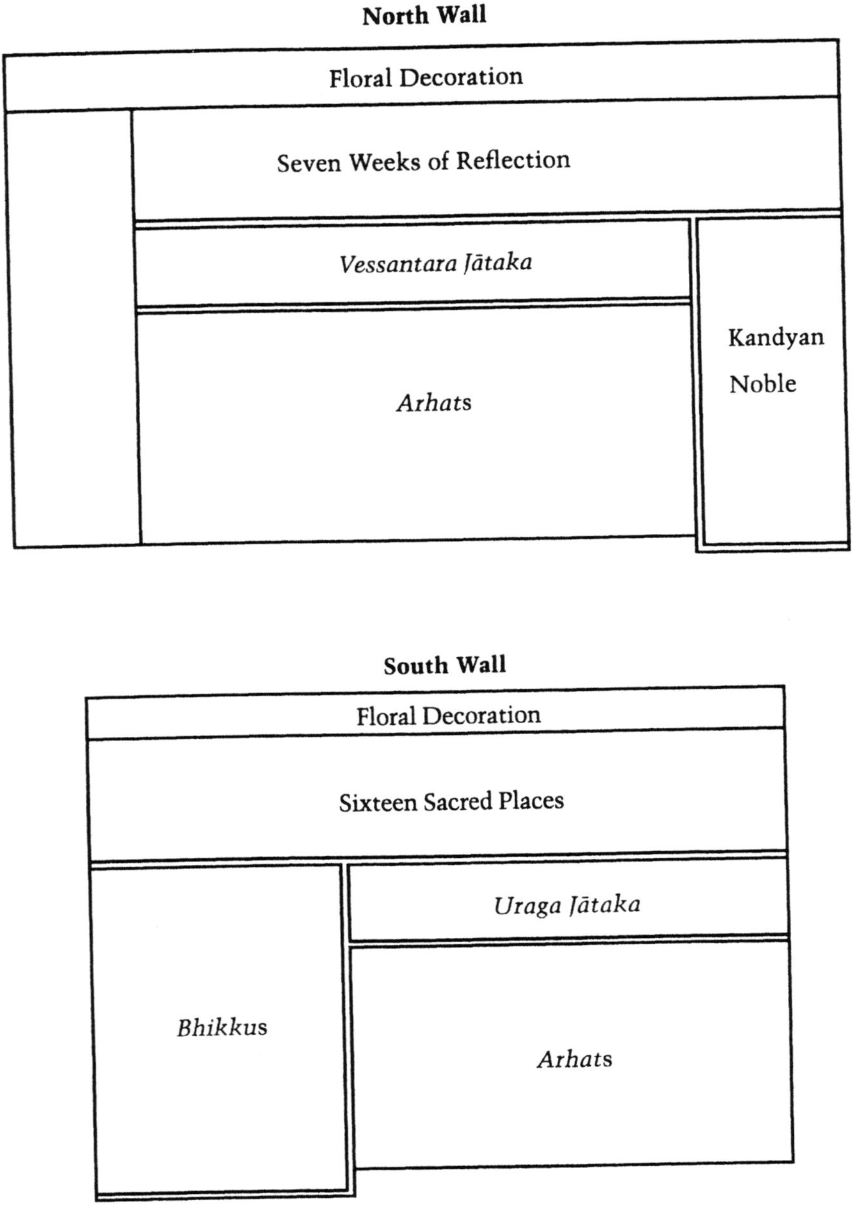

Figure 1 Image house in Mädavela; north wall (*top*) faces south wall (*bottom*).

ernors, or chiefs) who administered, on behalf of the king, the twelve districts that surrounded the boundaries of the central Kandyan district proper.

Soḷosmasthāna

While the central wood-carved *makara toraṇa* edifice can be interpreted to reflect the power structures of the socio-political world, it is the religio-historical meaning of the wall paintings that remains the focus. The wall paintings on the inside of the Mädavela image house are arranged as indicated in figure 1. The upper tier of the south wall contains the most novel constituent portion of what becomes the Kandyan visual liturgy: the *soḷosmasthāna*, or sixteen sacred places of Sri Lanka. There, at Mädavela, we find the oldest extant version of their portrayal. What they represent are the destinations of ritual pilgrimage associated with either the mythic visits of the Buddha to the island after his enlightenment experience, or the monumental efforts—usually massive *stūpa* constructions—by past great Sri Lankan kings to enshrine the Buddha's relics. The inspiration for the sixteen sacred places is drawn from the *Mahāvaṃsa* and other important textual sources, such as the *Butsāraṇa* and the *Pūjāvaḷiya*. Indeed, the *soḷosmasthāna* may be taken as shorthand for the intended function of the *Mahāvaṃsa*: to show that Sri Lanka is the island abode of the pure and true *dhamma*—predetermined by the Buddha himself—and that its kings have defended and supported that identity through their righteous efforts throughout history. The constellated *soḷosmasthāna* appear in every one of the other temples that are considered here. After their introduction at Mädavela, they became a staple element in virtually every other royally sponsored temple cave- or wall-painting project.

The *soḷosmasthāna* are usually represented in a series of register paintings. (See plate 35, which illustrates their iconic representation at Gangārāma; there, they appear as two sets of eight registers that flank the entrance to the image house, but in other image houses they may form a single unbroken linear representation, as at Mädavela.) The *soḷosmasthāna* are to be viewed in a certain order.[22] The sequence of the first eleven corresponds to the order found when they are first mentioned in the *Mahāvaṃsa*'s mythic account (3–9) of the Buddha's three magical aerial visits to the island during the course of his missionary career, after his enlightenment experience. Hence, Mahīyangana always appears first and is represented in iconographically distinct fashion: as seven *stūpas* within each other, which symbolize the number of times that the collarbone relic of the Buddha—miraculously brought to Sri Lanka by the Thera Sarabhu (a disciple of Sāriputta) after the cremation of the Buddha (*Mahāvaṃsa* 5)—has been encased throughout history, beginning with Uddhacūlābhaya, son of Devānampiya Tissa (the first of the Anurādhapura kings who were converted to Buddhism), and then followed by Duṭṭhagāmiṇi, who "was dwelling there [Mahīyangana] while he made war on the Damilas [Tamils]." Both plate 36 (a painting at Mädavela) and plate 3 (a painting at Ridī Vihāra) graphically depict Mahīyangana in a stylistically unique mode.

Because the *Mahāvaṃsa*'s account of the Buddha's three visits to the island serve as the major inspiration for much of the symbolism expressed in the *soḷosmasthāna* constellations, and because the prelude to this account expresses themes and events that are absolutely central to understanding the Kandyan visual liturgy, it is important to summarize chapter 1 of the *Mahāvaṃsa*. In the process not only am I able to account for and to illustrate the sequential appearance of eleven of the sixteen sites that constitute the *soḷosmasthāna* but also I can identify precisely the source of literary reference for most of what comes together to form the entirety of the Kandyan visual liturgy.

The *Mahāvaṃsa* (1–2) begins with its famous first paragraph that has been made known and handed down to "awaken serene joy and emotion," and it immediately proceeds to note how "the Conqueror resolved to become a Buddha, that he might release the world from evil" while he was paying homage to the previous twenty-four Buddhas and receiving "from them the prophecy of his (future) buddhahood." The Buddha's interchanges with these twenty-four Buddhas, all listed serially in the *Mahāvaṃsa*, are referred to collectively as *sūvisi vivaraṇa*, and their artistic portrayal comprises another central ingredient of the visual liturgy.[23] So do the following episodes, which, in the *Mahāvaṃsa*'s narrative (2–3), are inserted just before the account of the Buddha's three visits to Lanka: the seven weeks of meditation that the Buddha engaged in immediately after his enlightenment, pictorially portrayed in temple wall paintings as *sat sati*; his "rolling of the wheel of law" (his first sermon: *Dhammacakkappavattana*) at Benares, also frequently given a central place in the liturgy; and the conversion of his first disciples (first five and then sixty). I will illustrate how each of these events is depicted in the relevant temple wall and cave paintings that constitute this visual liturgy, after my discussion of the *soḷosmasthāna* is concluded.

The *Mahāvaṃsa*'s description (3–5) of the Buddha's sacralizing visit to Mahīyangana is fraught with symbolism. In the ninth month that followed his enlightenment, during a great sacrificial gathering of ascetics, the Buddha "set forth for the isle of Lanka, to win [or purify] Lanka for the faith" (3). Knowing that *yakkhas* (demons) were holding a gathering of their own at the Mahānāga garden, the Buddha, magically "hovering in the air over their heads, at the place of the (future) Mahīyangana-thupa, . . . struck terror to their hearts by rain, storm, darkness and so forth" (3–4). The *yakkhas* ask to be released from their terror, and the Buddha obliges when given a place to sit. The Buddha then causes a ring of flames to surround his seat, thereby terrifying the *yakkhas* again, and then, through his magical power, moves the island known as Giridipa into proximity. The *yakkhas* are then settled on this island and the island then is made to return to its original place somewhere off in the far regions of the sea. The *yakkhas* have departed Lanka. Gods then assemble, the Buddha preaches the *dhamma* to them, and they are converted, take refuge, and vow to keep the precepts. Buddhism has a home, a purified, safe place where it may thrive.

There are at least two levels of related interpretation that are notable, in addition to the *Mahāvaṃsa*'s own ostensible intention to identify Lanka as the purified abode in which the *dhamma* of the Buddha will thrive. In the first instance, this story, along with the stories of his next two visits, might be read as a civilizing myth wherein the Buddha and his actions can be construed as symbols for the eviction or domestication of the aboriginal peoples on the island—the establishment of moral order. The eviction of the *yakkhas* may also serve as a harbinger of the manner in which the Tamils will later be regarded in the *Mahāvaṃsa* (Clifford, 1978: 43). Alternatively, the story may be read in such a way that the *yakkhas* represent the fears of the mind that are finally displaced or quelled once the pacifying and purifying *dhamma* of the Buddha is made known. In this instance, Lanka itself represents the mental field of the religious adherent, and the departure of the demons represents the overcoming of fear and malevolence.

The second visit of the Buddha to Lanka is very similar to the first in plot, scope, and meaning. The events it describes are alleged to have occurred during the fifth year after his enlightenment experience, when the Buddha, in his mind's eye, "saw that a war, caused by a gem-set throne, was like to come to pass between the *nāga*s Mahodara and Cūlodara, uncle and nephew, and their followers" (*Mahāvaṃsa* 6). The Buddha, again by means of his magical aerial power, alights on Nāgadīpa (the site of the conflict), preaches the *dhamma*, and converts both royal *nāga*s, who, in turn, offer up their throne in giving thanks to the Buddha. While this myth may also express the same historical memories of the process of establishing moral order on the island, through the Buddhist civilization, and/or the domestication of its pre-Buddhist inhabitants, it also makes the key point that the true kingship of this island (symbolized by the throne) has been dedicated to the Buddha, thereby foreshadowing a long tradition of Sinhala kings who would project their intentions of gaining future Buddhahood as *bodhisatta*s.

The second visit of the Buddha to Lanka blends into the account of his third: The uncle of the *nāga* Mahodara is Maṇiakkhika of Kälaṇiya, one of the many converted *nāga*s, who invites the Buddha and the *sangha* to be honored at a feast at Kälaṇiya,[24] some three years after the occasion of his second visit; the feast is held on the Vesak full-moon day. This account in the *Mahāvaṃsa* (8–9) then proceeds to describe how the Buddha, after his Kälaṇiya visit, sanctified many other sites on the island by his presence:

> When the Teacher, compassionate to the whole world, had preached the doctrine there, he rose, the Master, and left the traces of his footsteps plain to sight on Sumanakūṭa. And after he had spent the day as it pleased him at the foot of this mountain, with the brotherhood, he set forth for Dīghavāpi. And there the Master seated himself with the brotherhood at the place where the cetiya (thereafter) stood, and gave himself up to meditation to consecrate the spot. Then arose the great sage from that place, and knowing well which places were fit and which unfit, he went to the place of the (later) Mahāmegha-vanārāma. After he had seated himself with his disciples at the place, where the sacred Bodhi-tree came afterwards to be, the Master gave himself up to meditation; and likewise there where the Great thūpa stood (in later days) and where (afterwards) the thupa in the Thūpārama stood. Then when he rose up from meditation he went to the place of the (later) Silācetiya, and after the Leader of the assembly (of bhikkhus) had uttered exhortation to the assembly of devas, he, the Enlightened, who has trodden all the paths of enlightenment, returned thence to Jetavana.

In this manner, the fifth-century C.E. *Mahāvaṃsa* refers to eleven of the sixteen sacred places precisely in the order in which they always appear in the *soḷosmasthāna* constellations in eighteenth-century temple wall and cave paintings. Following the depiction of the Mahīyangana *stūpa*s encased within each other, the *soḷosmasthāna* then include representations of the *stūpa*s at Nāgadīpa and Kälaṇiya. These two *stūpa*s that symbolize Nāgadīpa and Kälaṇiya are, stylistically, the same as the *stūpa*s used to symbolize the Great Stūpa (Ruvanvälisäya), Thūpārāma, Silācetiya, and Jetavana (all located in or near Anurādhapura), and Dīghavāpi. The five remaining sacred sites of the *soḷosmasthāna* that are symbolized by *stūpa*s are Abhyagiriya and Mirisaväti (both in Anurādhapura), Tissamahārāma, Mutīyangana (in Badulla, and Kiri Vehera (in Kataragama). (See the map.) These are also rendered indistinctly. The only way to identify any of them is to know their order of appearance in the *Mahāvaṃsa*, or, more likely, to know them from a *vandanagāthā* (pilgrimage song).

The other three sites, Śrī Mahābodhi in Anurādhapura, Śrī Pāda (Sumanakūṭa, or Adam's Peak), and Divyāguhā, especially the last two, have been the subject of much artistic license. Plate 37 (a painting at Mädavela), illustrates how the Buddha's foot has left an imprint on top of the mountain. Plate 38 contains a painting at Ridī Vihāra that combines Śri Pāda with Divyāguhā. There, Saman (Sumana Deviyo), the god of the mountain, is seen worshiping the Buddha's footprint, as is the wont of pilgrims today, while Divyāguhā is represented in the lower left portion by curtains that shielded the Buddha during his restful midday sleep.

What remains in this discussion of *soḷosmasthāna* is to account for the textual or historical sources of those places not accounted for in the first chapter of the *Mahāvaṃsa*. Mutīyangana derives its sanctity from the fact that it is mentioned in the *Samantapāsādikā*, also a fifth-century C.E. text and therefore contemporaneous with the *Mahāvaṃsa*, as yet one more place that the Buddha visited after his feting at Kälaniya. There is also a tradition that Devānaṃpiya Tissa, the first of the Buddhist Anurādhapura kings, who was converted to Buddhism by Aśoka's *bhikkhu* son Mahinda, built a *stūpa* on this site to commemorate the Buddha's visit (Gatellier, 1991: 1:218). The building of the Mirisaväti *stūpa* in Anurādhapura, allegedly in the second-century B.C.E. by the warrior-king Duṭṭhagāmiṇī, whose own image was commissioned by Kīrti Śrī to be sculpted (or resculpted) at Ridī Vihāra in the eighteenth century, is described in the *Mahāvaṃsa* (170–181); its construction was commenced when, after the Tamils and their own great king Eḷāra had been defeated, Duṭṭhagāmiṇī declared that the building of the *stūpa* was a merit-making act to expiate his actions that had resulted from war. Building the *stūpa* in Tissamahārāma, by King Kākavaṇṇatissa, is mentioned in passing within the *Mahāvaṃsa*'s account (148) of Duṭṭhagāmiṇī's birth. Abhayagiriya, in Anurādhapura, according to the *Mahāvaṃsa* (232–235), was built by King Vaṭṭagāmaṇī (the same king responsible for the foundations of Mädavela, according to the temple's *sannasa*) after he had returned from exile. Jain ascetics who were unsympathetic to Vaṭṭagāmaṇī had been occupying the site on which this great *stūpa* and monastic complex were eventually built. Finally, Kiri Vehera, in Kataragama, is adjacent to an ancient seat of the cult of Skanda (Śiva's son in Hindu myth and perhaps the most important deity in the Tamil Śaivite religious culture). Kataragama is first mentioned in the *Mahāvaṃsa* (132) as a site at which one of the saplings of Śrī Mahābodhi was distributed after its arrival with Mahinda. Tradition holds (Gatellier, 1991: 1:222) that the *stūpa* dates from this time. The *Cūlavaṃsa* (1:93) says that a prince by the name of Aggabodhi, who ruled over Rohana, constructed a monastic *vihāraya* at this site in the seventh-century C.E.

Further comments regarding the sacred sites that comprise the *soḷosmasthāna* are in order. Apart from the eleven sites associated with the visits of the Buddha in the *Mahāvaṃsa*, all of the remaining sites are understood as having achieved their fame as the result of great *stūpa*-building by pious kings. Indeed, virtually all of the sixteen sites are associated with kingship, as all eleven mentioned in the accounts of the Buddha's visits were later venues for the construction of *stūpa*s or other forms of royal patronage. More specifically, I have already noted how Kīrti Śrī, in his campaign to revive the *śāsana* by making a pilgrimage to sacred sites, revoked the license of Śaivite Brahmans to operate their ritual trade at Śrī Pāda and restored the sacred places at Anurādhapura. In addition, Mirisaväti, Ruvanvälisäya, and Abhyagiriya are all associated with stories in which Buddhist kings defeat Tamil forces to reestablish Lanka as the abode of the Buddha's *dhamma*, reminiscent of the mythic pattern first established in the *Mahāvaṃsa* when the Buddha drives the *yakkha*s from the island. I have noted how this penchant for depicting enemies was also applied to the Dutch in eighteenth-century Kandy.

Finally, the geographical distribution of the sixteen sacred places, though concentrated in Anurādhapura (which contains five, or six if nearby Silācetiya at Mihintale is counted), ensures that pilgrimage sites of sacred renown are distributed in virtually every region of the island (see the map). There could be two reasons for this. The first is that such a distribution ensured accessibility for Buddhists living all over the island; sacred places of pilgrimage are thus always near. The second is that, because of their association with royal support, the *soḷosmasthāna* collectively symbolize religio-political overlordship in each region of the island.

Sat Sati

Having explored some vicissitudes of myth and symbolism associated with the *soḷosmasthāna*, I will again discuss the Mädavela image house, where, on the south wall, directly opposite the *soḷosmasthāna* depiction on the north wall and occupying the same parallel space in juxtaposition, is the *sat sati* (see figure 1): an artistic rendering of the seven weeks of reflective meditation engaged in by the Buddha following his enlightenment experience. During this time, the Buddha is said to have pondered the implications of his newly discovered enlightened state, the profundity of the four noble truths, and whether or not he should try to propagate a *dhamma* so rare and perhaps too difficult for others to understand. We have already noted the passing reference to *sat sati* in the *Mahāvaṃsa*'s first-chapter account of the Buddha's three visits; there, the reference is given with no details. The original literary reference made is probably to the postenlightenment account of the Buddha's activities that is given in the *Mahāvagga* of the *Vinayapiṭaka*, which was later embellished in the *Nidāna Kathā*.

In describing, week by week, this critical forty-nine-day period in the life of the Buddha, I can note the crucial moments reflected distinctively in temple wall paintings at Mädavela and the other early Kandyan school venues.

The Buddha spent the first week of his postenlightenment experience by reflecting on the profundity of his discovery. He is almost always depicted in stylized fashion under a pipal (*ficus religosa*) tree in a manner not very different from the way his enlightenment itself is usually depicted. In plate 4 (a painting at Mädavela), his hand is raised in the *vitarka mudrā* position, which distinguishes this portrayal from the *samādhi* (meditational) pose normally used in enlightenment characterizations.

More dramatic iconographic variation occurs in the portrayal of the second week, when the Buddha first elevates himself to assure the gods, particularly Brahma, that he has decided to make the *dhamma* known. Plate 5 (a painting at Gangārāma) reflects this moment in utter simplicity: The Buddha is posed with his begging bowl, suggesting his decision to embark on a *dhamma* tour, as Brahma looks on, rejoicing at just having heard about the Buddha's decision to preach.[25] But plate 39 (a painting at Ridī Vihāra) illustrates the other event of the second week: how the Buddha returned to gaze in wonderment at the *bodhi* tree underneath which he had gained his enlightened insight. The *mudrā* here is exceptional. Within the iconographic world of Sri Lankan painting and sculpture, it is found only in portrayals of the second week of the *sat sati*, except for its puzzling use in the monumental standing figure overlooking the reclining Buddha in the magnificent rock-hewn sculptures at Gal Vihāra in Poḷonnaruva.

During the third and fourth weeks, the Buddha engaged in a meditational walk between the place where he had been meditating the week before and the *bodhi* tree, before taking his rest in the *ratanaghara* (jeweled-throne) shrine.

In the fifth week, under the *ajapāla* tree, an event occurs that is the most dramatically rendered episode of the *sat sati*. Māra, the lord of death, who had been defeated earlier by the Buddha during the night of his enlightenment experience, returns with his three daughters (named Discontent/Depression, Delight/Lust, and Thirst/Craving) to attempt, one last time, to seduce the Buddha. The defeat of Māra (*māra yuddhaya*) on the night of the Buddha's enlightenment became a favorite episode depicted by the artists who worked in these temples, as it allowed them the greatest degree of creative expression. Within the context of the *sat sati*, this is also the case. Plate 40 (a painting at Daṁbulla) reflects its most exquisite stylization and its most creative rendition. It is interesting to note that at Daṁbulla Māra's three daughters would seem to appear no less than six times as a trio,[26] each trio being roughly separated by stylized clouds, which, in the conventional language of Kandyan-school paintings, usually demarcate the boundaries between the various realms of *samsara*. It may be possible that the artist was seeking to symbolize the fact that the three mental conditions represented by the daughters' names are present in all conditioned realms of being. The banishment of the conditions is symbolized in all three paintings by the *samādhi* pose of the Buddha, who remains thoroughly undistracted.

Plate 41 (a painting at Daṁbulla) shows the Buddha's being sheltered by the *nāga*-king Muchalinda, who protected him from a storm that consisted of rain, lightning, and thunder, sent by Māra to distract the Buddha from his clarification pursuit.

Finally, during the seventh week, a deity appeared to two traveling merchants, Tapussa and Bhallika, and pointed out the figure of the Buddha, who was then meditating under the *bodhi* tree again. Plates 6, 7, and 42 (paintings at Ridī Vihāra and Daṁbulla) illustrate this scene. The merchants present an offering of food while the four *lōkapāla* guardian deities of the four directions are seen providing bowls for the Buddha to accept food; he has said that he is "thus come" (*tathāgata*), which, according to tradition, means he is not allowed to accept food with his hands (plate 7 shows a close-up of the *lōkapāla* at Daṁbulla). At first, the Buddha refuses their gesture, but the divinities point out that in the future he will need to have some means of accepting food from ordinary human beings. So he acquiesces and takes his nourishment. What follows, then, is symbolically very significant. The Buddha proceeds to preach for the first time and converts the two merchants, who become his first followers and then take refuge in the Buddha and the *dhamma*.[27] He then offers them hair and nail relics.[28] What can be seen in this simple sequence of events is the basic outline of the relationship between the Buddha, his *sangha*, and the laity, which will become normative throughout Buddhist tradition. In exchange for food and material support, the *sangha,* in this case the Buddha, preaches the *dhamma*. The laity in turn venerates the Buddha by honoring his presence, as symbolized by relics encased in *stūpa*s. It is also worth noting that in the *Vinayapiṭaka*'s *Mahāvagga* account, the Buddha preaches two different kinds of sermons, one for the laity and one for prospective monks. In the first, for the laity, he preaches about the merit derived from morally virtuous actions and gift giving that lead to a favorable rebirth. This is the sermon he preaches to Tapussa and Bhallika. In the second, for the monks, he presents the "four noble truths" and the "noble eightfold path" that lead to *nibbāṇa*. This story, therefore, articulates the nature of the symbiotic relationship that will obtain between monk and layman and also clarifies relative and ultimate soteriological aspirations (favorable rebirth and *nibbāṇa*).

I will conclude my discussion of the elements that constitute the visual liturgy of Kandyan temple wall paintings, as it was first expressed at Mädavela, by briefly pointing out the three remaining constituents of the paintings there. First, the north and south walls of the Mädavela image house contain, at the same level (see figure 1) and in symmetrical juxtaposition to one another, illustrations of *jātaka* stories—in this case, the *Uraga Jātaka* on the south wall and the *Vessantara Jātaka* on the north. As I have indicated earlier in this chapter, the paintings of the narrative *jātaka* stories are the most engaging constituent of the liturgy. In the next chapter, I shall closely examine the didactic function of these paintings, along with those *jātaka*s that appeared on the temple walls of Degaldoruva in the later phase of work accomplished during Kīrti Śrī's reign. The second remaining constituents expressed at Mädavela is the stylized characterization of *arhat*s and *bhikkhu*s. What is curious about Mädavela is that while the *arhat*s are conspicuously portrayed, there are no references to the Buddha's career of preaching *dhamma*, apart from the *sat sati* portrayal of his conversion of the two merchants, Tapussa and Bhallika. In addition, the portrayal of his first sermon, given at Deer Park to his five former ascetic companions who became *arhat*s, is also missing. Also, there are no renditions of the twenty-four previous Buddhas, the other element incorporated from the formulaic *Mahāvaṃsa* prelude to the Buddha's three visits to Lanka. But what is included is a third element, which also became a standard feature of the Kandyan visual liturgy: a ceiling painting of the next Buddha-to-be, Bodhisatta Metteyya. (See plate 43 for the manner in which Metteyya is portrayed [in Tusita heaven, preaching the *dhamma*] at Daṁbulla, cave 3.)[29]

The paintings at Mädavela are stunning in their simplicity and economy. They laid the basis for the development of a more expansive liturgy painted on the walls of temples in the so-called middle and later phases of art work during Kīrti Śrī's reign. The directions that this expansion took are seen in the elements that were introduced at Ridī Vihāra, Gangārāma, Degaldoruva, and Daṁbulla.

Ridī Vihāra contains wall paintings that depict both the twenty-four Buddhas and the preaching of the first sermon. So does Gangārāma. These would seem to be the first temples to have completed the fundamental liturgical constellation, based largely on the first chapter of the *Mahāvaṃsa* and other sources. In fact, the five converts who became the first five *arhat*s of the Buddhist *sangha* are shown in two different paintings at Ridī Vihāra (see plates 8 and 9). Stylistically, *arhat*s are distinguishable from *bhikkhu*s in that their heads are always silhouetted with a halo.

Sūvisi vivaraṇa

With regard to the twenty-four Buddhas, another interesting phenomenon begins to appear at Ridī Vihāra. One finds not only the twenty-four Buddhas and attendant figures that represent the Buddha in various guises (see, for example, plate 10, a Degaldoruva painting, in which the Buddha appears, during his rebirth, as a lion to receive his prophecy),[30] but also veritable fields of Buddhas inaugurated in what later comes to be known as the thousand-Buddhas motif. Plates 44 and 11 illustrate how this motif was stylized at Gangārāma and Daṁbulla, respectively. The symbolic function and religious meaning of the twenty-four Buddhas are clear: to express the truth of the Buddha's *dhamma* and the path to *nibbāṇa* as being cosmologically normative for all known time and space; the suggestion is that these truths of existence and this method of spiritual attainment are ontologically intrinsic to the way in which things really are and always have been.[31] But what is the meaning of the thousand-Buddhas motif?

There is no canonical basis for this representation, nor is it discussed in the monastic chronicles except in a reference to its illustration. So unlike the other elements that became part of the visual liturgy, I cannot regard it as having textual origins. It is certainly not a part of orthodox Theravāda doctrine and seems more reminiscent of the Mahāyāna imagination. Whatever its origins, I am more interested in its effect. Is it but an extension of the meaning of the twenty-four Buddhas that is designed to create a sense of truth (symbolized by the Buddhas) that is eternally realized? That is, is it designed to create the sensation that all space is ultimately filled with the reality that the Buddha has come to represent? While the thousand-Buddhas theme may share in the cosmological symbolism evident in the representations of the twenty-four Buddhas, its sensational effect on the meditative beholder may be even more spectacular. Representations of the thousand-Buddhas theme are basically iconic in character, without any narrative content, except for the possibility that they might refer to an episode in the *Pūjāvaḷiya* where the Buddha miraculously multiplies his presence to demonstrate his wondrous powers.[32] They do not constitute a story, and therefore are probably not aimed at cultivating a cognitive or intellectual awareness. Rather, they seem designed to produce a psychological or spiritual state—either emotional (a sense of joy or well-being) or beyond emotions (an equilibrium).[33] In either case, the thousand Buddhas would appear to be objects of meditation par excellence. Unlike the narrative tropes I have already discussed, which form related pieces of visual liturgy for the benefit of both monks and the laity, the thousand-Buddhas theme would seem to be a device for serious-minded monastic meditators. Their appearance in these temple wall and cave paintings may very well signal the revival of the meditation practice in the *sangha*—a finding not so surprising when we remember that virtually all forms of Buddhist practice seem to have been revitalized during the reign of Kīrti Śrī, including *vipāssana* meditation.

Buddhacārita

At the same time that the thousand Buddhas were making their first appearances in Kandyan temples, the practice of illustrating the *Buddhacārita* (life of the Buddha), also seems to have been revived. At Mädavela, the life of the Buddha, except for his *jātaka* rebirths and the *sat sati*, was not represented at all. At Gangārāma and later at Daṁbulla, it receives a full and detailed treatment. Plate 45 (a Gangārāma painting) represents just a small number of the events that form the Buddha's career of preaching *dhamma* following his enlightenment. Plate 46 (also a Gangārāma painting) shows the return of the Buddha's horse, Channaka, after failed entreaties had been made by representatives of his father's (the king's) court to get him to reconsider and return to the royal palace, following his great renunciation. Specific events of the *Buddhacarita* are then represented in detail at both of these temple venues, including spectacular illustrations of his defeat of Māra (the *Māra yuddhaya*) on the night of his enlightenment experience. This becomes a scene that is almost always repeated in wall paintings of the Kandyan school. Plate 47 (a Gangārāma painting) illustrates Māra and elements of his army as they are attacking the Buddha in an effort to prevent his enlightenment. Plate 12 shows the same theme at Daṁbulla. It is worth noting that in the Daṁbulla portrayal, Māra's army consists of *yakkha*s and *nāga*s, precisely the same mythological creatures he defeats in the *Mahāvaṃsa*'s first chapter. The most spectacular illustrations of this favorite scene are found on the ceilings of the caves at Daṁbulla (cave 2) and Degaldoruva.[34] In plate 13 (a Degaldoruva portrayal) Bhū Devi, the earth goddess, responds to the Buddha's touching of the earth as his witness to Māra's defeat. Plate 14 (a Daṁbulla portrayal) depicts just a few from the pantheon of deities that attended the Buddha's first sermon at Deer Park in Sarnath, when he converted his first disciples.[35]

In the middle (Gangārāma) and later (Daṁbulla and Degaldoruva) phases of painting during the reign of Kīrti Śrī, events from the *Buddhacarita* proliferated. For instance, plate 15 (a Gangārāma painting) and plate 16 (a Daṁbulla painting) show the conversion of one of the Buddha's two chief disciples (Moggallānna) and the Buddha's final *parinibbāṇa* under the two sal trees at Kapilavatthu, respectively. In the paintings at Gangārāma, I can note two further developments. The first is the presence of rectangular blocks of white paint that, at one time, served as background contrast for brief Sinhala explanations for accompanying scenes (see plate 17, for example). This convention was subsequently utilized at many other Kandyan and low-country venues, including Degaldoruva and Lankatilaka. Second, from this expanded treatment of the *Buddhacārita*, especially at Gangārāma, it can be seen that Kīrti Śrī's artists drew inspirations for their subjects from the local Kandyan culture that surrounded them. The manner of dress given to sixth-century B.C.E. noblemen (see plate 18), laymen (see plate 19), and laywomen (see plate 17) at Kapilavastu (North India) in the Gangārāma linear paintings that form part of the *Buddhacārita* is distinctively and classically Kandyan in style.

The Liturgical Extension at Daṁbulla

The *sūvisi vivaraṇa* (twenty-four Buddhas), the elaborated thousand-Buddhas motif, the *sat sati* (seven weeks of reflective meditation after the Buddha's enlightenment), the *Buddhacārita* (life of the Buddha), and the *soḷosmasthāna* (sixteen sacred places of Sri Lanka) had been established as constituent forms of the Kandyan visual liturgy by the time of Kīrti Śrī's efforts to repaint the famous Daṁbulla caves, a massive undertaking in its own right. The sheer magnitude of space that could be utilized in the Mahārāja *lena* (cave 2) afforded his artists an opportunity to complete a project wherein a definitive statement could be made regarding the essential conceptions of Buddhist thought and the history of Buddhist tradition. All of the major elements that I have noted and discussed above were included in this expansive project. The added elements were painted in order to amplify or provide more detail for the trajectory of this liturgy, particularly with regard to those elements that depicted the *Buddhacārita* and the mythic/historical memory compiled in the *Mahāvaṃsa* or such other sources as the *Mahābodhivaṃsa*, the *Thūpavaṃsa*, and the *Pūjāvaliya*. Sequentially, these additions not only increase the number of important moments of the liturgy, but they also stretch the time frame. Specifically, the additional scenes portrayed in cave 2 at Daṁbulla include renderings of the Buddha as a *bodhisatta* in

Tuṣita heaven before his final birth as Siddhārtha; the forty-five rain-retreat seasons (*vassa*) that the Buddha and his *sangha* experienced during the Buddha's forty-five-year career of preaching *dhamma*;[36] the enshrinement of the Buddha's relics, following his death, in eight *stūpas* erected by the eight republican clans in the northern India of his day (see plate 48); the convocation of the *sangha*'s First Buddhist Council, after the death of the Buddha, to settle on a canonical version of the Buddha's teaching; the *Mahāvaṃsa*'s story of King Vijaya and the arrival of the prototypical Sinhalese from North India; the moments surrounding the beginnings of Buddhism in Anurādhapura; and King Duṭṭhagāmiṇī's epic victory over the Tamil King Eḷāra. With these additions, the process of telescoping becomes ever more detailed and intensified. In particular, I want to focus on the paintings that comprise a brilliantly executed constellated mural that has the beginnings of Buddhism in Anurādhapura as its principal theme, for the moments depicted by the mural become the most paradigmatic for the subsequent evolution of public cultic life in Buddhist Sri Lanka.

Several important moments are indeed illustrated in the mural that depicts the advent of Buddhas at Daṁbulla,[37] including the conversion of Devānaṃpiya Tissa by Mahinda at the future site of the cultic complex of modern Mihintale (including Ambatthala Cetiyagiri and nearby Silācetiya), Mahinda's preaching of the *Petavatthu* (stories of the departed); the plowing of the *sīmā*, or monastic boundaries for the establishment of the Mahāvihāra (orthodox Theravāda) *sangha* (see plate 20); the bringing of the *bodhi* sapling (see plate 21); and the enshrinement of relics in the *Thūpārāma* (see plate 22), the first *stūpa* that was constructed in Sri Lanka (according to the *Mahāvaṃsa*). All of these moments, of course, are roundly celebrated in the *Mahāvaṃsa* and other literary sources I have mentioned. I single them out at this point in the discussion to underscore the link in mythical/historical memory that they supply in terms of portraying the beginnings of Buddhist kingship and the institutional life of the *sangha* and because they really do symbolize the origins of cultic life as they were articulated in every Buddhist *vihāraya* during the eighteenth-century reign of Kīrti Śrī, and as expressed today in the Sri Lankan Sinhala Buddhist culture. Specifically, the *stūpa*, the Buddha image, the *bodhi* tree, and the *sīmā* are the primary symbols of the *śāsana*'s (Buddhist tradition's) *triratna* (triple-gem: Buddha, *dhamma*, and *sangha*). That is, the *stūpa*, perhaps more so than the Buddha image, has become the symbol par excellence of the

Buddha's continuing presence in Sri Lanka; the *bodhi* symbolizes his *dhamma*; and the consecrated *sīmā* refers to the sacralized space of the *sangha*'s activities. A Buddhist *vihāraya* is not truly a Buddhist *vihāraya* without all four. They remain the bedrocks of cultic life in the Sinhala Buddhist temple culture.

Summary

To summarize, I want to emphasize what I see as the major function of the visual liturgy by Kandyan temple wall paintings, and, in the process, to again note its telescoping effect. I will proceed not in terms of the historical appearance or development of these constellated works, but, rather, will seek to interpret the liturgy as it unfolds in its completed state.

In entering a Kandyan temple, one is overwhelmed by repetitive representations of the Buddha, especially if the thousand-Buddhas motif or *sūvisi vivaraṇa* have been invoked. Whether or not the effect was intended for monastic meditators or not, the consequence is an awareness of the Buddha's presence or of the cosmic reality he symbolizes ad infinitum. The expressions of the Buddha's truth seem limitless, only to be interrupted by its particularization in time and space, which is the function of the remaining motifs of the liturgy, beginning with the moments that constitute the *Buddhacārita*. In the *Buddhacārita* and *sat sati* depictions, the Buddha's temporal realization of enlightened truth (made possible through his conquering of the lord of death [Māra]) and his decision to disseminate this truth (turned into concrete action by his conversions of Tapussa and Bhallika) introduce the reality of this truth into this world's time and space. The *soḷosmasthāna* and the more detailed depictions that appear at Daṁbulla link this truth directly to the vicissitudes of historical perceptions of Sinhalese Buddhist kingship and civilization in Sri Lanka. The telescoping effect is simply this: from infinite cosmic reality to Lankan temporal history, and finally to the existential context of the observer.

But there is one other element of the liturgy that we have not yet specifically addressed in detailed fashion: the *jātaka*s. If we were to follow an interpretation of this liturgy based solely on a sequential or temporal framework, the *jātaka* paintings would form a unit that would precede the *Buddhacārita* because, ostensibly, they relate the anterior lives of the Buddha as a *bodhisatta*, before his final birth as Gotama

Siddhārtha. That may indeed be a valid way to proceed. But the centrality that the *jātaka*s are accorded in the temples refurbished during Kīrti Śrī's time and in the temples that contain the proliferated Kandyan school of art in the nineteenth and twentieth centuries, indicates that another approach is warranted.

Each of the scholars who (as I have noted earlier in this chapter) has studied the paintings of the Kandyan school rightly observes that the *jātaka* portrayals are the most engaging paintings of the lot. This is not just because they often occupy a central eye-level space, but chiefly because they are didactic narratives about how the path of *dhamma* is to engage the nonmonastic layman who has not yet renounced the world. Indeed, *jātaka* literature remains the most popular religious literature in Theravāda Buddhist societies today. It is the most accessible form of the Buddha's teachings and the most fundamental to understand. In a way, *jātaka*s are the literary corollary to the style of Kandyan school paintings. In short, they were, and continue to be, existentially engaging to the masses of agrarian-based Buddhist folk. That is, the *jātaka*s afford an opportunity for the telescope to train its focus on the religious possibilities for these particular people.

Furthermore, within the last series of stories that comprise *jātaka* literature, the *bodhisatta* is reborn as a king, a fact that probably made these stories very appealing to kings like Kīrti Śrī, whose endeavors were aimed at training the telescope on himself. It is to a discussion of the *jātaka* paintings extant at Mädavela and Degaldoruva that I will turn my own attention in chapter 5.

Details of the Liturgy: Wall Paintings from the Time of Kīrti Śrī

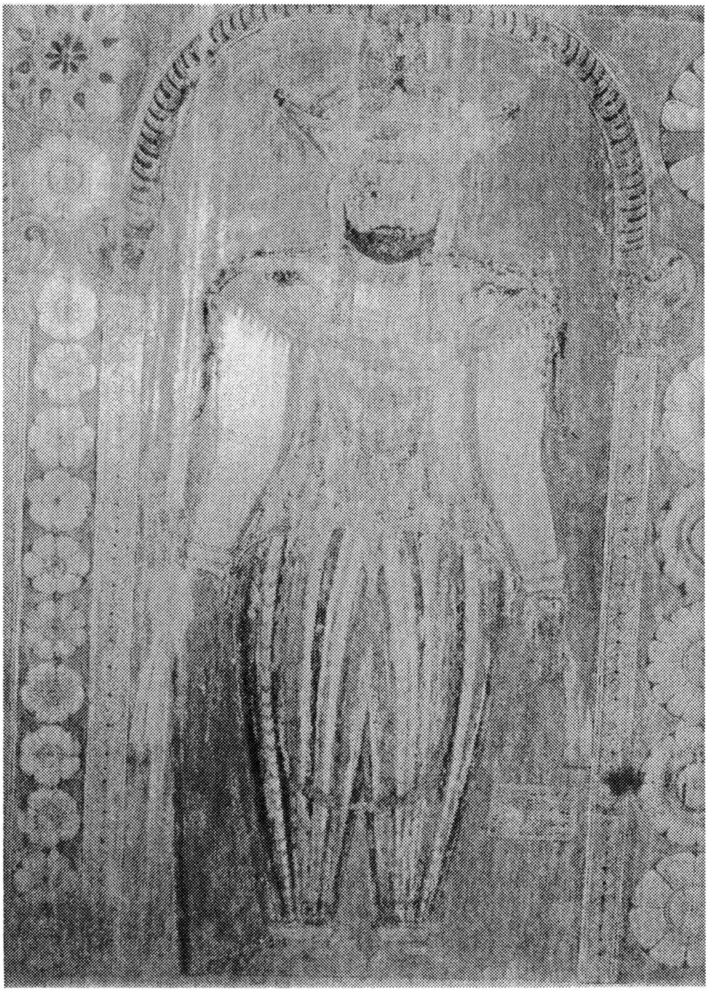

Plate 1. This portrait of Kīrti Śrī is on a wall of the *buduge* (shrine room for venerating the Buddha) at Dodaṇtale. Late eighteenth century. 54″ × 30″.

Plate 2. This free-standing painted stucco-and-rock sculpture of Kīrti Śrī is in the southwest corner of cave 3 at Daṁbulla. Late eighteenth century. 70˝ in height.

The *Soḷosmasthāna* Mural

Plate 3. These *stūpas* within *stūpas* symbolize the reliquary at Mahīyaṇgana (the first of the sixteen sacred places), mentioned in mythic accounts of the Buddha's visits to Sri Lanka. An upper *buduge* wall at Ridī Vihāra, within a section of the *soḷosmasthāna* mural; late eighteenth century. 9″ × 13″.

Sat Sati Depictions

Plate 4. The Buddha, in *vitarka mudrā*, is sitting under the *bodhi* tree during his first week of contemplation following his enlightenment experience. A *buduge* wall at Mädavela; mid-eighteenth century. 30" × 24".

Plate 5. Brahma rejoices at the Buddha's decision to preach his newly discovered *dhamma* during the second week. A *buduge* wall at Gangārāma; mid-eighteenth century. 6" × 10".

Plate 6. The two merchants and the four *lokapala* deities are offering alms to the Buddha during the seventh week. A *buduge* wall at Ridī Vihāra; late eighteenth century. 9″ × 13″.

Plate 7. The four *lokapala* deities are offering alms bowls to the Buddha during the seventh week. On the ceiling of cave 2 at Daṁbulla. Late eighteenth century; 36″ × 24″.

Bhikkhu Conversions

Plate 8. The Buddha is preaching to his first five *bhikkhus* following their conversion at the Deer Park in Sarnath (India). A *buduge* wall at Ridī Vihāra; late eighteenth century. 9″ × 13″.

Plate 9. The first five *bhikkhu* converts have become enlightened *arhats*. A *buduge* wall at Ridī Vihāra; late eighteenth century. 48″ × 64″.

Sūvisi Vivaraṇa

Plate 10. In his previous reincarnation as a lion (one of the twenty-four manifestations of previous Buddhas), the Buddha receives the prophecy of his eventual Buddhahood from another of the twenty-four. On the ceiling of a cave *buduge* at Degaldoruva; late eighteenth century. 14″ × 21″.

The Thousand Buddhas

Plate 11. This thousand-Buddhas motif is on the ceiling of cave 2 at Dam̆bulla. Late eighteenth century. 48″ × 64″.

Scenes from the *Buddhacārita*

Plate 12. Māra's army is attacking the Buddha on the night of enlightenment. On the ceiling of cave 2 at Daṁbulla; late eighteenth century. 84″ × 52″.

Plate 13. Bhū Devi is witnessing the Buddha's victory over Māra. On the ceiling of the cave *buduge* at Degaldoruva; late eighteenth century. 12″ × 8″.

Plate 14. Deities are witnessing the Buddha's first sermon at Deer Park in Sarnath. On the ceiling of cave 2 at Daṁbulla; late eighteenth century. 36″ × 54″.

Plate 15. This shows the Buddha's conversion of one of his most important disciples, Moggallana. A *buduge* wall at Gangārāma; late eighteenth century. 10″ × 6″.

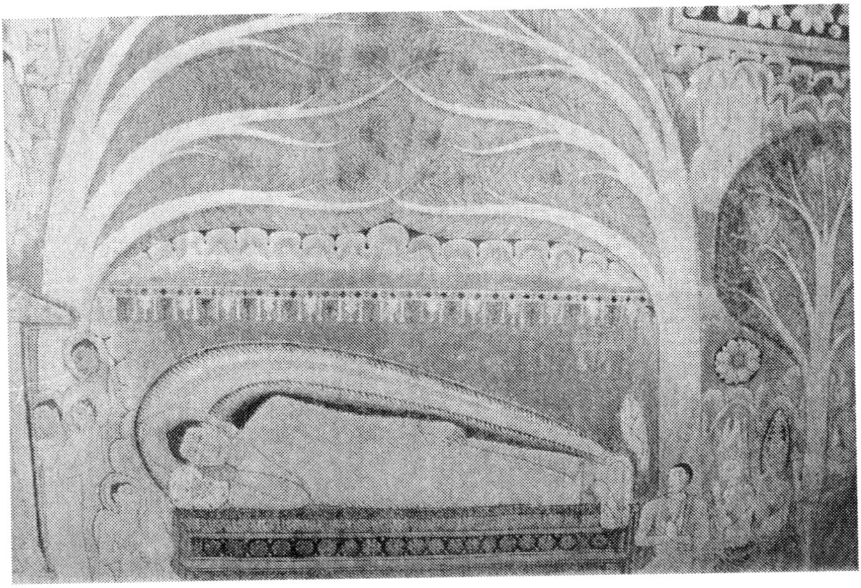

Plate 16. This shows the *parinibbāṇa* (great decease, or liberation) of the Buddha. A wall in cave 2 at Daṁbulla; late eighteenth century. 50″ × 80″.

Plate 17. Laywomen (styled in Kandyan dress) are shown, at Kapilavatthu, honoring the Buddha's return to his native place. A *buduge* wall at Gangārāma; late eighteenth century. 6″ × 10″.

Plate 18. Noblemen (styled in Kandyan dress) are shown, at Kapilavatthu, honoring the Buddha's return to his native place. A *buduge* wall at Gangārāma; late eighteenth century. 6" × 10".

Plate 19. Laymen (styled in Kandyan dress) are shown, at Kapilavatthu, honoring the Buddha's return to his native place. A *buduge* wall at Gangārāma; late eighteenth century. 6" × 10".

Scenes from the *Mahāvaṃsa*

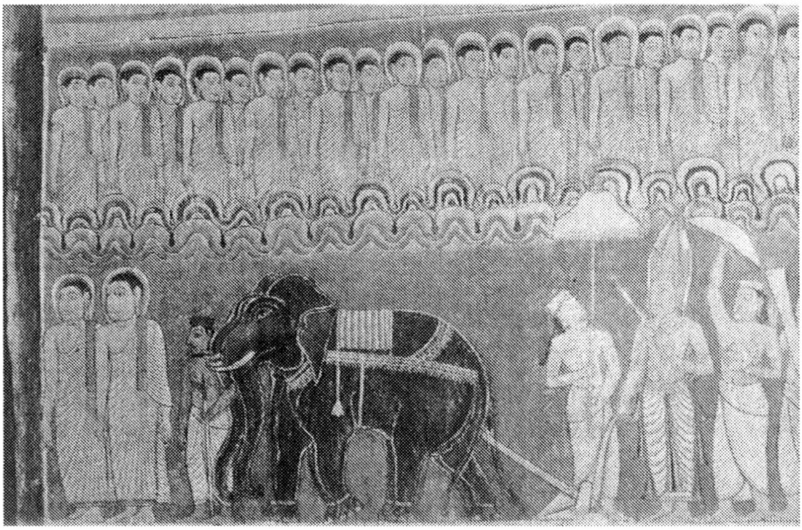

Plate 20. This depicts the plowing of the *simā* (boundaries) for the establishment of the Mahāvihāra *sangha* in Anurādhapura in the third century B.C.E. A mural on the back of a boulder in the southwest corner of cave 2 at Daṁbulla; late eighteenth century. 36″ × 54″.

Plate 21. This depicts the planting of a graft from the *bodhi* tree that was brought by Aśoka's daughter, Sanghamitta, and later became Śrī Mahābodhi in third-century B.C.E. Anurādhapura. A mural on the back of a boulder in the southwest corner of cave 2 at Daṁbulla; late eighteenth century. 36″ × 54″.

Plate 22. This shows the enshrining of relics of the Buddha at the Thūpārāma in third-century B.C.E. Anurādhapura. A mural on the back of a boulder in the southwest corner of cave 2 at Dam̆bulla; late eighteenth century. 36″ × 54″.

Scenes from the *Uraga Jātaka*

Plate 23. The *bodhisatta* is shown as a Brahman with his family and servant. A *buduge* wall at Mädavela; mid-eighteenth century. 30″ × 16″.

Plate 24. The *bodhisatta*-as-Brahman and his son are plowing while the son is being bitten by a serpent. A *buduge* wall at Mädavela; partially retouched; originally painted in mid-eighteenth century. 18″ × 12″.

Plate 25. This shows the pyre of the *bodhisatta*-as-Brahman's son, which attracts Sakka's attention. A *buduge* wall at Mädavela; mid-eighteenth century. 18" × 12".

Plate 26. Sakka, in disguise, is inquiring as to the family's equanimity in the face of death (*right*), and then is revealing his true identity to the *bodhisatta* (*left*). A *buduge* wall at Mädavela; mid-eighteenth century. 24" × 16".

Scenes from the *Sutasoma Jātaka*

Plate 27. The hundred princes of India are being sacrificed to the *yakkhini* in the tree by the deranged Benares prince. Exterior wall a cave *buduge* at Degaldoruva; late eighteenth century. 9" × 15".

Plate 28. The royal cook prepares a human victim for the Benares prince. Exterior front wall of a cave *buduge* at Degaldoruva; late eighteenth century. 15″ × 9″.

Plate 29. The *bodhisatta,* as Prince Sutasoma, is being transported by the deranged Benares prince. Exterior wall of a cave *buduge* at Degaldoruva; late eighteenth century. 9″ × 15″.

Scenes from the *Vessantara Jātaka*

Plate 30. This shows the distribution of the "gift of seven hundreds." Exterior wall of a cave *buduge* at Degaldoruva; late eighteenth century. 9˝ × 15˝.

Plate 31. Vessantara gives away his horses and chariot to Brahmans while the gods look on. Exterior wall of a cave *buduge* at Degaldoruva; late eighteenth century. 9˝ × 15˝.

Plate 32. Jujaka, the Brahman to whom Vessantara has given his children (who are now tied to the tree), is hiding from King Sanjaya's (Vessantara's father's) men (*left*); King Sanjaya is offering Jujaka a ransom for the two children (*right*). Interior right wall of a *buduge* at Mädavela; mid-eighteenth century. 12" × 16".

Plate 33. Queen Phusati is measuring out gold equal to the weight of Vessantara's children while Sakka looks on (*left*); King Sanjaya is declaring his rescue of the children (*right*). Interior right wall of a *buduge* at Mädavela; mid-eighteenth century. 12" × 12".

Plate 34. This shows the reunion of the royal family as Prince Vessantara pays homage to his father, King Sanjaya. Exterior wall of a cave *buduge* at Degaldoruva; late eighteenth century. 9″ × 15″.

The *Soḷosmathāna* Mural

Plate 35. Eight of sixteen sacred places of Buddhist Sri Lanka are portrayed. Interior wall of a *buduge* at Gangārāma; mid-eighteenth century. 72″ × 30″.

Plate 36. (*At right*) *Stūpas* within *stūpas* symbolize Mahīyaṇgana. Left interior wall of a *buduge* at Mädavela; mid-eighteenth century. 12″ × 8″.

Plate 37. (*Below*) This shows the Buddha's foot imprint on Śrī Pāda (Adam's Peak). Left interior *buduge* wall at Mädavela; mid-eighteenth century. 8″ × 8″.

Plate 38. Sakka is venerating Śrī Pāda (*right*) and Divyaguhā (where the Buddha rested). Interior wall of an upper *buduge* at Ridī Vihāra; late eighteenth century. 9″ × 15″.

Plate 39. The Buddha admires the *bodhi* tree during the second week following his enlightenment. Interior wall of an upper *buduge* at Ridī Vihāra; late eighteenth century. 9″ × 15″.

Plate 40. The temptation is offered by Māra's daughters during the fifth week following his enlightenment. Ceiling mural of cave 2 at Daṁbulla; late eighteenth century. 60″ × 84″.

Plate 41. Nāga-king Muchalinda shelters the Buddha during the sixth week after his enlightenment. In cave 2 at Daṁbulla; late eighteenth century. 30″ × 24″.

Plate 42. This depicts the two merchants (one offering alms and the other receiving *stūpa* with a hair relic) and the four *lokapala* deities during the seventh week after enlightenment. Ceiling mural of cave 2 at Daṁbulla; late eighteenth century. 48″ × 64″.

The *Bodhisatta* Metteyya

Plate 43. Metteyya is preaching in Tusita heaven. Ceiling of cave 3 at Daṁbulla; late eighteenth century. 60″ × 84″.

The Thousand Buddhas

Plate 44. The thousand-Buddhas motif is seen. Interior *buduge* wall at Gangārāma; late eighteenth century. 54″ × 80″.

Scenes from the *Buddhacārita*

Plate 45. These scenes are on an interior *buduge* wall at Gangārāma. Late eighteenth century. 36˝ × 54˝.

Plate 46. Channaka, the *bodhisatta*'s horse, returns without its rider following the Great Departure. Interior *buduge* wall at Gangārāma; late eighteenth century. 9˝ × 15˝.

Plate 47. Māra and his army attack the Buddha on the night of his enlightenment. Interior *buduge* wall at Gangārāma; late eighteenth century. 6˝ × 9˝.

Enshrinement of the Buddha's Relics in India

Plate 48. These are the eight *stūpas* erected by the eight republican clans of northeastern India to house the relics of the Buddha. Ceiling of cave 2 at Dam̆bulla; late eighteenth century. 30˝ × 54˝.

Scene from the *Khāntivāda Jātaka*

Plate 49. The *bodhisatta*-as-ascetic is given alms by the Benares commander in chief. Interior wall of a cave *buduge* at Degaldoruva; late eighteenth century. 12" × 18".

Scene from the *Vessantara Jātaka*

Plate 50. Vessantara ministers to the Brahman Jujaka before giving away his children. Right interior wall of a *buduge* at Mädavela; mid-eighteenth century. 12" × 12".

4

Royalty Reborn

Karmic retribution, the force of human action that fuels the stream of continuous personal rebirths in the various realms of existence throughout the multitiered, conditioned cosmos of *saṃsāra*, is a bedrock principle of the classical Buddhist world view. Karma is a notion that is not just an archaic and quaint belief of past Buddhist times; it is also a continuing concept of pivotal contemporary importance for almost all Buddhists (and Hindus) in the modernizing cultural contexts of both South and Southeast Asian societies. Though literally volumes of Buddhist apologetic and Western scholarly literature have been devoted to karma's elucidation over the centuries, and while it continues to attract serious and copious academic attention in the present, karma basically remains a profound yet very simple doctrine: the quality of actions in the present determines the quality of existence in the future. The reason that the 547 *jātaka* stories of the Pali Theravāda Buddhist canon have been, and remain, so popular with the Buddhist laity is that they recount the lessons of karmic retribution so clearly and in such a positive light. That is, they constitute the Buddha's own karma.

The *jātaka* stories recount actions of the *bodhisatta*'s past rebirths, actions that eventually led to his final rebirth, which culminated in the experience of enlightenment and the attainment of *nibbāṇa*. These are stories about how the *bodhisatta* perfected various human qualities of a moral and spiritual nature: loving-kindness, perseverance, even-mindedness, empathy, charity, and wisdom. The realization of these qualities or perfected actions empowered the *bodhisatta* through a series of favorable rebirths that made possible the opportunity for him to become the Buddha of our current time. The *jātaka*s offer tangible illustrations to the laity of what they too might achieve: if not enlightenment in this lifetime, at least favorable rebirths and progress along the path to eventual enlightenment in the future. These stories, therefore, may be the most didactic in all Buddhist literature. They have been, certainly, the most accessible. Because of this, they have come to form an important constituent of the Buddhist temple culture, an inspiration for a good deal of Buddhist art and Sinhala poetry.[1] The *Vessantara Jātaka*, for instance, was sculpted in central India at Bharhut perhaps as early as the second century B.C.E., at Sanchi in the first century B.C.E., and in South India at Amarāvati from the first through the third centuries C.E., and it was painted at Ajānta in the fifth century. Gombrich and Cone (1977: xxxv) rightly assert that "there is hardly a major Buddhist site in India which has no representation of Vessantara."

Of the collected 547 *jātaka*s in the Theravāda Buddhist Pali canon, about forty were painted on the temple walls by artists of the Kandyan school in the eighteenth and nineteenth centuries.[2] Of the forty, by far the most popular was, and still is, the *Vessantara Jātaka*. Since this is indisputable, the *Vessantara*'s significance is the centerpiece of discussion in this chapter. The painted illustrations of the *Vessantara* became almost a normative feature of the most important Kandyan Buddhist temples in the eighteenth and nineteenth centuries, not only because this *jātaka* purports to be the story of the *bodhisatta*'s next-to-last life before his final rebirth, when he became the Buddha, but because it is also, indirectly, an important discourse pertaining to Buddhist kingship.

Other *jātaka*s also functioned in a fundamentally didactic manner in inculcating basic moral and religious teachings for the benefit of lay Buddhist *religieux*. Before addressing the *Vessantara Jātaka* per se, we will examine three of these other *jātaka*s painted on the walls of the Mädavela and Degaldoruva image houses, the earliest and latest Kandyan temples that were patronized and refurbished by Kīrti Śrī. As I have stressed, *jātaka*s formed a central part of temple liturgy because they represented fundamental Buddhist teachings, especially karma, at their most accessible level. This is also true spatially, for the *jātaka*s were always strategically located within the visual liturgy so that they could be easily observed. Herein, the *bodhisatta* is usually presented not as a great, almost superhuman, all-knowing monastic teacher who enunciated sophisticated and esoteric philosophical truths to advanced religious virtuosos, but as a layman (or sometimes even as an animal), albeit an extraordinary one, who is resolutely struggling to make progress on his own path to the ultimate goal, through the virtue of his actions performed in everyday life.

Uraga Jātaka

This story, painted beautifully at Mädavela (the first temple renovated by Kīrti Śrī), tells of the *bodhisatta*'s rebirth as a cultivated Brahman, happily married, and living with his son (who was also married).[3] One day, while the *bodhisatta* and his son were working in the fields, his son, after setting fire to a rubbish heap, disturbed a nearby snake living in an anthill, was bitten by the snake, and suddenly died. Observing this dreadful mishap, the *bodhisatta*-as-Brahman dispassionately told a passing wayfarer to inform his wife that only one meal would be needed at midday—a message through which she understood the tragic demise of her son. When the family gathered to cremate the son's body, the intense heat from the fire awakened Sakka (Indra, king of the gods in heaven), who then descended to the human realm, assumed a disguise, and appeared serially to the *bodhisatta*, then to his wife, then to the wife of his deceased son, and, finally, to the family servant, asking them, in turn, why they did not weep for the departed loved one who had died so tragically. Each one replied that there is no reason for lamentation when death and rebirth are understood to be the fundamental facts of life.

The religious meaning of the *Uraga Jātaka* is quite clear and recalls a famous scene from the *Mahāparinibbāṇa Sutta* of the *Dīgha Nikāya* (3:175–179), in which the Buddha asks his followers not to weep on the occasion of his own death; death is not a finality, but only a transition to another life or the moment of life's liberation itself. Further, death is an occasion on which to meditate on the truth that whatever is subject to an uprising is also subject to a cessation. To be overcome with grief is not only to succumb to attachment but also to reflect a lack of understanding of death's ultimate significance. This *jātaka*, therefore, is a meditation on the attainment of mental equipoise. What happens in the normal course of life is sometimes unpredictable or tragic, but it must be recognized and accepted nevertheless.

The *Uraga Jātaka*'s illustration at Mädavela is unique, for it is not found in any of the other temple wall paintings in Sri Lanka. Plate 23 (the right-hand portion) depicts the entire family, sans the son, as the *bodhisatta* sets off for the day's labor. The left-hand portion shows the women as they, too, are beginning their day's work. Plate 24, which shows some evidence of the painting's having been slightly retouched (especially around the eyes of the *bodhisatta* and his diminutively rendered son), portrays the *bodhisatta* as he plows in the field, while his son is being bitten on the foot by a snake that has emerged from the ground. Plate 25 depicts the funeral rite as it is being observed by the deceased son's wife. The right-hand portion of plate 26 illustrates the visit of the disguised Sakka, who is inquiring about the family's equanimity in responding to the death of a family member, while the left-hand portion represents the *bodhisatta*, in *añjali mudrā*, as he is paying homage to the revealed Sakka, who, at the conclusion of the story, praises the family's understanding and even-mindedness.

As can be seen in figure 1, the *Uraga Jātaka* occupies the same central, eye-level space on the north wall of the image house at Mädavela that the *Vessantara Jātaka* occupies on the south wall. I will again refer to the paintings at Mädavela within the context of the later discussion of the *Vessantara*. But here I will discuss two other *jātaka*s, found at Degaldoruva Viharaya.

Sutasoma Jātaka

The *Sutasoma Jātaka* is one of the most dramatic stories in the entire collection of this genre of literature.[4] Along with the *Uraga Jātaka*, it has death as a central theme. But rather than focusing on how to respond to the unpredicted death of a loved one, the *Sutasoma*'s attention is given more specifically to the problem of killing and flesh-eating. It illustrates how proclivities or karmically efficacious actions during a previous rebirth may have a continuing dispositional effect in a future life and may require the apprehension of *dhamma* to assuage the dangerous consequences. The lesson of this *jātaka* constitutes a teaching in *ahiṃsā* (non-injury) and is linked in its colophon to the legend of Angulimala, the murderer and thief who was converted by the Buddha, according to the *Majjhima Nikāya*.[5] The story line of the *Sutasoma Jātaka* runs as follows.

The *bodhisatta* was given the name Sutasoma because, as a child of the chief queen, he exhibited a great fondness for juice pressed from the ancient *soma* plant.[6] As part of his education as a youth, Sutasoma was sent to Benares along with one hundred other princes from throughout India to learn the *dhamma* of the *kshatriyas* (warrior, or royal caste). There, he excelled over all others, became the master of all the other princes, and proclaimed, as they were departing after completing their studies, that they should always abstain from taking a life on *Uposatha* (new- and full-moon) days, the traditional days of performing sacrifices or preaching in ancient India. But soon after their dispersal, his good friend and companion, the prince of Benares, became fond of eating meat on a daily basis. One day, when the palace supply of meat was left unattended and was eaten by dogs, the royal cook prepared human flesh instead, which the prince found had a dramatic, exhilarating effect on his body. In his previous birth, the Benares prince had been a flesh-devouring *yakkha* (subhuman demon). Having tasted human flesh and having reawakened this ravenous appetite, there could be no satiating the prince's desire for more, and soon, due to the work of the cook (who was acting on royal instructions), a panic occurred in the city as more and more people suddenly disappeared without explanation. The commander in chief of the royal army, however, while lying in wait, discovered that it was the royal cook who was responsible for the killings. He then confronted the prince with his evidence and the prince, in turn, confessed that his craving for human meat was the cause of the killings. (Several stories, then offered by the commander in chief and, alternatively, by the prince himself, are meant to illustrate the folly of consuming one's fellow humans because of an uncontrolled appetite.) Still, the prince, in spite of his knowledge, could not desist. Along with his cook, he left his kingdom for the forest to continue his habit of eating men, including, eventually, the unfortunate cook himself! Later one day, finding no one to kill and eat, the prince, in desperation, made a vow to the local tree-inhabiting *yakkhi* that he would sacrifice all one hundred princes of India to her if he, in exchange, could gain her assistance in continuing to satiate his habit. He then proceeded to round up all the princes of India with the exception of Sutasoma and, hanging them by their hands from the *yakkhi*'s tree, then traveled to Sutasoma's town for the final capture. Having been detained by the Benares prince, Sutasoma requested that, before going with him, he first be allowed to hear *dhamma* verses that, he had just learned, had been originally taught by the earlier Buddha Kasyapa and now were known by a local Brahman. If given the chance to hear these verses, he promised to return with the Benares prince to the forest and the scene of sacrifice. The prince reluctantly agreed. The verses were as follows:[7]

> In union with the saints just once, O Sutasoma be,
> And ne'er consort with evil men and peace shall encompass thee.
> With holy men consorting aye, as friends such only know,
> From holy men true doctrine learn and daily better grow.
>
> As painted cars of royalty wax dim and fade away,
> So too our bodies frail wear out and suffer swift decay.
> But faith of holy men abides and never waxes old,
> Good men proclaim it to the good through ages yet untold.
>
> The sky above us stretches far, far stretches earth below,
> And lands beyond the boundless sea far distant are we know,
> But greater still than all these and wider in its reach
> Is dhamma whether good or bad that saints or sinners preach.
> (Cowell, 1895–1913: 5:264)

Paying a thousand pieces of gold for each verse, to the Brahman who recited these verses (originally uttered by the Buddha Kasyapa), Sutasoma left his kingdom and returned with the royal flesh-eater, who himself now demanded to know these verses. The prince then declared that he would grant Sutasoma four boons in return for knowledge of these verses. The four boons Sutasoma asks for are that the man-eater might live for a hundred years, that the hundred captive princes will not be eaten, that they will be restored to their own realms, and that the man-eater desist from eating flesh in the future. The *jātaka* then plays out each of these developments, with the man-eater being restored to his former royal position in his own kingdom through the intervention of Sutasoma. In the end, all the princes, including the Benares prince, attained heavenly rebirths.

Commenting on the basic significance of this *jātaka*, Jones (1979: 70–71) writes:

> The most striking thing about it is that, although there is much preaching of *ahiṃsā* in the effort to convert the man-eater, the dominant interest is in the fate of the man-eater himself. When he does finally surrender his cannibalism, he is restored to his kingdom. In view of the law of karma, and in view of the extent and seriousness of the man-eater's crimes, this might seem to be a genuine miscarriage of justice. However, the man-eater is always depicted as the slave of his appetites—rather like an alcoholic who does not so much will to drink as

> feel driven to it. The obsessive nature of his crime, which has a karmic cause, requires a process of behavioural therapy before moral instruction can be usefully imparted. Once the craving has been overcome, the will, which never was intentionally wicked, is set free to revert to the practice of normal morality. Throughout the story, the bodhisatta exhibits a spirit of sacrificial concern for others which seems much closer to Mahāyāna in its ethos than to Theravāda.

Jones's commentary is quite apt and requires little in the way of amplification. It is true that the plight and recovery of the protagonist, the prince of Benares, represent the healing power of the *dhamma* (symbolized by the verses made known to Sutasoma) to overcome karmic propensities caused by behavior in previous rebirths. The actions of the *bodhisatta* also reveal the perfection of compassion for those who are ostensibly wicked.

The *Sutasoma Jātaka* is given an extensive treatment on the exterior walls of Degaldoruva Vihāraya (see figure 2). Plate 27 depicts the deranged prince's rounding up of the one hundred princes of India and his hanging of them as a sacrifice on the *yakkhi*'s tree. Plate 28 shows the royal cook of Benares as he is preparing the prince's human victim for a meal in the palace. Plate 29 shows the man-eating Benares prince's transporting of Sutasoma to the place of sacrifice before the verses that symbolize the liberating *dhamma* are spoken. In all of these paintings, the Benares prince is aptly represented as mentally ill or intoxicated by his craving.

Khāntivāda Jātaka

In addition to its painted portrayal at Degaldoruva, the *Khāntivāda Jātaka* was also artistically rendered later at six other *vihārayas* during the nineteenth century in both the low and up-country regions.[8] The Degaldoruva rendition, however, is the earliest one still extant. This story, the colophon tells us, is about controlling anger and enduring a long period of suffering. It runs as follows.

The *bodhisatta* was born into a Brahman family of great wealth, and, on the death of his parents, gave away all his inherited wealth to those lay *religieux* who had virtuously practiced almsgiving. He then renounced the world and took off for the Himalayas to become an ascetic who would live on wild berries. In search of salt and vinegar, he came to Benares and, on going on alms rounds to the commander-in-chief's

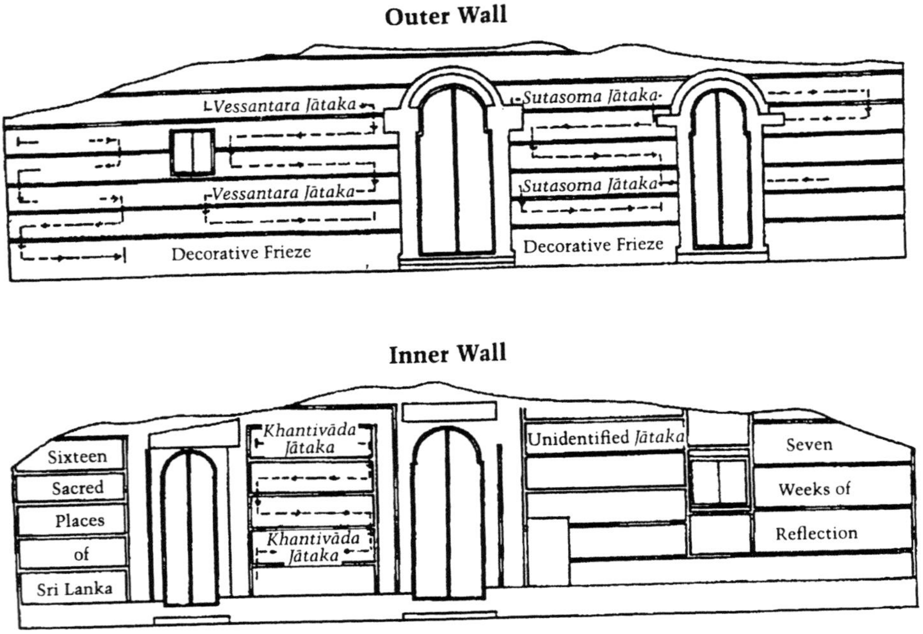

Figure 2 Image house in Degaldoruva; outer wall (*top*) and inner wall (*bottom*).

house, he was invited in, fed, and asked to live in the royal park. One day the king, having drunk too much, came to the park with his harem and, while listening to music, fell asleep. While the king slept, his musicians asked the ascetic to preach, at which time they heard the *bodhisatta* preach a sermon on the *dhamma* of patience and nonanger. On awaking, the king was enraged to find that his harem had deserted him for the attention of the newly arrived ascetic and proceeded to ask the ascetic what he was preaching. On hearing the discourse on patience and nonanger, the king ordered his executioner to lash the ascetic on all sides. After the beating, the ascetic responded by saying that his patience was not skin-deep. The king, enraged by this insolence, then had the ascetic's hands, feet, ears, and nose cut off, but each time got a similar response from the *bodhisatta*: patience lies in the heart. Finally, after crushing the ascetic's heart, the vicious king departed the scene, only to have a great earthquake occur that split the ground and dropped him into the worst of all hells, Avici. The *bodhisatta*/ascetic still lived for a while, despite his amputated and pummeled condition, and yet showed no anger whatsoever toward the king. Later that day, the *bodhisatta* expired.

Again, the meaning of this *jātaka* is rather straightforward insofar as the actions of the *bodhisatta* are realizations of the *dhamma* that he preached; in this case, the *dhamma* is not only about patience and even-mindedness but also about giving. Giving consists not simply of giving away wealth, thus illustrating nonattachment to the pleasures of the material world (again illustrated by the *bodhisatta*'s presence in the king's harem and pleasure garden), but a willingness to sacrifice his very life in order to make manifest the truth of his teaching. Unlike many other *jātaka*s that end on a happy note of positive rebirth, this one ends rather abruptly and hence conveys no utilitarian ethic.

The *jātaka* paintings on the inner wall of the image house at Degaldoruva are in a very serious state of dilapidation. While portions of the *Khāntivāda Jātaka* that are located to the left of the main entrance are still visible (see figure 2), the *jātaka* located to the right of the door is so obliterated that it is now unidentifiable. Only one scene from the *Khāntivāda* remains in a condition that makes photographic reproduction worthwhile. Plate 49 shows the *bodhisatta*/ascetic as he is being received and given alms by the Benares commander in chief at his house. The Benares people, male and female, are costumed in eighteenth-century Kandyan styles of the nobility.

Vessantara Jātaka

Richard Gombrich begins the introduction to Margaret Cone's splendid translation of the *Vessantara Jātaka* with these comments:

> The selfless generosity of Vessantara, who gave away everything, even his children and his wife, is the most famous story in the Buddhist world. It has been retold in every Buddhist language, in elegant literature and in popular poetry; it has been represented in the art of every Buddhist country; it has formed the theme of countless sermons, dramas, dances, and ceremonies. In Theravāda Buddhist countries, Ceylon and South-East Asia, it is still learnt by every child, even the biography of the Buddha is not better known. (Gombrich and Cone, 1977: xv)

While it is debatable that this, the longest and best known of all *jātaka*s, is the most famous story in the Buddhist world, as well known as the biography of the Buddha (technically, it is actually part of the extended life of the Buddha), Gombrich is right in emphasizing the ubiquity and vast popularity of this epic story.[9] Aside from the *Buddhacarita* itself, there is no other story as renowned as this one in the traditional Sinhalese culture. In modern Sri Lanka, in addition to its reading or telling on various ritual occasions, references to Vessantara are sprinkled in the contemporary vernacular;[10] the story line has been made into a popular Sinhala film, and it has also enjoyed successive runs in Colombo Theaters as a staged play. I have already mentioned that it is the most favored of all *jātaka* stories depicted on the walls of Buddhist temples in Sri Lanka.

The story begins by recounting the rebirths of the *bodhisatta*'s mother. During the Buddha Vipassin's time in the cosmic past, she had made a gift of sandalwood powder to that Buddha and, as a result of the merit that accrued from her generosity, had been reborn as Sakka's wife, the queen of heaven. When the merit of her virtuous action had finally dissipated and she was ready for rebirth, Sakka granted her the boon of being reborn as Princess Phusatī in the family of the king of Sivis, and, in time, she married the crown prince Sañjaya, who later became Vessantara's father. When Phusatī was pregnant with Vessantara, she began to experience powerful cravings to have almshouses built and to give away, every day, six hundred thousand gold coins. The more that Phusatī gave away her father's wealth, the more it multiplied.

When Vessantara was born to Phusatī and Sañjaya, he immediately asked: "Mother, I want to give a gift; have you anything to give?" At the age of four, he gave his nurses a gold ornament worth one hundred thousand coins. At eight, he declared that he was not content with the giving away of mere externalities, but that, if asked, he would given even his ear, eyes, flesh, and blood. At sixteen, he is deemed worthy of kingship and is married to Princess Maddī. On his consecration as king, he begins the practice (like his mother) of giving away six hundred thousand gold pieces daily. In time, Maddī gives birth to a son (Jāli) and daughter (Kaṇhājinā). The real drama is then set to begin.

In the country of Kalinga, a famine has struck. Its king begins a fast in the hope that his austerity will coerce the gods into sending rain. But he is unsuccessful in his efforts. The Brahmans of his court tell him about a magical white elephant, owned by Vessantara in a neighboring country, that provides for his kingdom's prosperity. The king dispatches his Brahmans to Vessantara's city, where they explain the current misfortune in Kalinga and request the white elephant as a gift to alleviate the condition. Vessantara not only complies by giving away his precious elephant, but also gives away five hundred families and a great deal of wealth as well. As the Brahmans are leaving the city with the white elephant, they jeer the townspeople, who are dumbstruck and cannot observe what is transpiring. This signals the following turn of events.

The people of the town become very angry about Vessantara's gifts because they fear that, without the white elephant, they may fall into their own difficult times. They approach Sañjaya (Vessantara's father), demand that Vessantara give up his right to kingship, and that he be banished from the kingdom. Sadly, Sañjaya summons his son to inform him of the people's will. Vessantara accepts the judgment. Maddī refuses to be left behind and consoles Vessantara with a long song in which she opines that because of the joyful presence of his children and the wonders of nature in the Himalayas, he will soon forget his lost kingship.

Then Queen Phusatī, Vessantara's mother, offers a long song of lamentation about her son's impending departure, to which Sañjaya replies that banishing his son is so difficult for him because Vessantara "is dearer than life itself." Before departing, Vessantara vows to make the "gift of seven hundreds," which essentially means giving away seven hundred of everything he has owned: elephants, horses, chariots, *kṣatriya* women, male and female slaves, cows, bulls, and food and drink. While this brings thousands of beggars to the city to receive this unprecedented bounty, it also brings more criticism from the townsfolk, who are incredulous that Vessantara, banished for giving away the magical white elephant, gives away yet more before his departure.

Meanwhile, King Sañjaya and Queen Phusatī seek to dissuade Maddī and the children from going into exile with Vessantara. Long songs are exchanged but Maddī stands firm on her decision to accompany Vessantara, along with the children.

Before the moment of departure has arrived, Vessantara has made sure that he has given away everything he possibly can. The earth quakes. They leave the city, riding in a chariot drawn by four horses. Not far from the city, they encounter four Brahmans who are late for "the gift of seven hundreds" that they had heard about from afar. Meeting Vessantara, they ask for the four horses and Vessantara gladly responds.

The gods, knowing how far the family must travel on foot in order to reach their first destination, an uncle's city, shorten the distance so that Vessantara and his family can arrive within one day in the kingdom of the Cetans. There, having explained the recent past, Vessantara is offered the kingship of the Cetans, but he declines because it might cause war with the Sivis. After a rest, the family continues on toward their goal of the Crooked Mountain in the Himalayas, accompanied by a retinue of admiring Cetans until they reach the thick forest. At the forest's edge, the Cetans post a guard to ensure that no evil people will enter and do harm to the family. At the same time, Sakka, who, from heaven, has been observing all developments, instructs the divine architect, Vissakamma, to construct a hermitage for the family at their destination. When they finally arrive after a difficult and exhausting journey, they don ascetic clothes, and Vessantara announces that, in accordance with the lifestyle they have now accepted, he will live the celibate life, with Maddī living with the children in one of the two huts and the second being reserved only for his meditations. Maddī assumes the role of the dutiful housewife who spends her days gathering fruits and nuts in the forest for their daily evening meal. For seven months they live this life of austerity.

At this time, in another part of India, an old Brahman named Jūjaka leaves a sum of money with a neighboring family when he goes out to wander. On his return, he finds that the family has spent his money during his absence. When he discovers the family's inability to give back his money, he demands the beautiful young daughter as payment. She reluctantly becomes his mate but is ridiculed by the villagers whenever she goes out. She tells Jūjaka that unless he finds her a servant to do the outside chores, she will leave him. She has heard about Vessantara's magnificent giving of wealth and people and tells Jūjaka to find him, so he can give her a suitable servant. Jūjaka departs for the kingdom of the Sivis, learns that Vessantara has been banished with his wife and children, and sets out for the Crooked Mountain in the Himalayas. When he encounters the forest guard, he dupes the guard into believing that he has been sent by Vessantara's father to bring him back. The guard gives Jūjaka elaborate directions on how to find the seer Accuta, who, in turn, will know exactly where to find Vessantara.

As Jūjaka approaches, Maddī has a dream that indicates impending misfortune. In the morning, she tells Vessantara its substance. Though Vessantara is aware that the dream foretells separation from his family, he tells Maddī that its occurrence is nothing to fear. Maddī seems consoled and goes to the jungle to gather food, her daily routine. Jūjaka then promptly arrives, tells of his mission, and asks for Jāli (Vessantara's son) and Kaṇhājinā (his daughter). Vessantara doesn't hesitate to give them up but tells Jūjaka that if he brings the children to their grandfather, King Sañjaya, they will fetch a big price.

Jūjaka demurs and says he needs them as slaves for his wife. Hearing these words, the fearful children flee for the jungle while Jūjaka becomes very angry, accusing Vessantara of lying to him about agreeing to give them up. Vessantara goes in search of the children, finds them, and tells each of them, in turn, to go with Jūjaka. He says to them: "Come, my dear son (/daughter), fulfil my Perfection. Consecrate my heart; do what I say. Be a steady boat to carry me on the sea of becoming. I shall cross to the further shore of birth, and make the world with its gods cross also" (Gombrich and Cone, 1977: 58). Before Jūjaka sets off with the children, Vessantara sets a steep price for both of them in the event that Jūjaka tries to sell them. This ensures that only royalty will be able to purchase them. Jūjaka binds the children and beats them before setting off with them. Vessantara recoils in grief, yet remains steadfast. Shortly after their departure, Jūjaka trips and loses his grip, allowing Jāli to escape, return to Vessantara, and plead. Jūjaka returns while Vessantara watches his children disappear again into the forest with the evil Brahman. Again Jūjaka stumbles, and this time Kaṇhājinā escapes; the same scene is repeated. Again Vessantara is sorely tempted to free the children and experiences deep remorse, but in the end retains his equanimity.

The cries of the children are heard in heaven by the gods. Knowing that as soon as Maddī returns, she will immediately follow after them and suffer grief in her inability to free them from Jūjaka, the gods dispatch lesser gods to become lions, tigers, and leopards who then retard her return to the hermitage by that night. Maddī is indeed unable to reach Vessantara until late at night and when she does return, she is rebuked:

> Maddī, you are beautiful and attractive, and in the Himalayan forest live a lot of people like ascetics and magicians. Who knows what you have been doing. You left early; why do you return so late? Married women do not behave like this, going off into the forest leaving young children. You did not so much as ask yourself what was happening to your children or what your husband would think, but left in the morning and are returning by moonlight. My unfortunate state is to blame for this. (Gombrich and Cone, 1977: 70)

Maddī begs Vessantara to tell her what has become of the children, but he remains silent throughout the night. In the morning she launches her futile searches and returns to Vessantara three times before finally collapsing in utter fatigue and despair. Vessantara fears that perhaps she has died, is finally moved to pity, revives her tenderly, and explains the events of the day before. Miraculously, Maddī calmly accepts the fate of her children.

Sakka has been observing the unfolding of these events and begins to fret that Vessantara will also give away Maddī to an unseemly person. He assumes his disguise as an old man, approaches Vessantara, and asks for Maddī. Maddī assents without objection and Vessantara says: "Look, brahmin, omniscience is a hundred, a thousand, a hundred thousand times dearer to me than Maddī. May this gift be the means for me to realize omniscience" (Gombrich and Cone, 1977: 76–77). At this, Sakka reveals his true identity, gives Maddī back to Vessantara, and blesses them. He says he'll grant Vessantara eight wishes. Vessantara makes his choices: that his father will recall him; that he will never consent to a criminal's execution; that the old, young, and middle-aged will find refuge with him; that he will be faithful to his wife; that his son will conquer the earth with justice; that heavenly food will appear with the sun's rising; that he will never regret giving; and that he will end his cycle of rebirths.

In the meantime, Jūjaka has been marching for two weeks, treating the children with abject cruelty. King Sañjaya has a dream in which he understands what has become of his grandchildren; he then summons his ministers and demands that Jūjaka and the children be found and brought to him immediately. When Jāli tells the king what has transpired, the royal ministers react by further criticizing Vessantara, but Jāli defends his father's actions as noble insofar as his ultimate pursuit is for the benefit of all. Sañjaya then pays Jūjaka a huge ransom, including a palace, for the release of the children and sets forth, with a huge retinue, for the Crooked Mountain to retrieve Vessantara and Maddī. Jūjaka is elated about his largesse, eats more than he can digest, and dies from overconsumption. Since no relatives come to perform his funeral rites, the ransom paid to him for the children reverts to Sañjaya.

At the Crooked Mountain, the entire family is emotionally reunited as the mountains roar and the earth quakes. Sañjaya restores Vessantara to his place of kingship; all of the wealth that had been given away is regained; and health and prosperity reign throughout the kingdom as Sakka continuously showers them with riches from heaven.

The "gift of seven hundreds" is shown in plate 30. Plate 31 portrays Vessantara as he is ministering to the Brahmans encountered on the road just after his banishment; this is the moment when he gives away his horses and chariot. Plate 50 (a Mädavela painting) depicts Vessantara as he is providing comfort to Jūjaka on his first arrival at the hermitage, before Jūjaka takes away Jāli and Kaṇhājinā. Plate 32 (a Mädavela painting) shows Jūjaka hiding in a tree to avoid detection by the king's men, while the children have been bound; it also shows King Sañjaya's offering to buy back the children. In plate 33, Sakka is seen looking on as Queen Phusatī measures out the gold that will ransom the children (it equals Jāli's weight). Plate 34 (a Degaldoruva painting) illustrates the family reunion in the Himalayas, with Vessantara paying homage to his father, King Sañjaya.

Obviously, the *Vessantara Jātaka* has more than a fair measure of pathos. Giving away a kingdom's wealth and material well-being is seen as pathetic and objectionable by the townsfolk of Sivi. How much more so is the giving away of one's children and family? The townsfolk are not alone in their objections to Vessantara's behavior. Anyone who has seen a staging of *Vessantara Jātaka* in Sri Lanka, Burma, or Thailand will remember the agony that the audience experiences when Vessantara lets the children go off with Jūjaka, even though they already know perfectly well that ultimately the children will be rescued. What that anguish signals is what Gombrich (in Gombrich and Cone, 1977: xxii) has referred to as the basic moral problem of the story: Is it right to give away one's family? Jones (1979: 134), for his part, is clearly uncomfortable with the morality of this episode:

> The canonical basis for giving, especially from the throne, is that this establishes the well-being of the monks and ensures the supremacy of the *dhamma* in the administration of the state. In these stories, giving has become almost a self-indulgence. It is on such an extravagant scale that it bears little relation to the actualities of life, neither does it consider the possibly harmful effects of such lavish generosity on its recipients; it shows a total disregard for personal feeling and it retains a rather distasteful ulterior, contractual character. The giving is not really disinterested. It is *quid pro quo*, material "goods" (including one's family in this category) being exchanged for spiritual benefits. Though the giving seems so costly at times, its costliness is largely offset by the donor's bland confidence that it must pay off.

Jones finishes his commentary by referring to this radical experience of giving as a "clear distortion of the canonical teaching."

Gombrich, having clearly identified the graphic displays of patriarchy and misogyny in the *Vessantara* (elements that surely alienate many Western and Asian readers/observers alike in an increasingly posttraditional age) approaches the central moral problem in a different manner:

> The point for the Buddhist lies not in the measure of Vessantara's gifts, but in his becoming so free from attachment that he doesn't mind parting with anything. Of that detachment his gift of his family is only the culminating demonstration. It is certainly not that he wants to be rid of them: for the Buddhist, dislike is just as great an evil as attachment, for both are manifestations, positive or negative, of desire. Enlightenment is attainable only by freedom from all desire whatsoever.
>
> When this has been said, the view that it is selfish to hand over one's family into slavery for, or as a sign of, one's own spiritual advancement still remains. . . . Preoccupation with one's own Enlightenment to the exclusion of concern for others was of course the accusation levelled against the older schools of Buddhism by the new school, Mahāyāna, which developed around the beginning of the Christian era. Mahāyāna Buddhists held that a true Bodhisattva would not attain Enlightenment, and thus achieve release from rebirth, before he had brought all other beings to the same salvation; that is why they gave less emphasis to the historical Buddha. In our text too there is a trace of the same idea: when his children run and hide, so that he cannot present them to the brahmin, Vessantara calls to them: "Come, my dear son (/daughter), fulfil my Perfection. Consecrate my heart; do what I say. Be a steady boat to carry me on the sea of becoming. I shall cross to the further shore of birth, and make the world with its gods cross also." (Gombrich and Cone, 1977: xxii–xxiii)

Gombrich makes the precise point that needs to be emphasized for gaining a perspective on the meaning of the *jātaka*s within the context of the visual liturgy of Kandyan temples. The *jātaka*s, on the whole, are didactic indeed, but the majority of those depicted in Kandyan temple wall paintings also reflect the manner in which the ethic of kingship in the Sinhala Theravada Buddhist culture had been idealized. In another book,[11] I have detailed the manner in which the two powerful images of the *bodhisatta* and kingship were combined, in historic and cultic terms, in Sri Lanka, a development due in part to the assimilation of Mahāyāna *bodhisattva* conventions.[12] Moreover, many kings in the history of Sri Lanka unabashedly claimed the status of *bodhisattva* for themselves, as future Buddhas. In making this claim, the king wishes to impress the following parallel on his people: just as the *bodhisattva* is ultimately concerned with ensuring the well-being of all sentient beings, so, too, the king is primarily dedicated to securing the welfare of his people. This brings me to the fundamental point of this discussion: the king gives in order to express his selfless altruism, an altruism that, at the same time, provides for the present well-being of his people, secures his own spiritual destiny, and, in turn, benefits the future spiritual well-being of all.

As I noted in chapter 2, what stands out in popular memory, and from the perspective of considered historical insight, is the manner in which Kīrti Śrī gave from his own resources. His kingdom had been pauperized by the Dutch and their monopolistic economic policies, yet Kīrti Śrī managed to rebuild the entire infrastructure of Theravāda Buddhism in a manner rarely matched in the history of Sri Lanka. Expedient or not, the historical legacy of his untiring efforts to promote the well-being of the *sangha* and to refurbish temples for the laity speaks for itself in this regard.

While it is impossible to know, with absolute certainty, whether the *Vessantara Jātaka* provided the specific, conscious motivation for Kīrti Śrī Rājasinha's generous endowments, the fact is that *jātaka* stories about the *bodhisatta*-as-king predominate as the central, eye-level elements of most visual liturgies in the temples that he restored. Clearly, Buddhist kingship and its identification with the religious path that led to *nibbāṇa* were afforded the highest profiles in these contexts. They articulate yet another discourse of legitimation, one that, Kīrti Śrī must have hoped, would not be wasted on his people. Since he was the giving king of the present time and place, these stories of the *bodhisatta* were also his stories; that is, they were royally didactic ones and, by inference, trained the telescope of consciousness indirectly on his own religious efforts.

As I have noted, the *Vessantara Jātaka* has been a constant staple of Buddhist artistic expression for more than twenty centuries. Though its illustration on the walls of Kandyan temples rehabilitated by Kīrti Śrī was prolific, we cannot really credit Kīrti Śrī with an innovation in this instance. By including the *Vessantara Jātaka* so often within these visual liturgies, Kīrti Śrī was only following a very well established Buddhist tradition. That, however, is exactly what needs to be underscored in this context. Kīrti Śrī was not at all interested in being understood by his people as a royal deviant. To the contrary, he hoped his constituents would understand him as a quintessential Buddhist sovereign, as a *Vessantara*-inspired *bodhisatta*.

In general then, the *jātaka* stories within the visual liturgies of Kandyan temple wall paintings trained the telescope not only on the human world of *saṃsāra*, within which the dynamics of karmic retribution are played out, but also, in most instances, on the figure of Buddhist kingship, a figure traditionally regarded as the ideal layman in his highest estate. The measure of that highest estate clearly seems to have been the cultivated capacity and pure intention to give selflessly.

5

Implications for Theory and Method

Why Kīrti Śrī sought legitimacy, and how, by his various appeals to symbolic discourse of Buddhist kingship, and by his articulation of a classical Buddhist world view expressed through painting, he ultimately succeeded, are subjects for a separate historical analysis of social and religious dynamics. There are, however, other serious implications of this work that are more political, philosophical, or methodological in character, implications that transcend the historical context of the specific issues that have been scrutinized here. One of these is discussed as the focus of this chapter, and a second is considered in the postscript, chapter 6.

The first of these theoretical issues is indeed methodological in character. It has to do with the types of sources selected and examined in attempts to answer some very basic questions about religious meaning. In both the past and the present, the systematic study of the history of religions, and, in particular, the study of Buddhism, has been focused almost exclusively on interpretations of sacred literature. What it means, or has meant, to be a Buddhist, or what constitutes the Buddhist religious identity, has been understood through an almost complete reliance on the translations and exegeses of written texts deemed, by Buddhist tradition, to be normatively authoritative either because these texts are traditionally ascribed to be *Buddhavācana* (words of the Buddha) and hence canonical, or because they are the scholastic products of revered monks of historical importance, whose efforts are regarded as constituting an accepted commentative tradition. On the whole, interpretative studies of these materials have been philosophical and philological in character, and aimed at unpacking a subtle and sophisticated system of religious thought designed to answer compelling existential, soteriological, and cosmological questions. These studies assume that canonical texts should be regarded as definitive statements that articulate the normatively accepted religious world view of tradition.

Alternatively, a growing number of recent studies of another type have sought to answer the same question—what it has meant to be a Buddhist—by means of symbolic interpretations of centrally important religious rituals and myths that, as often as not, are also prescribed or discuss in the same sacred literature studied by the more philosophically and philologically inclined. These studies have often been inspired by anthropological inquiries and, to a great extent, complement, rather than contradict, the findings of the first type of study noted. (Indeed, there has even been a very successful hybrid study done specifically on Sinhalese Theravāda Buddhism in the up-country Kandy region of Sri Lanka; it is aimed at determining whether or not the teachings of the Buddha that are articulated in the Pali canonical literature are essentially the same as, or at least consistent with, the religious truths realized in village myths, folklore, and ritual.)[1] While the first type of study seems to focus on ascertaining what the Buddha is believed to have *taught*, the second type focuses on determining what it is that Buddhists formally *do*.[2]

Both kinds of approaches have not been wrongheaded. But they have been, for many reasons, overvalued and repeated far too often (engendering formidable schools of academic thought that have taken on existences of their own), on the one hand, and are somewhat limited in what they can really reveal historically, on the other. This is not to argue that the *dhamma* (teaching of truth) and the *vinaya* (social and moral behavior) of the Buddha, which the Buddhist order of monks has preserved in the Pali *Tipiṭaka* for many centuries, do not contain important answers to fundamental religious questions about what it means to be Buddhist. It is also not to suggest that an understanding of the Buddhist religious quest, as it has been systematically articulated by figures like the great fifth-century C.E. orthodox Theravāda commentator Buddhaghosa, is irrelevant. Nor is it to belittle the importance of myth and ritual in understanding the dynamics of the cosmos from the perspective of Buddhist tradition. Rather, what is being suggested is that, as students of religion, we need to explore, more fully, other types of sources as well, sources that have been routinely ignored in the past because of predispositions on the part of Western scholars;[3] and sources that, because of their very nature, have been regarded by both modern scholastic Buddhists and Western scholars as being merely popular in character and hence unworthy of serious attention, because they supposedly lack philosophical profundity, and express ecclesiastical sanction or the intricacies of symbolic rites. Whatever the reasons that these sources have been eclipsed in previous considerations, what is now required in the study of religion in general, and the study of Buddhism in particular, is a recognition of, and a cultivated sensitivity to, precisely those forms of religious expression that house or generate a variety of religious experiences and religious world views within the historical context of the subject under study.

The primary sources used in this book consist mainly of royal inscriptions and temple wall paintings that depict those elements and moments in Buddhist tradition that were regarded in the eighteenth century by Kīrti Śrī as contributing to an understanding of the meaning of religious life and tradition, past and present. Modest and simple in terms of style and design, and usually categorized as folk art, the paintings discussed here functioned preeminently as the most important didactic devices to instill the classical Buddhist world view in the vast majority of Sinhalese Buddhist religious adherents. My argument here is very simple: that more than any other form of cultic religious expression, these paintings clearly illustrate, through their obvious accessibility, not only the fundamental mythic history of Theravāda Buddhist tradition but also the basic behavioral actions and cognitive tenets that explain what it meant to be Buddhist during this time. They do not stand in marked contrast to the sacred texts or mythic literature of Pali tradition, but, rather, they summarily incorporate them in a way that made fundamental teachings and understanding vastly more accessible to the general and nominally Sinhalese Buddhist populace.

As I have noted, many of the paintings discussed are illustrated narratives of the *jātaka* stories. One, in particular, the *Vessantara Jātaka*, stands out among them all and has gotten special attention. Many paintings are narrative references to mythic events described in the *Mahā-*

vaṃsa or other important sources of Sinhala Buddhist inspiration. Other paintings, I have noted, are inspired by episodes or teachings found in canonical literature itself. The selection of themes expressed in these paintings formed a kind of canon of its own, or a visual orthodoxy. By virtue of their very arrangement in temples, they comprised a visual liturgy for a classical Theravāda Buddhist world view. These paintings provided the means by which a visual understanding of Buddhism could be achieved, without the intervention of sermons preached by monks or the authoritativeness of an ancient language (Pali) in largely undistributed hallowed texts that very few (only learned monks) could understand.[4]

The didactic importance of temple wall paintings as a means of propagating a normative religious world view is further underscored when we consider that most Sinhalese Buddhists of the eighteenth century could not read, let alone decipher (when they heard), the Pali verses that comprised sacred literature or were chanted on ritual occasions. It is true that a considerable efflorescence of Pali literature occurred during the reign of Kīrti Śrī, owing to the notable efforts of the venerable monastic scholar, Välivita Saranaṃkara. But the meaning and significance of these religious treatises were limited to a small, albeit important, circle of monastic scholars, whose influence was only gradually felt, especially in the latter part of the nineteenth century. The fact of the matter is that most Sinhalese Buddhists, especially women, in the eighteenth century did not read. And if they did read, they read Sinhala, and probably not Pali.

British census figures in the nineteenth century, in addition to accounting for the population, ethnic distribution, religious affiliations, and gender breakdowns of various districts and subdistricts of the island, attempted to determine the numbers of men and women who were able, or not able, to read. For example, in 1881 in the lower Dum̆bura Valley, just northeast of Kandy, out of a population of almost 50,000, only 13 percent, or 6,500 (of which only 400 were women), were able to read (Lawrie, 1898: 1:188). Since Buddhist *vihārayas* (temples) and *pirivenas* (monastic schools) were the chief venues for formalized education in precolonial and Kandyan Sri Lanka, and since it was necessary for Kīrti Śrī to import *bhikkhus* (ordained monks) from Thailand to reconstitute the *sangha* and its moribund institutions (as no Sinhalese *bhikkhus* could be found at that time to carry on the teachings and discipline of the monastic community), it is safe to assume that literacy during the earlier part of his reign (in the middle of the eighteenth century), could scarcely have been higher than the 13 percent rate noted above, and was likely far less.

While Kīrti Śrī sought to revive the Pali literary traditions of the *sangha*, his attempt to impart his understanding of the Buddhist world view, through the rehabilitation and repainting of temples, was of even more fundamental importance for the vast majority of Buddhistic people in his realm. Therefore, in examining what was understood to be the Buddhist world view, or what it meant to be Buddhist, during this particular time and in this particular culture, I have focused primarily on the most accessible and, consequently, probably the most easily understood expressions of that religiosity: temple paintings. And the relevant questions that have been raised are: Which mythic events and *jātaka* stories were selected under Kīrti Śrī's direction for illustration in his rehabilitated temples? What are the themes and patterns that emerge from a consideration of the temples that we know he reconsecrated? What is their message? How do they answer the fundamental question of what it means to be Buddhist? How did they foster a Buddhistic religious experience? What is their relation to conceptions of Buddhist kingship?

Very often in the study of Asian religions, we (meaning Western or Westernized students of religion) have unwittingly selected materials for analysis that are more germane to our own personal experiences or philosophical inclinations, or materials of a more familiar genre that resonate with those religious traditions with which we have been more accustomed.

In studying the Theravāda Buddhism of Sri Lanka, this problem is compounded by a tendency among some modern Buddhist apologists who, quite unaware of how their perspectives have been radically impacted by a Western understanding of religion, seek to rid Buddhism of what they now regard as nonessential cultural accretions. The result of this phenomenon has been aptly dubbed "Protestant Buddhism" by two incisive Sinhalese social scientists (Malalgoda and Obeyesekere),[5] who have described the various social, cultural, and ideological processes behind the manner in which Sinhala Buddhist religious innovations of the late nineteenth and early twentieth centuries emulated patterns intrinsic to Protestant missionary movements of the same period. The early- to mid-twentieth-century legacy of Protestant Buddhism has been mapped out carefully and systematically by a leading American scholar.[6] The religious by-product is a disposition that is very antiritualistic, antisymbolic, extremely individualistic, and is characterized further by what Max Weber referred to as "inner-worldly asceticism" (in terms of both psychological and social ramifications), which is focused on the assurance of spiritual salvation and material well-being in the here and now. Few of these urbanized, Westernized modern Buddhist types would be interested in understanding the classical world view of Kīrti Śrī as it was expressed through the paintings of the Kandyan school of art. They are not so interested in what the study of culture and history can teach. They express a rather timeless view of Buddhism, assuming that what it has meant to be a Buddhist has always remained the same throughout the ages. Sinhalese Theravāda Buddhists of this type would seem to lack a mythohistorical awareness of, or a cultural sensitivity to, their own traditional roots.

Religions do, however, change their contours and their emphases over time. History, society, and culture condition religious understanding in such a way that transformations in meaning and expression do, in fact, occur. This book has been a study of what Buddhism meant two-and-a-half centuries, ago, in the waning phases of a medieval world that was about to be hit directly by a colonial experience, a world then only glimpsed through an appreciation of those expressions that were then alive and relevant and have survived as precious indices and icons. But what can also be seen, in the postscript in chapter 6, is how the various dynamics that operated in the time of Kīrti Śrī have an important relevance even today. Not only did the reforms and rehabilitations undertaken by this great king become paradigmatic of ritual, liturgy, and artistic expressions of religious experience and meaning for a great number of today's traditional up-country Kandyan Sinhalese, but it is also now clear that some of the same socioeconomic patterns and dynamics that operated during Kīrti Śrī's eighteenth-century reign continue to operate in principle in the present.

6

Postscript: Ethnic Identity and Alienation

A second theoretical issue raised by this book, this one more implied than direct (so I have decided to write about it in this postscript), is pertinent for understanding the nature of conflicts between various communities in multiethnic societies. It has to do with the question of what exactly has constituted ethnicity within the variegated culture of Sri Lanka, and how, if at all, these elements or forces are linked (or not) to the outbreaks of communal violence that plague Sri Lanka and other multiethnic countries today. Can this study of an eighteenth-century king and his social, religious, and political context contribute to an understanding of the contemporary scene?

When I first began research for this book, I was intrigued by Kīrti Śrī's predicament and by the question of how a king of Tamil Śaivite Hindu origins could become so highly regarded by Sinhala Theravāda Buddhists. From the beginning and throughout my research, I hoped that I might learn something important about the relationship between religion and ethnicity, so that I might be able to better understand the nature of Sri Lanka's contemporary ethnic conflict, especially since I had seen (and consequently been affected by), on several occasions, some brutal acts of violence and had experienced some of the fears that had touched the lives of many Sri Lankan colleagues and friends in 1983–1985, 1987, and again in 1989–1990.

In thinking analogically about Kīrti Śrī's context and the recent tragic events in Sri Lanka, I have come to the conclusion that the role of religion in the current ethnic conflict has been somewhat overemphasized by many and that, given the high profile religion has received in the press and in scholarly literature regarding the causes of Sri Lanka's turmoil, it needs to be deemphasized. That is, while religion is certainly a force in forging ethnic identity in Sri Lanka, and while some segments of the Buddhist community have definitely aggravated, rather than ameliorated, the tense relations between the Tamil and Sinhala communities, I now contend that the deep-seated causes of ethnic alienation are more economic in nature than religious. In this chapter I want to explain why.

Since the mid-1950s, and thus shortly after independence from British colonial rule, when the Western-educated, Christian-raised, and low-country-elite politician S. W. R. D. Bandaranaike opportunistically raised the political stakes of ethnic consciousness in Sri Lanka by advocating (to the majority of Sinhalese Buddhist voters) a platform of instituting "Sinhala only" as the official national language of the country and "restoring Buddhism to its rightful place," tensions between the Sinhalese and Tamil communities have erupted sporadically, simmered, and then spectacularly exploded (especially in the early 1980s), before degenerating into what has amounted to a protracted civil war.[1] The ongoing political debate and military confrontation over the de facto or de jure division of the country by Tamil militants in the north and east of the island, along with the recalcitrance, evident in both communities, that prevents a negotiated political solution, is but an expression of a deeper fundamental problem that has now come to be known in Sri Lankan local parlance as "the ethnic conflict." The mounting number of violent deaths, including, in 1993, the assassination of the president of the country, Ranasinghe Premadasa (and, before that, of many other important government officials and politicos); the continuous disintegration of what was at one time a socially segmented and yet relatively stable and somewhat ethnically cross-fertilized society; the deterioration and distortion of an economy that was already in a state of transitional development; the resulting increased brain drain of talented Tamil and Sinhalese youth from the country; the often desperate plight of Sri Lankan Tamil expatriates as refugees or as seekers of political asylum throughout the world—these events have motivated an avalanche of recent academic studies, from a variety of disciplinary perspectives, that are aimed at ferreting out the root causes and tragic significance of the ethnic conflict in modern Sri Lanka.[2] The subject is very complex indeed, and this postscript does not pretend to offer any facile solutions; nor, in fact, does it propose any radically new insights. This book has been only partially concerned with exploring the problems and forces related to ethnicity in an earlier historical epoch, but this has been done in the hope that it might contribute some depth and wider scope to an understanding of the issues that continue to trouble Sri Lanka. Just as it can be seen that religion had a part in the political events of the eighteenth century, so, too, Buddhism has had a part in the political events of the recent past. However, one of the implications of this work is that the gravity of responsibility sometimes assigned to the role of Buddhism in the contemporary ethnic conflict in Sri Lanka may have been overemphasized or partially misunderstood by some scholars or journalists.[3]

The academic analysis of ethnicity in Sri Lanka has rightly revolved around a discussion of how language and religion are regarded as the two most powerful factors that create ethnic identity. These were precisely the very aspects of ethnicity that Bandaranaike appealed to when, in an impassioned and short-sighted attempt at seeking election as the country's prime minister in 1956, he unwittingly unleashed what was to become an uncontrollable force of modern historic proportions for postcolonial Sri Lanka. By appealing to the Sinhala ethnic sentiment of the masses, he also thoroughly alienated and frightened the Tamil minority. That the chord struck by Bandaranaike is historically deep-seated can be gleaned from a study of many other eras of Sri Lankan history, including the mid-eighteenth-century reign of Kīrti Śrī. That is, Sinhala ethnic consciousness and identity, represented primarily by linguistic and religious identities—despite extensive merging of Hindu and European Christian elements, over many centuries, into the Sinhala Buddhist community—has a very protracted history in the island's politics.[4]

In my recounting of the history of Kīrti Śrī's reign, it was noted that the factors of religion, language, and kinship weighed heavily on the minds of major political players of his time. That Kīrti Śrī understood the importance of religion in the Sinhala Buddhist identity, and that he projected a religio-political understanding of his kingship, primarily in terms of normative mythic symbolizations rooted in royal discourses that appealed to Sinhala Theravāda Buddhists, was clearly seen in chapters 2–4, in which I emphasized the importance of the Aśokan and other royal discourses. There, it was made clear that Kīrti Śrī framed his royal discourses in the most graphic of mythic terms, ritual conventions, and artistic expressions that were inherently meaningful to the Theravāda tradition in Sri Lanka, in an effort to consolidate the foundation of his power in the face of the internal and external threats (which I previously had delineated in chapter 1). I noted that Kīrti Śrī is now generally considered in Sri Lanka, by peasant and academician alike, to have been one of the most ardent supporters of Buddhism in the history of the religion on the island. To be perceived in that manner during his own time had been precisely his aim. While Sinhalese Buddhist historical consciousness eventually cleared him of blame for his Tamil Śaivite Hindu origins (and perhaps private religious orientation), I have also noted that some of his eighteenth-century contemporaries (Buddhist monks and members of the Sinhalese aristocracy) and some nineteenth-century monastic chroniclers of religious history could not. They simply remained unconvinced or alienated. Why was this the case? Did they reject him only on grounds of ethnicity (language and religion)? Why would they plot to assassinate a king so intent on the restoration of their own religious tradition? In turn, this raised further questions: If Kīrti Śrī's religious works that publicly professed Buddhism were not convincing enough, why weren't they? Was language the real wedge, rather than religion?[5] Or was the conspiracy against Kīrti Śrī hatched by higher levels of the Kandyan nobility and the *sangha*, "where there were *strong ties of blood* between the two" (Dewaraja, 1971: 114; italics mine), indicating that kinship might have been a decisive factor.[6]

While language, religion, and extended kinship ties were, no doubt, contributing factors, this study, though primarily focused on myth, symbol, ritual, and art, has also suggested that economic issues provided a chief motivation for ethnic alienation among the Sinhalese nobility and the Tamil royalty of eighteenth-century Kandyan society. What is being suggested here is that the factors (language and religion) that gave rise to ethnic *consciousness* need not be regarded as the same factors (economic issues) that led to ethnic *alienation*. What I would like to suggest here is that the same kind of economic irritation that existed between Sinhalese and Tamils in the eighteenth century remains a critical factor in the contemporary acrimonious relations that exist between Sinhalese and Tamils. The difference now is one of degree: the irritation is much more intense. Moreover, economic rivalry might be understood as the most aggravating issue, not only between Sinhalese and Tamils, but also among the various classes of both ethnic communities.

The tragedy of the ethnic conflict between the Sinhalese and Tamils is born of the social fact that both communities have now developed the perception that they are economically disadvantaged in relation to one another. They both have suffered from minority complexes with regard to perceived economic opportunity.

With regard to current Tamil alienation, Gerald Peiris (a Sinhalese scholar) has described the contemporary situation in the following terms:

> The increasing politicization of administrative processes and what it has meant in respect of the disbursement of benefits of development among the people appear to have had an even more profound impact upon ethnic relations in Sri Lanka, especially on the increasing alienation of the Sri Lankan Tamils from the economic mainstreams of the country. . . . Almost throughout the period after independence, the Sri Lankan Tamils have been in "opposition" which, in turn, meant that their interests and aspirations . . . have not been adequately represented in the vital day to day affairs of government. Though some of the frequently articulated Tamil claims seem to lack substance and objectivity, it cannot be denied that, especially since the early 1970s, the working of the political in respect of economic affairs placed them permanently in the position of a disadvantaged segment of the electorate. To some extent the emergence of a militant separatist movement among them can be attributed to this phenomenon.[7]

One could read Peiris's description of the contemporary dynamics of Sri Lanka's political economy and imagine its accuracy, in principle, if it were used to depict the dynamics afoot in the Kandyan kingdom some 250 years ago, except that the group being precluded from participating in the administration of the economy would be the Kandyan Sinhalese nobles and the group in control would be the kin of Tamil royalty. About 250 years ago, Sinhalese nobles, largely alienated by economic disenfranchisement, attempted to assassinate a Tamil head of state. In 1993, Tamil militants, though they deny it publicly, may have been responsible for the murder of a Sinhalese head of state, and of several other leading Sri Lankan government officials and the prime minister of India.

On the Sinhalese side of contemporary perception, it is taken as a social fact of history that when the British finally gave up on their colonial intrusion, they left behind, as part of their legacy, a socioeconomic milieu in which the Tamil community had come to dominate the civil service, the medical and legal professions, and most of the institutions of higher learning in Sri Lanka.The Tamils had also become a major force in the business community, not only in the metropolitan area of Colombo, but also in many good-sized towns in the Sinhalese ethnic regions of the south and the up-country. Sinhala apologists never tire of reminding us that, at least until 1983, the Tamil community, collectively, was in control of a far greater percentage of the country's economic wealth than a simple noting of the Tamil's percentage of the population would seem to indicate. It would not be grossly inaccurate to say that Sinhalese-dominated democracies in postcolonial Sri Lanka have passed laws that affect the use of language, the special state recognition of Buddhism (including the restoration of so many sites of archaeological importance, for political purposes) and the procurement of educational opportunities, chiefly as means for seeking redress for what they perceived (rightly or wrongly) as the relative social and economic disenfranchisement that the Sinhalese people had suffered, on the whole, under British colonial rule.

While religion and, especially, language are certainly ethnically definitive and have functioned as a basis for powerful political rallying cries that guarantee votes in popular elections, perceived economic deprivation may produce an even more powerful emotion. Again, language and religion are formative for ethnic *identity*, but perceptions of who has more and who has less, and of who controls access to the group that will have more, or less, in the future, foster *alienation* or envy per se, whether or not it is alienation along ethnic lines or among classes within ethnic communities. Economic deprivation certainly was the deep-seated motive in the failed, but extremely bloody, intraethnic conflicts or revolutionary movements launched by the Sinhalese Janata Vimukta Peramuna (JVP) in 1971 and again in 1988–1990, in which masses of rural and economically disadvantaged and, therefore, alienated Sinhala youth sought to disestablish what was perceived as an elite Sinhala-dominated government that was acting, preferentially, in the vested interests of those with political and economic power (radical JVP Buddhist statements about protecting the motherland notwithstanding). Economic deprivation was also a key motivation in the rise of the revolutionary Tamil militants—the Liberation Tigers of Tamil Eelam—who have displaced the traditional political leadership of the Sri Lankan Tamil community, which was formerly provided by the more well-to-do landowning castes of the Jaffna peninsula. It is significant that in neither

Sinhala nor Tamil revolutionary contexts has Buddhism or Hinduism played the most significant role in either the formation or ideology or in the claims of special identity. Only on the Sinhala JVP side in the late 1980s did some even attempt to directly link religion (Buddhism) to the cause, and only very sporadically have attempts been made to link the cause of the Tigers to religion (Christian liberation theology).

To illustrate and further frame the importance of the economic factor in creating alienation between the Sinhalese and Tamil communities and in deemphasizing the religious factor, I will cite a personal experience.

During the last week of July 1983, one day after riots had erupted throughout the neighborhoods of the Borella district in Colombo, on the night following funerals for thirteen Sinhalese government soldiers who had been blown up by a land mine that, allegedly, was planted by Tamil revolutionaries on the Jaffna peninsula the week before, I arrived in Sri Lanka to begin a two-year stint as teacher and researcher. On my way from the airport to the city, I could see, in all directions, plumes of smoke streaming skyward from burning factories, stores, and houses (which, I later learned, were owned by Colombo Tamils). Shattering glass and scattered screams punctuated the eerie silence of the normally bustling Pettah market area of the city, and a fiery chaos reigned amid many of the shops on Galle Road (to the south of central Colombo, in Bambalapitiye and Wellawatte). Quite clearly, Colombo was "up for grabs" as Sinhalese goon squads and unruly crowds attacked the defenseless Tamils in the area and destroyed their properties. Backtracking on major thoroughfares in order to reach Negombo (30 kilometers north of the heart of the city), and safer environs, I observed a scene that, in hindsight, was important in the way I eventually came to understand the other bewildering events (or, as it has now become fashionable to say, "ethnic cleansings") that occurred during the rest of a week that was filled with killing and arson throughout the Sinhalese regions of the island. It also sheds light on the root causes of the conflict, which, I would argue, are parallel, in principle, to the reasons an attempt was made to assassinate Kīrti Śrī.

While nearing Negombo, a horde of young men were throwing stones at a nearby hotel, tentatively breaking into its premises, retreating, and then stoning it again. About half an hour later, the hotel under siege had been set ablaze and its occupants and employees sent fleeing to the beach or to the road, while the young men who had been throwing stones finished their work. I was but one of several Westerners who simply stood paralyzed and watched as the hotel was looted and almost totally destroyed by fire.

Now, most academicians and journalists have emphasized how the politicization of religion and language are the deep-seated reasons for Sri Lanka's continuing pattern of communal violence over the past forty years and have cited, as I have done in this chapter, the pivotal election campaign of 1956 (filled with rhetoric about language and religion) that has fundamentally changed the political landscape of the island ever since. Furthermore, especially in Europe and the United States, the spectacular week of violence in July 1983 was initially reported or typified by journalists and, later, often misrepresented by some academicians (almost all of whom were not in Sri Lanka at the time) as a Sinhala Buddhist/Tamil Hindu conflict. Even now, many years later, media reports of armed conflicts between the Sri Lankan military forces and the Liberation Tigers of Tamil Eelam (Tamil Tigers) almost always include a reference to the fact that the Sinhalese are Buddhists and the Tamils are Hindu. In the academic context, it is still often asked whether or not the Buddhist religion itself, a religion known throughout Asia and the rest of the world for its teachings of peace, has not been betrayed by Sinhalese adherents, not only in the context of 1983 but also more generally in the period that led up to and followed political independence from Britain.[8] Buddhist militancy has certainly been on the rise during this time and has sharply delineated the lines of ethnic identity. But one has to ask, Is it Buddhism that is really responsible for the violence in Sri Lanka? Some Buddhist monks may have helped to inflame passions and some have been so bizarre in their public statements as to justify violence. In this instance, it can be said that the teachings, and especially the monastic discipline of the Buddha, have been seriously manipulated and wrongly understood.

However, an overemphasized and sometimes misplaced assumption in many of the scholarly attempts to sort out reasons for the 1983 conflagration has been that the perpetrators of the violence were all Buddhists and that the victims were all Hindus or Christians. Such a religious characterization of the participants can be somewhat misleading. Furthermore, because popularized Buddhistic sentiments—that is, the *dhammadipa* legacy that the Sinhalese people of Sri Lanka are destined to preserve Buddhism in its pristine purity—were (unfortunately) expressed by some misguided Buddhist zealots to rationalize or explain the heinous crimes committed in July 1983, the case against Buddhism has proceeded apace. What I want to note, however (before discussing the question about who was attacking whom in the Negombo hotel attack that I witnessed in 1983), is that the same kind of discursive rationalization was made by nineteenth-century Sinhalese Buddhists to explain the attempt to eliminate their "heretical Śaivite" king in the eighteenth century.

Certainly, it is the case that language, traditional mythic and ritualistic patterns, and assiduously asserted religious identity have all contributed to a heightened consciousness of ethnicity among Sinhalese Buddhists, especially since postindependence politicos in Sri Lanka have continuously pandered to language and religion as the distinctive features of Sinhala ethnicity, which, they paranoically imply, are threatened by the continued presence of other ethnic identities. But it does not follow that these critical elements of ethnic identity are the direct causes of ethnic violence of the type that characterized the 1983 pogrom; nor, perhaps, are they the essence of the conflict per se between these two ethnic communities since the 1950s.

Regarding the incident that I witnessed on that scorching Monday, during the last week in July 1983: those young men who looted and burned that Negombo hotel (owned and operated by Tamils) were not the same kind of organized (by chauvinistic sections of the government?) thugs who, on the following day, arrived in lorries to begin torching Tamil shops in up-country Peradeniya and Kandy. Rather, they were locals known to the employees and proprietors of the nearby hotel where I was staying. And, they were nominal Christians. (Negombo has the most Christians of all the towns in Sri Lanka; they comprise more than 90 percent of Negombo's population, with a good number of the remaining 10 percent living in a Muslim enclave immediately north of the town.) My point, obviously, is that I do not blame Christians or Christianity for the communal violence I witnessed; nor do I argue that most of the perpetrators of violence in 1983 were not nominal Buddhists. Instead, my point is that religion did not have much, if anything, to do with the immediate problem at hand. In this case specifically, and now, in general, the violence of the ethnic conflict is born of economic rivalry between ethnic communities who identify themselves primarily on the basis of language and, only secondarily, by religious affiliation. In Sri Lanka, being a Christian does not exclude one from being either Sinhalese or Tamil. One's linguistic ability is far more crucial in this regard. (This fact was cruelly revealed during the 1983 violence, when some groups of Sinhalese thugs stopped public and private buses to distinguish between Sinhalese and Tamil passengers; those who could not speak Sinhala satisfactorily were beaten and, in some cases, killed.) But while language, and to a much lesser extent religion, are key factors in defining ethnic identity, they need not be identified as the primary causes of violence. Indeed, genuine religious sentiment across Sri Lanka's religious communities remains one of the recognized hopes for ameliorating the continuing ethnic problem, though even the Roman Catholic Church has split along Sinhala and Tamil ethnic lines.

The immediate causes of the 1983 riots were, at first, emotional in nature. Violence (militant Tamil violence against Sinhala soldiers) itself incited the passions for revengeful Sinhala violence against Tamils in the south. Language and religion defined ethnic identity; aggressive, violent provocation generated even greater ethnic violence; but the primary underlying causes of the ethnic alienation that set the table for violence was economic in nature.

In addition to being the underlying cause, economic factors also did play a direct role in motivating some sections of the Sinhalese populace to join in the action during July 1983. Once it was apparent that government security forces were not resisting the pillaging and burning (and this was very apparent as early as the second day after I had arrived), much of the violence and looting was systematically orchestrated against economic targets by organized thugs (of urban origins) who intruded into communities outside Colombo (their governmental base?), or was inspired by local business rivalries and, finally, by individual attempts to take personal advantage of the chaotic situation. For instance, after outside (Colombo-based?) thugs had successfully invaded Kandy and Peradeniya on the Wednesday of the last week in July, it was open season in downtown Kandy, when some business rivalries were settled by torches and petroleum. This was then followed by looting by scores of poor people who took whatever remained in the stores as policemen simply stood by and watched, or, in some cases, joined the fracas. This was also the pattern for what had happened throughout metropolitan Colombo, but only a day or two earlier.

It is quite perplexing that the then president of the country, J. R. Jayewardene, did not go on the airwaves to make a public appeal for calm and order until Thursday night (the fifth night of uncontrolled violence in the streets). Indeed, a few of his government ministers were later widely suspected to have been quite actively responsible for some of the mayhem that followed the initial emotional outbursts. But in fact, no government military or police force was actively trying to prevent violence or to restore order, until the sixth day (Friday) of the rioting, when crowds of Sinhalese panicked and fled the Colombo Fort area in a mass hysteria, on the heels of a rumor that Tamil Tigers had arrived in Colombo and were then poised as snipers on the roofs of buildings in the downtown area. Only after that amazing demonstration of collective Sinhalese guilt (and cowardice?) was a nationwide curfew imposed that lasted some 72 hours and effectively ended the more than five days of riots. President Jayewardene then addressed the nation once more and called the week of violence "a moral crisis in civilization." While the moral emphasis of his historical perspective was well aimed, the fact is that, from a political perspective, that week of ethnic violence in which the police and the military remained generally passive, while thousands of Sri Lankan Tamil lives were snuffed out or shattered, also demonstrated Sri Lanka's lack of morally courageous political leadership.

(Although I want to stress that the property damage caused by the 1983 riots was extraordinary in comparison to the number of innocent people who died [and some two thousand to four thousand people were murdered, by most estimates], and although I am arguing that economic factors were the chief culprit in the ethnic alienation and the violence that followed between ethnic groups and classes in Sri Lanka, I do not mean to downplay the terrible loss of human life that resulted from the organized manhunts that fanned out, throughout Colombo and Kandy, in search of unprotected Tamils during those days when all civil order had broken down.)

Those terrible events that occurred during that week in 1983, in turn, have had the effect (as an example of karmic consequences) of refueling the determination of militant Tamil groups to strike back with vengeance, in ways equally as despicable, in the years that have followed. The Tamil militants, as I have already pointed out, are also driven by a hatred bred by an economic grouse. But I also want to stress again that Hinduism and Christianity have played no real part in the ideology of the Tamil Tigers (except perhaps only indirectly in their cult of martyrdom), just as Buddhism was not a major inspiration for the JVP or for the uncontrolled Sinhalese mobs or organized thugs in 1983. Religion, it has to be recognized, is not the primary culprit in this case. Only in a limited sense has the legacy of Buddhism been appealed to as an ex post facto rationalization by some deluded zealots, in the same manner in which, one hundred years earlier, a textual attempt had been made to rationalize the assassination attempt on Kīrti Śrī. Most truly religious Buddhists are genuinely peace-loving people, as are most truly religious Hindus and Christians. Many of them acted courageously in providing shelter to the desperate during the time when the police and the army had shirked their responsibilities. On the other hand, the politically inspired often misuse religious identity to further their nonreligious aims. Or, at best, they believe that history can be reversed, that the classical era can be reinvented to replace the modern or postmodern condition.

It may appear that, in this postscript, I am undermining my own argument. Why, after all, did the politically inspired Kīrti Śrī go to such great efforts to present himself as an ardent supporter of Buddhism, as a legitimate quintessential Buddhist king, if aligning himself with Buddhism, by restoring its vitality, was not the most important politically correct move of his day? In fact, it was the politically correct move of his (classical) era, but only because, in so doing, he used his wealth and economic power in a manner that was thoroughly approved by his Buddhist constituency. Not only was Kīrti Śrī concerned with presenting himself publicly, through orchestrated symbols, rituals, and art, as a pious Buddhist king, but his greatest legacy (as noted by Ananda Coomaraswamy), was how he put his wealth and energies to use. Because of the manner in which he used his economic resources, he was virtually unassailable, on religio-political grounds, by his noble Sinhalese rivals. He was, after all, from the perspective of those Sinhalese Buddhists who were loyal to him, a selfless giver, a pious layman acting in support of the *śāsana*, and possibly a future Buddha.

Appendix

The Religious Works of Kīrti Śrī at Gangārāma and Ridī Vihāra

The religious works of Kīrti Śrī at Gangārāma and Ridī Vihāra receive by far the most detailed descriptions of any temples cited in the entire Cūlavaṃsa. *Insofar as the Buddhist monk Tibboṭuvāve, who was assigned by Kīrti Śrī to update the chronicle from its thirteenth-century state, was originally from Ridī Vihāra, it is not surprising that his treatment of Kīrti Śrī's reign concludes with such an extensive description of the king's efforts to beautify this monk's own monastic home. The description is valuable precisely because it provides us with so many details about the various elements of artistic work carried out by Kīrti Śrī, details that Tibboṭuvāve could record at length because of his own intimacy with the place. Tibboṭuvāve's description of Gangārāma, while not as extensive, seems to have been given great emphasis so as to please Kīrti Śrī himself. Since it was located literally in the king's own backyard, Kīrti Śrī had spent enormous sums, as the chronicle reports, to make this temple resplendent, only to have it ruined by the Dutch invasion in 1765. It should be noted that Gangārāma had also been very*

Wilhelm Geiger, trans. and ed. (1953). *Cūlavaṃsa: Being the More Recent Part of the Mahāvaṃsa*. 2 vols. Colombo: Ceylon Government Information Department.

sacred for the monks of the Malvatta Vihāraya because it had been the site of their cremation ceremonies. The following descriptions of both temples allow us to examine what Kīrti Śrī considered his priorities in his rehabilitation exercises.

Description of Gangārāma (*Cūlavaṃsa* 2:289–291)

On a firmly fixed rock situated on a beautiful spot not too far to the east of the town of Sirivaddha [in Kandy] he had hewn out by skilful workers, masons and others a splendid standing image of the Victor nine cubits high and he had placed on the radiant, shining stone image gold plates so that it resembled the living Sage. Round about this Buddha statue he had erected a lofty, massive beautiful stone wall and superb stone pillars placed and splendid beautiful two-storeyed temple built fair to look at, as well as a roomy court, outer walls, maṇḍapas [porches for ritual chanting of scriptures] and so forth set up in the best way. Then he put thereon canopies and curtains of all kinds of coloured stuffs. Round about he placed arches one after another and provided them in every way with much ornament. Here and there he set up various flags and pennants and on the day of the sacrificial festival of the eyes he lit a row of lamps, placed filled jars (about) and carried out in blameless fashion the various customs prescribed for festivals. To the people who supplied the coloured paintings, he dispensed abundantly robes, ornaments and the like and satisfied their wishes in every way. Then he made the splendid long clang of the musical instruments, like shell trumpets, kettledrums and so forth resound, like the roar of a wide sea, and under a good constellation, at a good hour, on a good day determined as favourable he put in the eyes and celebrated a great festival. Numerous silver bowls and many silver vessels, costly necessaries and valuable monks' robes, banners, white umbrellas, shields, fly-whisks and fans—all these and other fair objects of sacrifice the Ruler offered, mindful of reward accruing from a sacrifice to the Buddha, with the thought that it was as if it took place in the presence of the still living Prince of the wise, with a heart full of the joy of faith, intent on merit. Many and manifold foods also such as sweet dishes, rice, solid dishes and others, sugar, honey, betel, lime, camphor and so forth, also remedies and perfumes of every kind like sandal and the like, beautiful flowers like jasmine, campaka blossoms and others—all these and other objects of sacrifice he offered in pious fashion. The makers of the Buddha image and other people he rejoiced by an offering of many animate and inanimate things, elephants, cattle, buffaloes and so forth. If one reckons the sums spent in the making of the Buddha statue and the other offerings of the occasion of this vihāra festival according to their money value, the result was sixteen thousand one hundred and fifty (kahāpanas).

The large beautiful vihāra, well worth seeing, which is known as Gangarama because it was built on a fair spot near the Mahāvālukagaṅgā [Mahāwēligaṅgā] was founded by the King under the name Rājamaha-vihāra. This vihara, thus superbly furnished with glory and splendour, was also destroyed by the enemy who had penetrated into the town. The King had it in the best way restored to its original condition, and just as he had held a solemn ceremony at the former eye festival, so now he held another eye festival. After the Ruler of Men had dispensed in great abundance to the painters and so forth garments, ornaments and other articles and had sacrificed with many sacrificial gifts, he erected nearby a fair monastery for the community and made a chapter of bhikkhus who devoted themselves with lasting zeal to the study and fulfillment of moral duties, take up their abode there, providing them in every way with what was necessary. Then by holding in the way described formerly, full of reverence for the Triad of jewels, a sacrificial festival for the Buddha, and at the same time sacrificing to the chapters of the bhikkhus, he increased the fulness of merit for himself and the laity.

Now in order that this beautiful vihara, worthy to be seen, that was erected in this manner, and all the numerous sacrificial ceremonies inaugurated there and the many meritorious works such as the offerings to the community—should be continued for a long time in the right way, the Ruler determined a village situated near the vihāra by the name Aruppala, and many other villages and fields, and gardens also, as well as the large populous village by name Udakagāma [now Diyagāma] in the district of Māyādhanu and granted them (to this monastery). And the King confirmed this in perpetuity by having an inscription graven on the beautiful mountain in stone.

In this way the King of Kings dowered with splendid virtues, since he realised the worthlessness of acquired wealth, in his piety and sacrificial festivals celebrated for the Buddha and sacrificial festivals for the community of the excellent sons of the Victor and so performed perpetually all valuable meritorious works. Therefore should ye all also perpetually perform without wearying, meritorious works.

Description of Ridī Vihāra (*Cūlavaṃsa* 2:293–299)

To the sāmaṇera called Siddhattha the Ruler granted the large Rajatavihara erected by King Duṭṭhagāmaṇī when inspired by the wish for the august position of a chief disciple of Metteyya, the King of the wise. After the Ruler of Lanka had caused the ceremony of admission to the Order to be performed on him, he granted this bhikkhu and all the sons of the Victor dwelling in the Uposathārāma rank and showed them favour in every way. Then in order to restore this vihāra which had long been in the state of a ruined house, the Ruler of men in Lanka assigned divers artisans, painters and others, as well as all handiwork and so forth. That prince among ascetics—Siddhattha—accepted all this and removed in the best possible way everything that had been destroyed by age. He had a lofty, massive stone wall and a fine plaster floor built in the house, and outside a maṇḍapa, as well as (a picture), the figure of the Buddha in combat with Māra above on the rock face. Then when he had caused creeper works of flowers to be applied in the best possible manner and had caused a vast image of the recumbent Buddha to be fashioned out of good bricks, lime and clay and also many sitting and standing images of the Victor, he had represented in the best way possible in painting on the beautiful inner wall, enlightened ones, a thousand in number. And at the foot of the vast statue of the recumbent Buddha he had placed one after the other beautiful images, that of the Buddha's constant servant and protector of the true doctrine—Ānanda, that of the bodhisatta Metteyya, that of the sublime patron deity (Viṣṇu) [In fact, here the text says *Nāthadeva*, clearly referring to Nātha/Avalokiteśvara rather than to Viṣṇu] and that of King Gāmaṇī. He overlaid the five great images of the Buddha with gold, and when he had thus in every possible way finished the works which were to be made in the inside (of the shrine), he had portrayed also outside on the wall a series of glorious figures of gods and Brahma figures with flowers in their hands, which look as if they had appeared for worship. Then too he caused a great, beautiful triumphal arch to be made, well worth seeing, further two lion figures on either side of the portal and in the empty interstices of the wall figures of demons. Also he had pictures portrayed in coloured painting of the sixteen holy places, Mahīyangana and the others, further of the famous footprint on the Saccabaddha mountain, of the ten pāramīs [perfections], of the three forms of (right) action, as well as of many Jātakas in which subjects like the five great renunciations are treated of. In the maṇḍapa he had all kinds of figures introduced, series of lions, series of elephants, series of geese and creeper work of flowers. In the delightful cave in the same rock he built a vast image house, well worth seeing, splendid, beautiful with many sculptures fashioned to perfection and so forth. There he made a beautiful, vast, life-like sitting Buddha made—splendid was this figure and fair to look at—on either side well-fashioned, upright standing statues of the Bodhisatta Metteyya and of the lotus-hued god [Uppalavanna]. He also caused many other figures to be set up: figures of sages, figures of many hundreds of the perfect, the four and twenty Buddhas, the whole of the Bodhi trees in the same number, the four and twenty intimations, the sixteen holy places, fair forms of spiritual beings and others, the five great Councils and yet diverse other beautiful pictures well worth seeing. Then he brought thither relics of the Sage and had a cetiya erected, adorned with a golden finial. In the image house itself he had placed on the lofty vaulted ceiling a sitting figure of the Sage surrounded by his five hundred followers, Sāriputta at the head. In the court he had walls and maṇḍapas erected at different places, as well as several gate-buildings and here and there stairs and other fine buildings, partly the restorations of much that had suffered by age, partly also many new (buildings).

All these fine structures the King dedicated (to the monastery) at the festival of the eyes by dignitaries whom he had sent, and in addition clothing, ornaments and much else. He had rows of various triumphal arches without gaps put up, placed on them the necessary ornament, gave orders for the sacred ceremonies and while celebrating in worthy fashion a great rite, he carried out the festival of the eyes under a lucky star and at a favourable hour.

From that time onwards there came hither many inhabitants of the whole kingdom from all quarters, like the sea when it overflows the land. When all the people who had gathered there beheld the many golden and other works of art which had been carried out, their hearts were filled with joy, as if they saw the Enlightened One at the miracle of the double appearances. In joyful and high spirits, they celebrated amid cries of Hail! a great festival and thus paved their way to Heaven. At the festival he invited the bhikkhu community of the vihāra, made bhikkhus who were preachers of the true doctrine sit down thereon, and had the Mahāmangalasutta and other sacred texts worth hearing recited by them and thus celebrated in worthy manner a sacrificial festival of the doctrine.

All the people who saw and heard this, in that they at one and the same time beheld the Enlightened One and heard the true doctrine, were filled daily in every possible way with the highest joy and ecstasy, as if by a sermon of the living Sage. Thus he made manifest both: the beauty of his form and the charm of his sermon.

Outside in the court he placed pillars of stone, erected a maṇḍapa, spread seats therein and after establishing the great multitudes gathered round the maṇḍapa in the five major and other commandments relating to moral discipline, he made them listen to abundant texts. Full of reverence he also invited the preachers of the doctrine repeatedly during the three watches of the night.

In the year two thousand three hundred and one after the final nirvana of the Enlightened One, he had the vihāra called Rājata restored and the great festival celebrated. He then thought of repairing the splendid cetiya erected on a clear, fine large slab of rock to the south of the vihāra but which was so dilapidated that it resembled a heap of dust. Therefore he had fetched from all quarters lime, bricks, stones and so forth. Hereupon he had a fine square throne built of stone in the best possible manner wherein he placed a relic of the sublime Enlightened One. At the restoration of the cetiya, he erected on a neighboring, particularly beautiful piece of land for the community whom he invited thither in fitting manner for the purpose, setting up a marked out boundary, a monastery with an Uposatha house and other (buildings) provided with a brick roof and so forth. On the land round about he laid out beautifully a large park adorned with divers blossoming trees, with divers blossoming creepers, and with divers fruit trees and the like, and where there were many bathing ponds. And full of zeal as he was, he piously made the sons of the Victor dwell there and devote themselves to study and religious exercises.

After the Ruler of men had in such wise stored up divers kinds of merit he passed in the thirty-fifth year of his reign from this world thither in accordance with his deeds.

When one reflects on the worthlessness of wealth and of the life of the flesh one utterly rejects the yearning thereafter. Ye also, revering the Triad of sacred things, ought to perform good works such as spiritual exertions and the like.

Notes

Preface

1. For an excellent discussion of the social and ideological foundations of ancient Indian Buddhism, see Stanley J. Tambiah, "The Institutional Achievements of Early Buddhism," in S. N. Eisenstadt, ed., *The Origins and Diversity of Axial Age Civilizations* (Albany: State University of New York Press, 1986).

Chapter 1. Kīrti Śrī's Predicament

1. For summaries of the Portuguese colonial experience in Sri Lanka, see Chandra Richard de Silva, *Sri Lanka: A History* (New Delhi: Vikas Publishing, 1987), pp. 116–128, or K. M. de Silva, *A History of Sri Lanka* (Berkeley: University of California Press, 1981), pp. 97–132. For detailed assessments on various aspects of their attempted political, economic, and religious hegemony, see T. B. H. Abeyasinghe, *Portuguese Rule in Ceylon* 1594–1612 (Colombo, 1966); C. R. de Silva, *The Portuguese in Ceylon 1617–1638* (Colombo: Lake House, 1972); on their expulsion from the island, see G. D. Winius, *The Fatal History of the Portuguese in Ceylon* (Cambridge: Harvard University Press, 1971). On the establishment and consolidation of Dutch power, see K. W. Goonewardene, *The Foundation of Dutch Power in Ceylon* (Amsterdam, 1958), and S. Arasaratnam, *Dutch Power in Ceylon* (Amsterdam, 1958).

2. S. Arasaratnam, "Dutch Commercial Policy in Ceylon and Its Effects on Indo-Ceylon Trade, 1690–1750," *Indian Economic and Social History Review* 4 (1967) 109–130.

3. See, for instance, E. Reimers, trans. and ed., *Memoir of Steivan Gollennesse for his Successor, 1751* (Colombo: Government Printer, 1935);

E. Reimers, trans. and ed., *Memoir of Joan Gideon Loten for His Successor, 1757* (Colombo: Government Printer, 1947); E. Reimers, trans. and ed., *Memoir of Joan Schreuder for His Successor, 1762* (Colombo: Government Printer, 1946); and J. H. O. Paulusz, trans. and ed., *Secret Minutes of the Dutch Political Council, 1762* (Colombo: Government Press, 1954).

4. Note Governor Schreuder's explicit confession to this effect: "The welfare of the Church and State are intimately connected" (Reimers, *Memoir of Joan Schreuder*, p. 95).

5. In contemporary Sri Lanka, over a million Sinhalese and Tamils, out of a population of some seventeen million, are Roman Catholics, while the number of Dutch Reformed churches that remain on the island are but a scattered handful. Even these are not well attended; for instance, the most historically important Dutch church in Sri Lanka (located within the Galle Fort) is currently open for services only twice a month. The question of why Sinhalese and Tamils in Sri Lanka took to Roman Catholicism and have remained loyal is very pertinent in light of the fact that among all Asian countries, excluding the Philippines, in Sri Lanka they form the largest Christian percentage of the population. Indeed, the percentage is seven times that in India. Malalgoda's argument that the success of Roman Catholicism was due to that tradition's affinity for ritualistic religiosity, an affinity or religious ethos more in common with South Asian traditions than with the Reformed Church's abhorrence of ceremonialism, however, is unconvincing. Kitsiri Malalgoda, *Buddhism and Sinhalese Society 1750–1900* (Berkeley: University of California Press, 1976), p. 34. How would one account for the relative success of Low Church Protestant missions in Burma, where Catholicism is concomitantly weak? How does one explain the situation in India, where Roman Catholicism did not succeed nearly as well, in that the Hindu religio-cultural context is given over much more to ceremonialism and ritual than it is in Buddhistic Sri Lanka? How does one account for the current successes of Low Church pentacostals in Sri Lanka?

6. Malalgoda points out that, in Sri Lanka, neither the Portuguese nor the Dutch made attempts like de Nobili made in South India and Ricci made in China to present Christianity in concepts and categories indigenous and therefore readily understandable to Asians. Ibid., p. 30.

7. Conversion was seen as a strategy that would help drive a wedge between the low-country Sinhalese and the Kandyan king. Moreover, the Dutch were clearly suspicious about, and demonstrably displeased with, the physical restorations and monastic appointments effected by Kīrti Śrī at the historically important Buddhist *vihārayas* (temples) at Kälaniya (just north of Colombo) and at Mulgirigala (about 15 miles east of Mātara), all of which had previously suffered serious, if not complete, denigration at the hands of the Portuguese and had been, for many decades, bereft of clerical incumbents.

8. It is interesting to note that Roman Catholics were more tolerated by the Buddhist community before the Nāyakkars' reigns, when Sinhalese kings were on the throne. It is quite clear, therefore, that the persecution of Roman Catholics under Śrī Vijaya and Kīrti Śrī had become an expedient act because of Buddhist suspicions regarding their commitment to the *śāsana*. Lawrie points out that "Kīrti Śrī continued the [policy of] persecution, but afterwards attributing a famine and plague, which afflicted the country, to this cause, he ordered the images which had adorned the church of Bogaṁbara [in Kandy], and which, on its destruction, had been deposited in his stores, to be given to the people of Vahakötte, with permission to rebuild their church and enjoy their religion." Archibald C. Lawrie, *A Gazeteer of the Central Province*, 2 vols. (Colombo: George J. A. Skeen, Government Printer, 1898), 1:104.

9. See K. W. Goonewardene, "Buddhism under the Dutch," paper presented at the Ceylon Studies Seminar, University of Peradeniya, 1990.

10. Governor van Eck, who led the expedition, describes the onslaught of the Kīrti Śrī's palace and the Daḷadā Māligāva as follows: "Shortly after it was inspected this castle was plundered and everything given up for booty. There was much treasure, consisting of gold, silver, precious stones, gold and silver cloths, velvets, silk stuffs, fine linen of all sorts in abundance. For three days the men did nothing else but roam and plunder so that everything had been ruined, both the walls and the doors, which were plated with silver, and now stripped of everything; it was a miserable spectacle." A. E. Buultjens, trans., "Governor van Eck's Expedition against the King of Kandy, 1765," *Journal of the Royal Asiatic Society* (*Ceylon Branch*) 16 (1899): 49. As for the indigenous perspective, the *Cūlavaṃsa* describes van Eck and his expedition in these terms: "Now when the enemy were thus tortured by fear a cruel and treacherous man placed himself at their head, low-minded, a villain, the end of whose life was near, and with a great following consisting of Javakas and many other people, he laid waste in every possible way the various provinces and villages, the viharas and the temples of the gods, the bridges, rest-houses and the like. . . . Thereupon the hostile hosts like cruel armies of yakkhas, forced their way into the town and destroyed the sacred books and everything else" (2:266–267).

11. For details and a translation of the treaty, see Lorna Dewaraja, *The Kandyan Kingdom 1707–1761* (Colombo: Lake House Publishers, 1971), pp. 160h–160n. Most significant, Kīrti Śrī lost complete control of access to ports and was effectively cut off from the outside world. For about six years, Kīrti Śrī lived with this isolated situation, until the first sign of unrest: a demand made by the Dutch for a share of the pearl fisheries off Mannar in 1772. See A. H. Mirando, *Buddhism in Sri Lanka in the 17th and 18th Centuries* (Dehiwala, Sri Lanka: Tisara Prakasakayo, 1985), p. 67. By 1776 he was asking for a return of some of the coastal districts.

12. The princess was the daughter of one Piṭṭināyakkar, who loomed as a major power broker in the affairs of the court. Indeed, it is possible that the origins of the cult of Pitiye, a god whose popularity arose in the Kandyan region during the reign of Narendra Sinha, can be attributed to his courtly eminence. See my *Buddha in the Crown* (New York: Oxford University Press, 1991), pp. 125–150.

13. For details of these two revolts, see Dewaraja, *Kandyan Kingdom*, pp. 72–90.

14. Dewaraja reports that "the idea of a Siamese prince on the Kandyan throne had seized the imagination of Governor Van Eck to such an extent that on his death bed on March 27, 1765, he dictated a letter to his council urging it to make one more attempt to secure Krumpty Pippit [the Siamese prince] for the Kandyan throne." Ibid., pp. 134–135, n. 131.

Chapter 2. Discourses of a Buddhist King

1. P. B. Meegaskumbura notes that the *Mandārampura Puvata*, as a work of several authors, which was written over a considerable period of time, might categorically be regarded as a royal *vaṃsa*, or chronicle, rather than a ballad. Personal communication.

2. Mirando, commenting on the *Cūlavaṃsa*'s portrait of the queens from Madurai, says that "the queens of Vijayarājasiṃha, who were also of foreign extraction, took steps to promote the Buddhist religion, calculated perhaps to gain popular support and confidence." Mirando, *Buddhism in Sri Lanka*, p. 57.

3. Verses 510–511, cited in K. N. O. Dharmadasa, "The Sinhala Buddhist Identity and the Nayakkar Dynasty in the Politics of the Kandyan Kingdom, 1739–1815," *Ceylon Journal of Historical and Social Studies*, n. s. 6 (1976): 11. The *Mandārampura Puvata* is a continuously written eighteenth- and nineteenth-century poem (this section was apparently written about two decades after Sri Vijaya's coronation. See K. N. O. Dharmadasa, *Language, Religion and Ethnic Assertiveness: The Growth of Sinhalese Nationalism in Sri Lanka* (Ann Arbor: University of Michigan Press, 1992), p. 9. It is, more likely, a historical ballad that recounts, in part, the legacies of Kandyan kingship. For a description, summary, and partial translation, see Julius De Lanerolle, "The *Mandārampura Puvata*," *Journal of the Royal Asiatic Society* (*Ceylon Branch*), n. s. 3 (1953): 153–160.

4. "Heroic" is used in the sense explained by Kemper, insofar as Kīrti Śrī's ritual actions, including his coronation and those that reflect his support of Buddhism, attempt to express a discourse on political unity and centralized power. Steven Kemper, *The Presence of the Past: Chronicles, Politics and Culture in Sinhala Life* (Ithaca, N.Y.: Cornell University Press, 1991), pp. 53–78, esp. p. 77.

5. See his *Rituals of the Kandyan State* (Cambridge, Eng.: Cambridge University Press., 1978).

6. This particular point is open to some debate, depending on how one views the religious activities of Narendra Sinha, the last of the ethnic Sinhalese kings. Scholars such as Dewaraja, Gunasinghe and, to some extent, Malalgoda have emphasized that institutional Buddhism experienced its nadir during Narendra Sinha's reign, from 1707 to 1739. However, it is also clear that while Narendra Sinha may have neglected the institutional *sangha*, he by no means ignored religious issues. In fact, his perspective on religion was probably far more eclectic or liberal than was usual for Kandyan kings. For instance, he is known to have been a patron of the cult of Pitiye, one of the twelve *baṇḍāra*-class deities of Sri Lanka, whose power is understood as more accessible to the laity for this-worldly assistance. The divine power attributed to these deities, who rank below the four national guardian deities (Nātha, Viṣṇu, Skanda, and Pattini) in Kandyan cosmology is regarded as jurisdictional and, hence, very accessible in character. Dewaraja, *Kandyan Kingdom*, pp. 83–84; Malalgoda, *Buddhism and Sinhalese Society*, pp. 57–58; and Siri Gunasinghe, *An Album of Buddhist Paintings from Sri Lanka* (*Ceylon*) (*Kandy Period*) (Colombo: National Museum of Sri Lanka, 1978), p. 6. See also, Deborah Winslow, "A Political Geography of Deities: Space and Pantheon in Sinhalese Buddhism," *Journal of Asian Studies* 43 (1984): 273–292. Piṭiye was regarded as the regional *bandara* deity, who had power that extended over the Duṁbara Valley area, part of which is Kuṇḍasāle, where Narendra Sinha himself built a royal residence. Narendra Sinha is also known to have sponsored a multireligious debate in 1712 between a Calvinist, a Catholic, a Muslim, and a Buddhist. Malalgoda notes that Saranaṃkara, who was later appointed *sangharāja* under Kīrti Śrī, first came to the attention of Narendra Sinha when he defeated a Hindu Brahman in a religious debate at the king's court. It would appear, therefore, that Narendra Sinha opened himself to a variety of religious ideas and practices at many levels—an approach to religion that may have alienated him from the legitimation discourses on kingship that appealed exclusively to Sinhala Buddhists. Nonetheless, in the *Cūlavaṃsa* (2:241–245), Narendra Sinha receives healthy praise (though in a very brief account) for his religious actions in support of Buddhism during his reign, actions which included making pilgrimages to the sacred places of the island and having the painting of thirty-two *jātaka*s completed within the confines of a newly rebuilt Daḷadā Māligāva. The rise of Saranaṃkara as an erudite *sāmaṇera* of great influence in the court is also noted in the *Cūlavaṃsa*'s account of Narendra Sinha's activities. Narendra Sinha's lack of support of the institutional *sangha* per se may have derived from the fact that in 1715 he endured a plot, hatched in part by monks, to assassinate him. It is very interesting to note that Saranaṃkara's own teacher, Sūriyagoda Rājasundara, was executed for his participation in this

treason. This event might be seen as a harbinger of Saranaṃkara's own later participation in the plot to assassinate Kīrti Śrī. H. L. Seneviratne's statement that the revival of Buddhism was already under way before the Nāyakkars came to power is most likely based on the appearance of Saranaṃkara as an influence in Narendra Sinha's court toward the end of this king's reign, for Saranaṃkara was the key monastic figure involved in the regeneration of Pali studies and the reestablishment of higher ordinations of *bhikkhus* during Kīrti Śrī's reign.

7. The subject of Theravāda Buddhist kingship has been explored very extensively. Among the more accessible general introductions, see Frank Reynolds, "The Two Wheels of Dhamma: a Study of Early Buddhism," in Bardwell L. Smith, ed., *The Two Wheels of Dhamma* (Chambersburg, Pa.: American Academy of Religion, 1972), pp. 6–30; B. G. Gokhale, "Early Buddhist Kingship," *Journal of Asian Studies* 26 (1966): 15–22; Joseph Kitagawa, "Buddhism and Asian Politics," *Asian Survey* 2, no. 5 (July 1962): 1–11; Robert Heine-Geldern, "Conceptions of State and Kingship in Southeast Asia," Southeast Asia Program Data Paper, no. 18 (Ithaca, N.Y.: Cornell University, 1956); A. L. Basham, "Society and State in Theravada Buddhism," in William T. de Bary, ed., *Sources of Indian Tradition* (New York: Columbia University Press, 1958), pp. 127–153; Richard Gard, "Buddhism and Political Power," in Harold Lasswell and Harlan Cleveland, eds., *The Ethics of Power* (New York: Harper and Bros., 1962), pp. 38–70; and U. N. Ghoshal, *A History of Indian Political Ideas* (Bombay: Oxford University Press, 1959), pp. 62–79, 258–309, and 337–349. For excellent studies that focus on the nature of Buddhist kingship in specific cultures influenced by the Theravāda tradition, see Stanley J. Tambiah, *World Conqueror, World Renouncer* (Cambridge, Eng.: Cambridge University Press, 1976), for an analysis of the Thai context; E. Sarkisyanz, *Buddhist Backgrounds of the Burmese Revolution* (The Hague: M. Nijhoff, 1965); and the collection of essays in Bardwell L. Smith, ed., *Religion and the Legitimation of Power in Sri Lanka* (Chambersburg, Pa.: Anima Books, 1978), especially Smith's "The Ideal Social Order as Portrayed in the Chronicles of Ceylon," Pp. 48–72, and his "Kingship, the Sangha, and the Process of Legitimation in Anuradhapura Ceylon: As Interpretive Essay," pp. 73–95.

8. Fivefold morality includes not injuring others, telling the truth, practicing sexual propriety, preaching nonintoxication, and taking only what is given. The canonical portrait of the *cakkavatti* in Pali literature is provided in the *Cakkavatti Sihanāda Sutta* and the *Mahāsudassana* Sutta in the *Dīgha Nikāya*. See T. W. Rhys Davids, trans., *Dialogues of the Buddha*, 3 vols., Sacred Books of the Buddhists, nos. 2–4 (London: Luzac and Co., for Pali Text Society, 1899–1921), 3:58–79, and 2:199–232. The myth of the "wheel-turning" universal monarch is also illustrated in the *Anāgatavaṃsa Deśanā*, where the appearance of such a king heralds the advent of the next Buddha, Metteyya.

See my and Udaya Meddegama's, *The Anāgatavaṃsa Deśanā: the Sermon of the Chronicle-to-be* (Delhi: Motilal Banarsidass, 1993). See also, Tambiah, *World Conqueror*, pp. 42–47, for an analysis that contrasts the Buddhist stress on dharma with the Hindu conception of *daṇḍa* as a means of ensuring social order.

9. For an excellent summary of how Aśoka came to be conflated with various aspects of the mythic *cakkavatti* ideal in early Buddhist literature, see John Strong, *The Legend of King Asoka* (Princeton, N.J.: Princeton University Press, 1983), pp. 38–56.

10. The chief *bhikkhu* (monk) of the third-century B.C.E. *sangha*, Moggalīputta is made to say to Aśoka: "Even in the lifetime of the Blessed One there was no generous giver like unto thee" (*Mahāvaṃsa*: 42). My portrait of Aśoka's fulfilling the cakkavatti ideal could be radically expanded by citing many other sources. However, I have limited my description to what can be gleaned from the *Dīgha Nikāya* and the *Mahāvaṃsa* because these are the two sources that were most likely known to Kīrti Śrī.

11. See Regina Clifford, "The Dhammadīpa Tradition of Sri Lanka: Three Models within the Sinhalese Chronicles," in Smith, *Religion and Legitimation*, pp. 36–47.

12. For a philosophically inclined discussion of the symbolism inherent in this dynamic cosmic tension between the *deva*s (gods) and the *asura*s, see F. B. J. Kuiper, "The Basic Concept of Vedic Religion," *History of Religions* 15 (1975).

13. See C. E. Godakumbura, "Sinhalese Festivals: Their Symbolism, Origins and Proceedings," *Journal of the Royal Asiatic Society (Ceylon Branch)*, n. s. 14 (1970): 91–134.

14. See my *Buddha in the Crown*, pp. 185–201.

15. For a brilliant discussion of the symbolism and significance of *axis mundi* in this religio-political, microcosm-macrocosm relationship, see Clifford Geertz's discussion of the "doctrine of the exemplary center" in his *Negara: The Theater State in Nineteenth Century Bali* (Princeton, N.J.: Princeton University Press, 1981).

16. See Gananath Obeyesekere, *The Cult of the Goddess Pattini* (Chicago: University of Chicago Press, 1984), pp. 50–70.

17. Strong, *Legend of King Asoka*, pp. 44–45, provides a convenient summary of this myth that comprises the *Aggañña Sutta*: "[In that primordial time], ethereal, self-luminescent beings live in bliss and know no discrimination between polar opposites such as male and female, good and evil, rich and poor, ruler and subject. The earth itself is made of a delightful soft edible substance that looks like butter and is as sweet as honey. Gradually, however, because of karma remaining from a previous world cycle, this Golden Age is lost. During a long period of decline that might, perhaps, best be described as a hardening

(in the literal and metaphorical sense) of the world and the beings in it, greed, grasping, sex, theft, violence and murder all come into the world. Finally sheer anarchy prevails, and in order to put an end to it, the beings get together to select from [the best] among their ranks a king to rule over them and maintain order. This is Mahāsammata, the Great-elect, and in return for fulfilling his functions as a monarch, the beings each agree to pay him a portion of their rice." Mahāsammata is again mentioned in the *Mahāvaṃsa* (10–13), where the lineage of the Buddha is traced directly to him—a lineage also meant to link Buddhist kingship to the lineage of kings in Sri Lanka. See R. A. L. H. Gunawardana, "The Kinsmen of the Buddha: Myth as Political Charter in the Ancient and Early Medieval Kingdoms of Sri Lanka," in Smith, *Religion and Legitimation of Power*, pp. 96–106.

18. See my *Buddha in the Crown*, pp. 57–71.

19. Dewaraja, in *Kandyan Kingdom*, p. 108, reports that Kīrti Śrī had been educated by a "*bhikkhu* preceptor" in his youth, a fact that might lend support to the view that he was intimately aware of the refinements of Buddhist religious thought. Though the *Cūlavaṃsa* repeatedly notes that Kīrti Śrī listened to the public chanting and sermonizing of Pali *sutta*s and that he had become familiar with the history of Buddhist kingship, it would seem highly unlikely that a *bhikkhu* was his tutor, if it is true that the last of the ordained monks (*bhikkhu*s) died in 1729 (which Dewaraja notes [ibid., p. 83]), and that the re-establishment of the *upasampadā* (higher ordination), making a *sāmaṇera* a *bhikkhu*, did not recur until 1753. Kīrti Śrī was born in 1731 and was not coronated until 1751. It is possible that the Pali term *bhikkhu* was used more generally at the time to refer to any Buddhist holy man, without a distinction being made between those who had received *upasampadā* and those who had not.

20. A second cause of the unrest in 1749 seems to have been related to Buddhist *sāmaṇera*s, who were upset about the return of Christian (Roman Catholic) missionaries who, four years earlier, had been accused of writing anti-Buddhist literature and were eventually put before a tribunal by Samanakkoḍi, the second *adigar* under the king, and by Saranaṃkara, who, under king Śrī Vijaya Rājasinha, had sustained the position of influence he had first gained under Narendra Sinha. "In this manner the uprising of the aristocracy in 1749 had in addition to the political motivation, racial and religious undertones as well. It is of interest to note that Samanakkoḍi and Saranaṃkara, two of the three Buddhist leaders who comprised the tribunal which tried the Catholic priests in 1745, were to participate later in 1760, in a conspiracy to replace Kīrti Śrī, who was branded a 'heretical Tamil.'" Dharmadasa, "The Sinhala Buddhist Identity," p. 12.

21. The *Cūlavaṃsa*, of course, attributes the rehabilitation of Buddhism almost solely to Kīrti Śrī's motivation, describing it as his attempt to fulfill the

duties of a king, which became apparent to him "when he learned the history of the many rulers of men who had formerly been kings in Lanka." (2:262).

22. The *Cūlavaṃsa* (2:256–257) mentions that Kīrti Śrī had *maṇḍapas* erected for the preaching of *suttas*, especially the *Dhammacakka Suttanta*, the Buddha's first sermon on the "four noble truths," which he preached at Deer Park in Sarnath, near Benares, to his first five converts—a scene frequently depicted in the visual liturgy of Kandyan temple paintings. It also refers to efforts he made to have the *Dīgha* and *Saṃyutta Nikāyas* copied by scribes, hired at considerable expense. Indeed, the list of literary works generated through royal support during Kīrti Śrī's reign is quite impressive. Not only was the *Mahāvaṃsa-Cūlavaṃsa* extended, from its thirteenth-century origin, to cover the reigns of kings through the time of Kīrti Śrī, but several other important works were finished, including *Śrī Saddharmovādasaṃgrahaya*, a work in which several *jātakas* are used to illustrate the duties (*rājadharma*) expected of a Buddhist king. Both of these projects were accomplished by Tibboṭuvāve Buddharakkhita, who, ironically, along with Saranaṃkara, was one of the chief conspirators involved in the attempt on Kīrti Śrī's life. Mirando mentions that during Kīrti Śrī's reign, the *Milindapraśnaya* and the *Vimānavatthu* were translated from Pali into Sinhala, as were several Pali *suttas* from the *Nikāyas*, which introduced a new class of literature, the *sūtra sannes*, a genre that became quite a standard part of the *sangha* thereafter. Other significant pieces of Sinhala literature that appeared during Kīrti Śrī's reign included the *Kāvyadīpani* (a poem based on the *Sutasoma Jātaka*, which was frequently illustrated in Kandyan temple paintings), and Sinhala poems based on the *Jayaddisa*, *Sonaka*, and *Dasaratha Jātakas*. Finally, it is interesting to note that the first anti-Christian Sinhala tract that countered Protestant propaganda, the *Āgamvādaya*, also appeared during this time at Mulgirigala, in the heart of the Dutch-held low country near Matara. Mirando, *Buddhism in Sri Lanka*, pp. 102–109.

23. For a summary of this successful mission, see Malalgoda, *Buddhism and Sinhalese Society*, pp. 61–63. Two other detailed accounts are P. E. Peiris, "Kīrti Śrī's Embassy to Siam," *Journal of the Royal Asiatic Society* (*Ceylon Branch*) 18 (1803): 17–41; and P. E. E. Fernando, "An Account of the Kandyan Mission Sent to Siam in 1750 A.D.," *Ceylon Journal of Historical and Social Sciences* 2 (1959): 37–83.

24. The Dutch seemed particularly concerned about attempts made to bring Kälaniya Rājamahāvihāraya, located just outside Colombo, back into the orbit of royal support. Kälaniya, like Śrī Pāda and Mahīyangana, was one of the sites purportedly visited by the Buddha, according to the *Mahāvaṃsa*. See Jonathan Walters, *History of Kälaniya* (Colombo: Social Science Association of Sri Lanka, 1995).

25. Dewaraja makes the interesting point that though this era was one of prolific literary activity, none of the Sinhala sources that date from that time

mention the assassination plot. She muses: "The reason is not far to see; for most of the literary works were produced by the pupils of Saranaṃkara or by monks of his school. As a result they were averse to recording any fact which would defile the saintly image of their master." She goes on to note, however, that Kīrti Śrī mentioned the assassination attempt in two of his land grants. Dewaraja, *Kandyan Kingdom*, p. 120.

26. This is the view expressed in the nineteenth-century *Śāsanavatīrna*.

27. A further example clearly reflects how appeals to the Śakran discourse served the purpose of making statements regarding Kīrti Śrī's place at the apex of the sociocosmic hierarchy, symbolic statements designed to create awe in the eye of the beholder. The example comes in the form of audiences granted by Kīrti Śrī to ambassadors of colonial powers. Duncan details how various British, Dutch, and French ambassadors were made to wait at least four days after their arrivals in Kandy; how they were made to enter Kandy "in bare feet, often in ankle-deep mud during the monsoon season without palanquin"; how seven boundary markers (emblematic of the seven mountain ranges that surround Mt. Meru in traditional Buddhist cosmography) had to be observed; how seven sets of curtains had to be negotiated within the palace to gain direct access to the king; and how only the king was allowed to ride on an elephant (the royal mount) within the city. Though the symbolic dynamics of these audiences were, no doubt, emphasized to impress foreign visitors, they also sustained a local impression. Duncan asks: "What was the impact of the audience upon those who witnessed it? For the Kandyans, the audience served as the most visible assertion that their king was a god on earth. It was . . . through public rituals that the divinity of South Asian monarchs was realized" (James S. Duncan, *The City as Text: The Politics of Landscape Interpretation in the Kandyan Kingdom* (Cambridge, Eng.: Cambridge University Press, 1990), pp. 144–153.

28. H. C. P. Bell, who collected many *sannasa*s during his tenure as head of the government archaeological survey in the nineteenth century, describes these inscriptions as "royal grants, engraved on copper-plates—occasionally on gold and silver—or written on olas [palm leafs], [that] were issued by Sinhalese kings to religious bodies, individual priests and laymen, usually 'to obtain merit' in accordance with Buddhistic dogma, or in acknowledgement of particular services rendered to the State. These grants frequently bear the royal sign of Sri, as a guarantee of their authority, and not infrequently other emblems significant of perpetuity.

"The issue of these *sannas* [*sic*] dates back certainly to the fourteenth century, and in all probability much earlier. From the seventeenth century onwards they became more numerous; and during the eighteenth century would seem to have been bestowed so freely as in a great degree to discount their special value and importance.

"*Sannas* were engraved at the royal charge by a branch of the *Abharana*

Pattale or 'Smiths Guild.' When ready for delivery, the grantees were usually summoned to court, and the *sannas* handed to them in person; more often they received them indirectly through Adigars [prime ministers].

"It is uncertain whether any register of these grants was kept at court—certainly not as a check on forgery, as no one would dare to approach the king or his ministers with a spurious document, on pain of instant death in the event of discovery. Forgery of *sannas*, like many other enterprises, sprung into existence only after the European occupation of the Island." H. C. P. Bell, *Report on the Kegalla District of the Province of Sabaragamuwa* (Colombo: George J. A. Skeen, Government Printer), p. 91.

Usually the *sannasa*s were granted in public ceremonies at which their contents were read in the presence of villagers. In this way, they were formally made a matter of public record. P. B. Meegaskumbura, personal communication.

29. Indeed, this *sannasa* seems quite formulaic insofar as it is found almost verbatim in the earlier *Ampiṭiye sannasa* and in the Ban̆baragala *sannasa* of 1759. Lawrie, *Gazeteer*, 1:46–47, 91–92.

30. Royal service was prescribed by kings to ensure labor on lands endowed for temples and/or to ensure that services required for the proper observance of ritual would be provided.

Chapter 3. A Visual Liturgy

1. For an elaboration of this point, see my discussion of pilgrimages to Kandy as a ritual statement of civil religion, in "Pilgrimage and the Structure of Sinhalese Buddhism," *Journal of the International Association of Buddhist Studies* 5 (1982): 23–40.

2. The best analysis of contemporary manifestations of this modern transformation is in Richard Gombrich and Gananath Obeyeseke, *Buddhism Transformed: Religious Change in Sri Lanka* (Princeton, N.J.: Princeton University Press, 1988).

3. This is meant in the sense invoked by Mircea Eliade, *Cosmos and History*, trans. Willard Trask (New York: Harper and Row, 1959): what is regarded as eternally true *in illo tempore* can be made present through ritual engagement and expression.

4. See, for example, Gunasinghe, *Album of Buddhist Paintings*, p. 2, and Ananda K. Coomaraswamy, *Mediaeval Sinhalese Art*, 3d ed. (New York: Pantheon Books, 1979), p. 170.

5. Coomaraswamy, in explaining the making and application of these colors, says: "The whole range of colours may seem very limited, but it will be found that a varied use of them can be made, and the very limitation was a safeguard and a stimulus to the inventiveness of the painter. . . . The apprecia-

tion of shades of colour is even in Europe a comparatively modern matter, and has gone to great extremes. The old appreciation of pure bright colour is almost lost, a fact not generally realised by persons who regard *pure* colour as barbaric." Coomaraswamy, *Mediaeval Sinhalese Art*, p. 165.

6. See ibid., pp. 77–79, for the distinction he makes between the two schools, which, he argues, have existed simultaneously throughout South Asian cultural history. Senake Bandaranayake seems to argue that the relationship between the two schools is rather more sequential, that the stylized forms of painting tend to give way to the more realistic, representational, or naturalistic forms. Bandaranayake and Gamini Jayasinghe, *The Rock and Wall Paintings of Sri Lanka* (Colombo: Lake House Bookshop, 1986), pp. 106–109.

7. I am tempted here to make much of the fact that Coomaraswamy was expressing the kinship of his own half-Tamil background (his father's side) with the alleged private Śaivite Hindu proclivities of the Nāyakkars; but I think this is far too presumptuous.

8. See, especially, the superb treatments in Marie Gatellier, *Peintures Murales du Sri Lanka: Ecole Kandyan XVIII–XIX siecles*. 2 vols. (Paris: Ecole Francaise d'Extreme Orient, 1991), vol. 1, chap. 2; and in Bandaranayake and Jayasinghe, *Rock and Wall Paintings*, pp. 25–216.

9. See Bandaranayake and Jayasinghe, *Rock and Wall Paintings*, pp. 79–103.

10. Von Schroeder describes how a number of Sri Lankan scholars have relied a great deal on this particular *Mahāvaṃsa* passage in order to stake the claim that the Buddha image has a veritable Sri Lankan origin. He also rightly points out that the *Mahāvaṃsa* is a fifth-century C.E. chronicle that, in this instance, describes events that it imagines took place some six centuries earlier. The conventional understanding of most historians of South Asian and Buddhist art is that Buddha images first began to appear in Gandhara (now northern Pakistan) or in Mathura (northern India). Ulrich von Schroeder, *The Golden Age of Sculpture in Sri Lanka: Masterpieces of Buddhist and Hindu Bronzes from Museums in Sri Lanka* (Hong Kong: Visual Dharma Publications, 1992), pp. 22–25.

11. Bandaranayake and Jayasinghe (*Rock and Wall Paintings*, pp. 109–112), cite *petikaḍa* cloth paintings from the seventeenth century; sixteenth-century carved, ivory-jeweled caskets; thirteenth- and fourteenth-century painted wooden boards used as covers for manuscripts; and stone carvings that date from the fourteenth century—these are the only surviving pieces of evidence that might yield some speculation as to the subject matter and style of paintings that might have been completed during this long period.

12. They were probably destroyed by the Dutch in their 1765 invasion.

13. Gatellier's exhaustive and wonderfully illustrated two-volume study (*Peintures Murales*) is the best source for determining how, and to what ex-

tent, the paintings done during the reign of Kīrti Śrī in up-country Kandy dominated the style and substance of all Buddhist temple wall paintings in Sri Lanka throughout the rest of the eighteenth century and most of the nineteenth century, with particular emphasis on its proliferation in the Southern and Western provinces in the nineteenth. On this point, N. B. M. Seneviratne has gone so far as to say: "In the temples earlier than the modern period, by far the preponderant style will be late 18th–early 19th century, the last of the important periods of temple art. But most of these are no more than competent imitations of the Medawela technique, sometimes in cliche." Seneviratne, "Medieval Sinhala Painting, 1150–1840," *Journal of the National Museums of Ceylon* 1: 5. Bandaranayake and Jayasinghe, however, are not quite as sure on this particular point: "What is not so certain, due to the lack of sufficient evidence, is the nature of the relationships between the two schools [Kandyan and Southern], in the period of about 1750–1830 and before, and the forms of art that were extant in the southern and western regions in the preceding phase of the 17th and 18th centuries." (*Rock and Wall Paintings*, p. 201).

14. See ibid., pp. 268–280, for superb photographs; see also, Marie Gatellier, "Les peintures due temple de Kälaniya a Sri Lanka," *Artibus Asia* 38 (1983): 49–70, and Stella Kramrisch, "Some Wall-Paintings from Kälaniya," *India Historical Quarterly* 1 (1925): 111–116, for discussions on how Western influences can be seen in the remarkable late-nineteenth- to early twentieth-century paintings of the (historically) very important temple at Kälaniya.

15. See Coomaraswamy, *Mediaeval Sinhalese Art*, p. 168; he adds this to what we know about the Degaldoruva painters: "Four painters worked at Degaldoruva, the work being completed in 1771, or at any rate before 1786, when the *sannasa* was granted. Their names were Nilagama Patabenda, who was the chief *gihiya* or foreman; Devaragampola Silvatenna Unnanse, who was an unordained priest of the acari [blacksmith] caste, and worked also at Ridī Vihāra, being still remembered as the best painter of his day; Kosvatte Hitaranayide, by whom the Sutasoma Jātaka is said to have been done. . . . [And] the work was overseen by Moratota Mahā Nāyaka of Malvatte. . . ."

16. For a bibliographic beginning, see Frank Reynolds et al., *Guide to the Buddhist Religion* (Boston: G. K. Hall, 1981), pp. 152–208, which contains a fairly comprehensive, categorized, annotated bibliography of iconographic studies pertaining to the cultural history of Buddhism throughout South, Southeast and East Asian cultures.

17. By far, the most valuable source for understanding the stylistic evolution of Buddha images throughout the history of Sinhala Buddhist traditions is the outstandingly comprehensive and lavishly illustrated massive tome published by Ulrich von Schroeder, *Buddhist Sculptures of Sri Lanka* (Hong Kong: Visual Dharma Publications, 1990). Von Schroeder's book also includes the most extensive bibliography on Buddhist sculpture in Sri Lanka that has been

compiled to date. He has also published a more condensed, focused, and accessible version of his extensive research in a beautifully illustrated book, *The Golden Age of Sculpture in Sri Lanka*.

18. Gatellier, *Peintures murales du Sri Lanka*.

19. A *makara torana* is an arch stylized as a "mythic and aquatic composite monster" (Bandaranayake and Jayasinghe, *Rock and Wall Paintings*, p. 298). The current Buddha image that occupies this seat is a late-nineteenth-century gift from Burma.

20. Alternatively, some image houses, especially in caves of temples, will have a reclining Buddha as the chief icon, or, in a few other instances, a standing Buddha in the *abhaya* (fear-not) *mudrā* (hand gesture).

21. Furthermore, two of the four gods mentioned by Bandaranayake and Jayasinghe are rarely, if ever, cited as national guardian deities of Lanka in this late medieval phase of Kandyan cosmology: the goddess Pattini and Nātha have replaced them by this time, as is evident from the manner in which Kīrti Śrī reorganized the *äsaḷa perahära* processions. The four cited by Bandaranayake and Jayasinghe comprised the national divine quartet during the Gampola (fourteenth-century) period.

22. In each of the *vihārayas* I visited during fieldwork, monks or laymen were found who were able to chant a popular *gātha*, in which the names of these sixteen sacred places were chanted in precisely the sequence in which they appear in these paintings. The *soḷosmasthāna* are frequently recited in various verses of *vandanagāthas* (pilgrimage songs).

23. There is, in fact, a text known as the *Sūvisi Vivaraṇa*—closely related to the *Buddhavaṃsa*—that contains the stories of the twenty-four occasions (during previous rebirths) when the Buddha as a *bodhisatta* vowed to become a Buddha, and when the Buddha on those occasions, to whom he proclaimed that vow, prophesied his future success. The text is the prologue to the *Saddharmaratnavaliya*, which Ranjini Obeyesekere chose to omit in her partial translation of that text. See her *Jewels of the Doctrine: Stories of the Saddharma Ratnavaliya* (Albany: State University of New York Press, 1991), pp. 3–4.

24. For an exhaustive account of the mythic "history" of Kälaniya, see Jonathan S. Walters, *A History of Kälaniya* (Kälaniya: Social Science Association of Sri Lanka, 1995).

25. In this painting, there is an anomaly regarding the begging bowl, because it is not until the seventh week that the Buddha receives his begging bowls from the four *lōkapala* guardian deities.

26. In fact, I have been able to identify only seventeen figures, rather than eighteen.

27. They could not take refuge in the *sangha* as it was not yet formed.

28. There are a number of legends connected to building various *stūpas*—

in Afghanistan, Burma (the Schwedagon in Rangoon), and Sri Lanka (in Tiriyaya) which claim to encase these relics.

29. The ceiling painting of Metteyya at Mädavela proved impossible to photograph.

30. The *Buddhavaṃsa* contains the stereotyped biographies of each of these Buddhas. They are all born into princely splendor, experience disillusionment through encountering the four signs (old man, sick man, dead man, and ascetic), renounce all, attain enlightenment under trees (which are also depicted in stereotypical style), and so on.

31. The notion of twenty-four Buddhas was probably originally taken from the Jain tradition of twenty-four *tirthāṅkaras*.

32. P. B. Meegaskumbura, personal communication.

33. Alex Wayman puts the matter this way: "The non-realistic [stylized] representations of the Buddha in time were combined with meditation exercises. Numerous benefits were set forth to be derived from contemplating the body of the Buddha which brought calming of the mind (*samatha*), and then from making offerings thereto, confession of sins, etc., before the so-contemplated Buddha. In this case the icon serves as a sort of prop to *assist in transferring the likeness to the mind*, since *samādhi* is not accomplished by what the outer senses are aware of but what the mind is aware of" (italics mine). See Alex Wayman, "The Role of Art among the Buddhist Religieux," in George Elder, ed., *Buddhist Insight: Essays by Alex Wayman* (Delhi: Motilal Banarsidass, 1984), pp. 296–297.

34. See Bandaranayake and Jayasinghe, *Rock and Wall Paintings*, pp. 144–145 (plate 70) and pp. 170–171 (plate 85), for unsurpassed photographs of the *Māra yuddha* scenes at Degaldoruva and Daṁbulla, respectively.

35. Again, see ibid., pp. 89–90 (plate 81), for a spectacular photograph of the entire setting rendered at Daṁbulla.

36. This refers to the three-month monsoon period of the year, when wandering ceased and mendicants took shelter. Many scholars believe that the transformation from the eremitic to the cenobitic monastic lifestyle evolved as the result of this observance. Simply put, monks ceased their itinerant wanderings in favor of dwelling in *ārāmas* (parks) provided through the support of the generous laity.

37. See ibid., p. 169 (plate 84), for a panoramic photo.

Chapter 4. Royalty Reborn

1. The following well-known Sinhala poetic works are inspired by various *jātakas*: *Kusada Kāva*, by Alagiyavanna, written in 1610 and based on the *Kusa Jātaka*; *Sandakinduruda Kāva*, by Vilgammula Thera, written in

1500–1520 and based on the *Candakinnara Jātaka*; *Vidhura Jātaka Kāvyaya, Mahājanaka Jātaka Kāvyaya, Sambulada Kāva, Padamanavaka Jātaka Kāvyaya, Muva Jātakaya, Vessantara Jātaka Kāvyaya*, and *Atpalda* (based on the *Hatthipala Jātaka*), all seventeenth-century works that bear titles very similar to the *jātaka* originals.

2. See Gatellier, *Peintures murales*, 1:110–111, where she lists each *jātaka*. Throughout her study she also indicates the temples in which each *jātaka* painted can still be found.

3. For the full version of the story, see E. B. Cowell, *The Jātaka; or, Stories of the Buddha's Former Births*, 6 vols. (London: Luzac and Co., for Pali Text Society, 1895–1913), 3:107–111.

4. For the full account, see *ibid*., 5:246–279.

5. See I. B. Horner, ed. and trans., *The Middle Length Sayings* (*Majjhima Nikāya*), 3 vols., Sacred Books of the Buddhists, vols. 29–31 (London: Luzac and Co., for Pali Text Society, 1954–1959), 2:97ff.

6. Just as the later central figure is plagued by the proclivities of his former rebirths, the reference here to the *bodhisatta*'s desire for *soma* is probably meant to signal his high-caste Brahmanical past as a *muni* (or seer) during the ancient Vedic period, when the drinking of *soma* juice was the means of producing great religious visions.

7. These verses are not exactly profound in their meaning, indicating that their function in the story is probably more symbolic than substantive; that is, they symbolize, more than constitute, the truth of Buddhist teachings.

8. For the full account, see Cowell, *Jātaka*, 3:26–29.

9. Indeed, an excellent translation and introduction that provide an analysis of the doctrinal significance, textual diffusion, and artistically rendered versions of the *Vessantara Jātaka* can be found in Richard Gombrich and Margaret Cone, *The Perfect Generosity of Prince Vessantara* (Oxford, Eng.: Clarendon Press, 1977).

10. For instance, if someone is asking for more than can reasonably be expected, he or she may meet with the rebuff, "What do you think this is, Vessantara's time?"

11. See my *Buddha in the Crown*, pp. 53–62.

12. I am using the Sanskrit term *bodhisattva* rather than the Pali *bodhisatta* when the context of usage refers to Mahāyāna rather than Theravāda.

Chapter 5. Implications for Theory and Method

1. Richard Gombrich, *Precepts and Practice: Traditional Buddhism in the Rural Highlands of Ceylon* (Oxford, Eng.: Clarendon Press, 1971).

2. The best example of this second type of anthropological study, which argues that what Buddhist do is much more important than what they believe,

is in Martin Southwold, Buddhism in Life: *The Anthropological Study of Religion and the Practice of Sinhalese Buddhism* (Manchester, Eng.: Manchester University Press, 1983).

3. What I am referring to specifically is the penchant of past Western scholars for assuming the primacy of the written word when studying religions other than Judaism, Christianity, and Islam—religions that have not attributed to their texts the same type or degree of sacred ontology. In Buddhism, there is no theology of the sort that bequeaths a sanctity to scriptures in the same way that Allah's revelation to Muhammad does for Muslims, or as Yahweh's commanded covenant does for Israel, or as the Logos becoming incarnate does for Christians. Further, while ritual is certainly important for expressing what it means to be a Buddhist, unless we take meditation and moral behavior to be primarily or essentially ritualized forms of behavior, ritual performance in the Theravāda Buddhist tradition does not assume the same degree of sacred gravity as prayer toward, or pilgrimage to, Mecca does for Muslims, or celebrating the Torah or the Eucharist does for Jews or Christians. Indeed, it has often been argued, even by the Buddha himself, that ritual behavior is not soteriological in its significance.

4. See John Garrett Jones, *Tales and Teachings of the Bhudda: The Jataka Stories in Relation to the Pali Canon* (London: George Allen and Unwin, 1979), pp. xi–xii. He takes my argument a bit further than is necessary regarding the overvalued primacy ascribed to the significance of the Pali canonical texts. But it is worth quoting at length from the opening paragraphs of his study of the *Jātakas*, in which he makes the case for the importance of this genre of popular literature (which serves as the inspiration for many of the paintings I have discussed) vis-à-vis the scriptures of the Pali Canon. He says:

> "Too often it has been assumed that a careful study of the Pali Canon will give an accurate indication of the beliefs, values and aims of the average Southern Buddhist. This overlooks the fact that the average lay Buddhist has only the sketchiest and most fragmentary acquaintance with the scriptures of his faith. He may have received some instruction at home or school during occasional visits to the monastery and this may, in part at least, have been based on passages from scripture. The chances are, however, that he will never, at any time of his life, have held any part of the canonical scriptures in his hand; he will only have encountered them through an intermediary. The reason for this may simply be that he is illiterate. Even if he can read, it is not easy for him to obtain more than brief anthologies of the scriptures since the Canon in its entirety would span upwards of forty volumes, many of them inaccessible. The scriptures, therefore, although they are treated with utmost veneration, encapsulating, according to widespread belief, the very words of the Lord Buddha himself, and therefore constituting the treasury of true Dhamma (teaching), are virtually unknown to the layman at first hand. Though treated with awe, they are regarded as hard to grasp and beyond the reach of the average

> person. Only the monk can normally be expected to have attained the refinement of mind and the long hours of leisure to grapple with them.
>
> For the layman, it is the *Jātaka* stories which provide the main source of Buddhist guidance and instruction. These stories are close enough to the Canon in their historical pedigree to enjoy something of its awe and veneration, but sufficiently different from the Canon in style and content to enjoy enormous popularity. With this kind of material, illiteracy is no bar. It is not necessary to ponder the written texts of the *Jātaka* in order to be able to fathom their meaning or even commit them to memory. These are stories which can live in a people's imagination. They can be told to small children as bed-time stories and provide much-loved texts for early ventures in reading at the village school; they can be enacted by travelling troupes of players, enchanting peasant audiences into the early hours of the morning; incidents from the stories can furnish an ever-fertile source of allusion for secular writers and dramatists, and have, for centuries, been depicted in beautiful paintings and carvings.

Jones's characterization of the "average Southern Buddhist" and literacy does not really ring true for contemporary Sri Lanka, where literacy rates are among the highest in all of Asia. A 1971 census revealed that 86 percent of all males and 71 percent of all females are literate in either Sinhala, Tamil, or English. See B. L. C. Johnson and M. Le. M. Scrivenor, *Sri Lanka: Land, People and Economy* (Exeter, N.H.: Heinemann Educational Books, 1981), p. 25.

5. See Malalgoda, *Buddhism and Sinhalese Society*, pp. 191–255; Gananath Obeyesekere, "Religious Symbolism and Political Change in Ceylon," in Bardwell L. Smith, ed., *The Two Wheels of Dhamma*, AAR Studies in Religion, no. 3 (Chambersburg, Pa.: American Academy of Religion, 1991); and Gombrich and Obeyesekere, *Buddhism Transformed: Religious Change in Sri Lanka* (Princeton, N.J.: Princeton University Press, 1988).

6. George Bond, *The Buddhist Revival in Sri Lanka: Religious Tradition, Reinterpretation and Response* (Columbia: University of South Carolina Press, 1988).

Chapter 6. Postscript: Ethnic Identity and Ethnic Alienation

1. Cogent analyses of Bandaranaike's impact on the Sri Lankan political landscape can be found in Howard Wriggins, *Ceylon: Dilemmas of a New Nation* (Princeton,: Princeton University Press, 1960); R. N. Kearney, *Communalism and Language in the Politics of Ceylon* (Durham, N.C.: Duke University Press, 1967); de Silva, *History of Sri Lanka*, pp. 510–524; and James Manor, *The Expedient Utopian: Bandaranaike and Ceylon* (Cambridge, Eng.: Cambridge University Press, 1989).

2. Among the many, if certainly not the most provocative, analyses of Sri Lanka's ethnic conflict are Jonathan Spencer, ed., *Sri Lanka: History and the*

Roots of Conflict (New York: Routledge, 1990); Spencer, *A Sinhala Village in a Time of Trouble* (Delhi: Oxford University Press, 1990); K. M. de Silva, *Managing Ethnic Tensions* (Lenham, Md.: University Press of America, 1986); the articles contained in *Ethnicity and Social Change in Sri Lanka* (Colombo: Social Sciences Association, 1984); Chelvadurai Manogaran, *Ethnic Conflict and Reconciliation in Sri Lanka* (Honolulu: University of Hawaii Press, 1987); Bruce Kapferer, *Legends of People, Myths of State* (Washington, D.C.: Smithsonian Institution Press, 1988); S. J. Tambiah, *Sri Lanka: Ethnic Fratricide and the Dismantling of Democracy* (Chicago: University of Chicago Press, 1986); and relevant articles in K. M. de Silva, Pensri Duke, Ellen Goldberg, and Nathan Katz, eds., *Ethnic Conflict in Buddhist Societies: Sri Lanka, Thailand and Burma* (Boulder, Co.: Westview Press, 1988).

3. Here, I want to say clearly that I do not mean to imply a criticism of S. J. Tambiah's provocative book *Buddhism Betrayed? Religion, Politics and Violence in Sri Lanka* (Chicago: University of Chicago Press, 1993), which has become the target of irresponsible interpretations in the Sri Lankan press. Nowhere in his analysis does Tambiah blame Buddhism per se for the ethnic crisis in Sri Lanka. Rather, his aim has been to describe and analyze the forces that gave rise to Buddhist militancy in the contemporary era. In fact, I find the book incisive and clarifying, a work that pinpoints the extent to which Buddhism can be distorted by ethnic chauvinists.

4. For an account and analysis of religious acculturation among the Sinhalese, see my *Buddha in the Crown*, especially chap. 1.

5. The best source for exploring the issue of how language has been politicized in late medieval and contemporary Sri Lanka, see K. N. O. Dharmadasa, *Language, Religion, and Ethnic Assertiveness: The Growth of Sinhalese Nationalism in Sri Lanka* (Ann Arbor: University of Michigan Press, 1992). Another excellent discussion—this one focuses on the period from the 1940s to the 1990s—can be found in K. M. de Silva, "Language Problems: The Politics of Language Policy," in K. M. de Silva, ed., *Sri Lanka: Problems of Governance* (Delhi: Konark Publishers, 1993), pp. 275–305.

6. For an excellent study of the manner in which caste and kinship have functioned in modern Sri Lankan politics, see Janice Jiggins, *Caste and Family in the Politics of the Sinhalese, 1947–76* (Cambridge, Eng.: Cambridge University Press, 1979).

7. G. H. Peiris, "Economic Growth, Poverty and Political Unrest," in de Silva, *Sri Lanka*, p. 268.

8. Again, for example, see the powerful analysis presented by S. J. Tambian in *Buddhism Betrayed?*

Bibliography

Abeyasinghe, T. B. H. (1966). *Portuguese Rule in Ceylon.* Colombo: Lake House.

Arasaratnam, Sinnappah (1958). *Dutch Power in Ceylon.* Amsterdam: Djambatan.

Arasaratnam, Sinnappah (1967). "Dutch Commercial Policy in Ceylon and Its Effects on Indo-Ceylon Trade, 1690–1750." *Indian Economic and Social History Review* 4: 109–130.

Arasaratnam, Sinnappah (1973). *Selections from the Dutch Records of the Government of Sri Lanka: Memoir of Julious Stein Van Gollenesse 1743–1751.* Colombo: National Archives of Sri Lanka.

Bandaranayake, Senake, and Jayasinghe, Gamini (1986). *The Rock and Wall Paintings of Sri Lanka.* Colombo: Lake House Bookshop.

Basham, A. L. (1958). "Society and State in Theravada Buddhism." In William T. de Bary, ed., *Sources of Indian Tradition*, pp. 127–153. New York: Columbia University Press.

Bell, H. C. P. (1904). *Report on the Kegalla District of the Province of Sabaragamuwa.* Colombo: George J. A. Skeen, Government Printer.

Bond, George (1988). *The Buddhist Revival in Sri Lanka: Religious Tradition, Reinterpretation and Response.* Columbia: University of South Carolina Press.

Buultjens, A. E., trans. (1899). "Governor Eck's Expedition against the King of Kandy, 1765." *Journal of the Ceylon Brarnch of the Royal Asiatic Society* 16: 36–78.

Campbell, L. D., ed. (1800). *The Miscellaneous Works of Hugh Boyd.* 2 vols. London: T. Cadell and W. Davies.

Chutiwongs, Nandana; Prematilleke, Leelanda; and Silva, Roland (1990a). *The Paintings of Sri Lanka*: Dambulla. Colombo: Archaeological Survey of Sri Lanka.

Chutiwongs, Nandana; Prematilleke, Leelanda; and Silva, Roland (1990b). *The Paintings of Sri Lanka*: *Gangarama.* Colombo: Archaeological Survey of Sri Lanka.

Chutiwongs, Nandana; Prematilleke, Leelanda; and Silva, Roland (1990c). *The Paintings of Sri Lanka*: *Medavela.* Colombo: Archaeological Survey of Sri Lanka.

Clifford, Regina (1978). "The Dhammadipa Tradition of Sri Lanka: Three Models within the Sinhalese Chronicles." In Bardwell L. Smith, ed., *Religion and the Legitimation of Power in Sri Lanka.* Chambersburg, Pa.: Anima Books.

Coomaraswamy, Ananda K. (1979). *Mediaeval Sinhalese Art.* 3d ed. New York: Pantheon Books.

Cowell, E. B. (1895–1913). *The Jātaka; or, Stories of the Buddha's Former Births.* 6 vols. London: Luzac and Co., for Pali Text Society.

De Lanerolle, Julius (1953). "The *Mandarampura Puvata.*" *Journal of the Royal Asiatic Society (Ceylon Branch)*, n. s. 3: 153–160.

de Silva, Chandra Richard (1987). *Sri Lanka: A History.* New Delhi: Vikas Publishing.

de Silva, K. M. (1981). *A History of Sri Lanka.* Berkeley: University of California Press.

de Silva, K. M. (1986). *Managing Ethnic Tensions.* Lanham, Md.: University Press of America.

de Silva, K. M. ed. (1993). *Sri Lanka: Problems of Governance.* Delhi: Konark Publishers.

Dewaraja, Lorna (1971). *The Kandyan Kingdom 1707–1761.* Colombo: Lake House Publishers.

Dhanapura, D. B. (1961). *The Story of Sinhalese Painting.* Dehiwala, Sri Lanka: Saman Press.

Dhanapura, D. B. (1964). *Buddhist Paintings from Shrines and Temples in Ceylon.* New York: Mentor Books, 1964

Dharmadasa, K. N. O. (1976). "The Sinhala Buddhist Identity and the Nayakkar Dynasty in the Politics of the Kandyan Kingdom, 1739–1815." *Ceylon Journal of Historical and Social Studies*, n. s. 6 (January–June): 1–24.

Dharmadasa, K. N. O. (1992). *Language, Religion and Ethnic Assertiveness: The Growth of Sinhalese Nationalism in Sri Lanka.* Ann Arbor: University of Michigan Press.

Duncan, James S. (1990). *The City as Text: The Politics of Landscape Interpretation in the Kandyan Kingdom.* Cambridge, Eng.: Cambridge University Press.

Eliade, Mircea (1959). *Cosmos and History.* Trans. Willard Trask. New York: Harper and Row.

Evers, Hans-Dieter (1969). "Monastic Landlordism in Ceylon." *Journal of Asian Studies* 23: 685–692.

Fernando, P. E. E. (1959). "An Account of the Kanyan Mission Sent to Siam in 1750 A.D." *Ceylon Journal of Historical and Social Studies*, 2: 37–83.

Gard, Richard (1962). "Buddhism and Political Power." In Harold Lasswell and Harlan Cleveland, eds., *The Ethics of Power.* New York: Harper and Bros.

Gatellier, Marie (1983). "Les peintures du temple de Kelaniya a Sri Lanka." *Artibus Asia* 38: 49–70.

Gatellier, Marie (1991). *Peintures murales du Sri Lanka: Ecole Kandyan XVIII–XIX siecles.* 2 vols. Paris: Ecole Française d'Extreme Orient.

Geertz, Clifford (1981). *Negara: The Theater State in Nineteenth Century Bali.* Princeton, N.J.: Princeton University Press.

Geiger, Wilhelm, trans. and ed. (1964). *The Mahāvaṃsa or The Great Chronicle of Ceylon.* London: Luzac and Co., for Pali Text Society.

Geiger, Wilhelm, trans. and ed. (1953). *Cūlavaṃsa: Being the More Recent Part of the Mahāvaṃsa.* 2 vols. Colombo: Ceylon Government Information Department.

Ghoshal, U. N. (1959). *A History of Indian Political Ideas.* Bombay: Oxford University Press.

Godakumbura, C. E. (1955). *Sinhalese Literature.* Colombo: Colombo Apothecaries.

Godakumbura, C. E. (1970). "Sinhalese Festivals: Their Symbolism, Origins and Proceedings." *Journal of the Royal Asiatic Society (Ceylon Branch)*, n. s. 14: 91–134.

Gokhale, B. G. (1966). "Early Buddhist Kingship." *Journal of Asian Studies* 26: 15–22.

Gombrich, Richard (1971). *Precepts and Practice: Traditional Buddhism in the Rural Highlands of Ceylon.* Oxford, Eng.: Clarendon Press.

Gombrich, Richard, and Cone, Margaret (1977). *The Perfect Generosity of Prince Vessantara*. Oxford, Eng.: Clarendon Press.

Gombrich, Richard, and Obeyesekere, Gananath (1988). *Buddhism Transformed: Religious Change in Sri Lanka*. Princeton, N.J.: Princeton University Press.

Goonewardene, K. W. (1958). *The Foundation of Dutch Power in Ceylon*. Amsterdam: Djambatan.

Goonewardene, K. W. (1990). "Buddhism under the Dutch." Ceylon Studies Seminar paper, University of Peradeniya.

Gunasinghe, Siri (1978). *An Album of Buddhist Paintings from Sri Lanka (Ceylon) (Kandy Period)*. Colombo: National Museum of Sri Lanka.

Gunawardana, R. A. L. H. (1978). "The Kinsmen of the Buddha: Myth as Political Charter in the Ancient and Early Medieval Kingdoms of Sri Lanka." In Bardwell L. Smith, ed., *Religion and the Legitimation of Power in Sri Lanka*, pp. 96–106. Chambersburg, Pa.: Anima Books.

Heine-Geldern, Robert (1956). "Conceptions of Kingship in Southeast Asia." Data Paper, no. 18. Ithaca, N.Y.: Cornell University.

Holt, John Clifford (1982). "Pilgrimage and the Structure of Sinhalese Buddhism." *Journal of the International Association of Buddhist Studies* 5: 23–40.

Holt, John Clifford (1991). *Buddha in the Crown: Avalokitesvara in the Buddhist Traditions of Sri Lanka*. New York: Oxford University Press.

Holt, John Clifford, and Meddegama, Udaya, trans. and eds. (1993). *The Anagatavamsa Desana: The Sermon of the Chronicle-to-be*. Delhi: Motilal Banarsidass.

Horner, I. B., trans. and ed. (1954–1959). *The Middle Length Sayings (Majjhima Nikāya)*. 3 vols. *Sacred Books of the Buddhists*, vols. 29–31. London: Luzac and Co., for Pali Text Society.

Johnson, B. L. C., and Scrivenor, M. Le. M. (1981). *Sri Lanka: Land, People and Economy*. Exeter, N.H.: Heinemann Educational Books.

Jones, John Garrett (1979). *Tales and Teachings of the Buddha: The Jātaka Stories in Relation to the Pali Canon*. London: George Allen and Unwin.

Kapferer, Bruce (1988). *Legends of People, Myths of State*. Washington, D.C.: Smithsonian Institution Press.

Kearney, Robert (1967). *Communalism and Language in the Politics of Ceylon*. Durham, N.C.: Duke University Press.

Kemper, Steven (1990). "Wealth and Reformation in Sinhalese Monastic Buddhism." In Donald Swearer and Russell Sizemore, eds., *Ethics, Wealth and Salvation*, pp. 152–169. Columbia: University of South Carolina Press.

Kemper, Steven (1991). *The Presence of the Past: Chronicles, Politics and Culture in Sinhala Life*. Ithaca, N.Y.: Cornell University Press.

Kitagawa, Joseph (1962). "Buddhism and Asian Politics." *Asian Survey* 2, no. 5 (July): 1–11.

Kramrisch, Stella (1925). "Some Wall-Paintings from Kelaniya." *Indian Historical Quarterly* 1: 111–116.

Kuiper, F. B. J. (1975). "The Basic Concept of Vedic Religion." *History of Religions* 15: 107–120.

Lawrie, Archibald C. (1898). *A Gazeteer of the Central Province*. 2 vols. Colombo: George J. A. Skeen, Government Printer.

Malalgoda, Kitsiri (1976). *Buddhism and Sinhalese Society 1750–1900*. Berkeley: University of California Press.

Manjusri, L. T. P. (1977). *Design Elements from Sri Lankan Temple Paintings*. Colombo: Sri Lanka Puravidya Sangamaya.

Manogaran, Chelvadurai (1987). *Ethnic Conflict and Reconciliation in Sri Lanka*. Honolulu: University of Hawaii Press.

Manor, James (1989). *The Expedient Utopian: Bandaranaike and Ceylon*. Cambridge, Eng.: Cambridge University Press.

Mirando, A. H. (1985). *Buddhism in Sri Lanka in the 17th and 18th Centuries*. Dehiwala, Sri Lanka: Tisara Prakasakayo.

Neusner, Jacob (1975). "The Study of Religion as the Study of Tradition." *History of Religions* 14: 191–206.

Obeyesekere, Gananath (1972). "Religious Symbolism and Political Change in Ceylon." In Bardwell L. Smith, ed., *The Two Wheels of Dhamma*. AAR Studies in Religion, no. 3. Chambersburg, Pa.: American Academy of Religion.

Obeyesekere, Gananath (1984). *The Cult of the Goddess Pattini*. Chicago: University of Chicago Press.

Obeyesekere, Ranjini (1991). *Jewels of the Doctrine: Stories of the Saddharma Ratnavaliya*. Albany: State University of New York Press.

Oldenberg, Hermann, trans. and ed. (1982). *The Dīpavaṃsa: An Ancient Buddhist Historical Record*. Reprint. New Delhi: Asian Educational Services.

Ono, T. (1978). *Mural Paintings of Buddhist Temples, Burma*. Tokyo: Kodansha International.

Paulusz, J. H. O., trans. and ed. (1954). *Secret Minutes of the Dutch Political Council 1762*. Colombo: Government Press.

Peiris, p. E. (1903). "Kirti Sri's Embassy to Siam." *Journal of the Royal Asiatic Society (Ceylon Branch)*, 18: 17–41.

Reimers, E., trans. and ed. (1947). *Memoir of Joan Gideon Loten for His Successor, 1757*. Colombo: Government Printer.

Reimers, E., trans. and ed. (1946). *Memoir of Joan Schreuder for His Successor, 1762*. Colombo: Government Printer.

Reimers, E., trans. and ed. (1935). *Memoir of Steivan Gollennesse for His Successor, 1751*. Colombo: Government Printer.

Reynolds, Frank E. (1972). "The Two Wheels of Dhamma: A Study of Early Buddhism." In Bardwell L. Smith, ed., *The Two Wheels of Dhamma*, pp. 6–30. Chambersburg, Pa.: American Academy of Religion.

Reynolds, Frank E. et al. (1981). *Guide to the Buddhist Religion*. Boston: G. K. Hall.

Roberts, Michael (1994). *Exploring Confrontations: The Political Culture of Sri Lanka*. New York: Harwood Academic Publishers.

Rhys Davids, T. W., and Folsy, C. A., trans. and eds. (1899–1921). *Dialogues of the Buddha (Dīgha Nikāya)*. 3 vols. *Sacred Books of the Buddhists*, vols. 2–4. London: Luzac and Co., for Pali Text Society.

Sarkisyanz, E. (1965). *Buddhist Backgrounds of the Burmese Revolution*. The Hague: Martinus Nijhoff.

Seneviratna, Anuradha (1983). *Golden Rock Temple of Dambulla*. Central Cultural Fund Publication, no. 14. Colombo: Ministry of Cultural Affairs.

Seneviratne, H. L. (1976). "The Alien King: Nayakkars on the Throne of Kandy." *Ceylon Journal of Historical and Social Studies*, n. s. 6 (January–June, 1976): 55–61.

Seneviratne, H. L. (1978a). "Religion and Legitimacy of Power in the Kandyan Kingdom." In Bardwell L. Smith, ed., *Religion and Legitimation of Power in Sri Lanka*. Chambersburg, Pa.: Anima Books.

Seneviratne, H. L. (1978b). *Rituals of the Kandyan State*. Cambridge, Eng.: Cambridge University Press.

Seneviratne, N. B. M. (1965). "Medieval Sinhala Painting, 1150–1840." *Journal of the National Museums of Ceylon* 1: 1–6.

Smith, Bardwell L. (1978). "The Ideal Social Order as Portrayed in the Chronicles of Ceylon"; and "Kingship, the Sangha, and the Process of Legitimation in Aunuradhapura Ceylon: an Interpretive Essay." In Smith, ed., *Religion and the Legitimation of Power in Sri Lanka*, pp. 48–72. Chambersburg, Pa.: Anima Books.

Southwold, Martin (1983). *Buddhism in Life: The Anthropological Study of Religion and the Practice of Sinhalese Buddhism*. Manchester, Eng.: Manchester University Press.

Spencer, Jonathan (1990a). *A Sinhala Village in a Time of Trouble*. Delhi: Oxford University Press.

Spencer, Jonathan, ed. (1990b). *Sri Lanka: History and the Roots of Conflict*. New York: Routledge.

Strong, John S. (1983). *The Legend of King Asoka*. Princeton, N.J.: Princeton University Press.

Tambiah, Stanley J. (1992). *Buddhism Betrayed? Religion, Politics and Violence in Sri Lanka*. Chicago: University of Chicago Press.

Tambiah, Stanley J. (1986). "The Institutional Achievements of Early Buddhism." In S. N. Eisenstadt, ed., *The Origins and Diversity of Axial Age Civilizations*, pp. 353–374. Albany: State University of New York Press.

Tambiah, Stanley J. (1985). *Sri Lanka: Ethnic Fratricide and the Dismantling of Democracy*. Chicago: University of Chicago Press.

Tambiah, Stanley J. (1976). *World Conqueror, World Renouncer*. Cambridge, Eng.: Cambridge University Press.

von Schroeder, Ulrich (1990). *Buddhist Sculptures of Sri Lanka*. Hong Kong: Visual Dharma Publications.

von Schroeder, Ulrich (1992). *The Golden Age of Sculpture in Sri Lanka: Masterpieces of Buddhist and Hindu Bronzes from Museums in Sri Lanka*. Hong Kong: Visual Dharma Publications.

Walters, Jonathan S. (1995). *A History of Kälaniya*. Kälaniya: Social Science Association of Sri Lanka.

Wayman, Alex (1984). "The Role of Art among the Buddhist Religieux." In George R. Elder, ed., *Buddhist Insight: Essays by Alex Wayman*. Delhi: Motilal Banarsidass.

Winius, G. D. (1971). *The Fatal History of the Portuguese in Ceylon*. Cambridge: Harvard University Press.

Winslow, Deborah (1984). "A Political Geography of Deities: Space and Pantheon in Sinhalese Buddhism." *Journal of Asian Studies* 43: 273–292.

Wray, E.; Rosenfeld, C.; and Bailey, D. (1972). *Ten Lives of the Buddha: Siamese Temple Paintings of Jataka Tales*. New York: Weatherhill.

Wriggins, Howard (1960). *Ceylon: Dilemmas of a New Nation*. Princeton, N.J.: Princeton University Press.

Index

Abhaya mudrā (hand gesture indicating "fearlessness"), 128 n. 1
Abhayagiriya (*see* map; one of the 16 sacred places), 61–62
Adigar (prime minister of the Kandyan kingdom), 27
Āgamvādya (Sinhala text of the 18th century), 123 n. 22
Aggabodhi (a prince of Rohana in the 7th c. C.E.), 62
Aggañña Sutta (text of the *Dīgha Nikāya*), 121–22 n. 17
Ahiṃsā ("noninjury"), 76, 78
Ajānta (cave temple complex in Maharastra, India), 74
Amarāvati (archaeological site in Andhra, India), 74
Anāgatavaṃsa Deśanā (textual prophecy of Metteyya), 120 n. 8
Ānanda (disciple of the Buddha), 112
Añjali mudrā (hand gesture paying homage), 76; plate 26
Anurādhapura (*see* map), 33, 36, 49, 60–62, 70
Ārāma (monastic park), 129 n. 36
Arhat (Buddhist monk who experiences enlightenment), 66
Äsaḷa Perahära, 20–21, 31–32, 128 n. 21
Asgiriya Vihāraya (Kandyan monastery), 30
Aśoka (3rd c. B.C.E. Indian emperor), 25–26, 33, 36, 61, 121 n. 10
  Kirti Sri's appeal to the Aśokan discourse of Buddhist kingship, 18–19, 20–21
Asuras (demi-gods), 20, 36, 121 n. 12
Atpalda (18th-c. Sinhala text), 130 n. 1
Axis mundi (ritual center of the world) 121 n. 15
  Kandy as the capital city functioning as, 20, 32

Bambaragala (temple in Kandyan village), 39
Bandaranaike, S.W.R.D. (prime minister in 1956–59), 98, 99
Bandaranayake, Senake, 47–48, 50–51, 55, 126 nn. 6 and 11
Bell, H. C. P., 124–25 n. 28
Bharhut (archaeological site in Madhya Pradesh, India), 49, 74
Bhikkhu conversions, plates 8–9
Bhu Devi (earth goddess), 68; plate 13
British colonialism, affects, 101–102
Bodhisatta (Sanskrit *bodhisattva*), 69, 71–72; plate 43. *See also Khāntivāda, Sutasoma, Uraga,* and *Vessantara*
  Gotama in *jātakas*, 73–90
  Royal Buddhist identification with, 21, 35, 72, 88–89

Bond, George, 132 n. 6
Borobudur (Buddhist monument in Indonesia), 49
Brahma (creator deity of Hindu pantheon), 64
Buddha. *See also Bodhisatta* and *Buddhacārita*
  as central figure represented in Kandyan art, 53, 70
  mythical visits to Sri Lanka, 56–63
  seven weeks of postenlightenment reflection, 63–66
Buddhacārita (life of the Buddha), 68–69, 71; plates 12–19, 45–47
Buddhagosa (5th-c. C.E. Theravāda Buddhist commentator), 92
Buddhavaṃsa (Pali Buddhist chronicle of the previous Buddhas), 53, 128 n. 23, 129 n. 30
Buddhism
  as a civil religion, 4
  "classical," vii–ix
  Kīrti Śrī's reform of, 17–39
Buddhist kingship. *See* Aśoka, *Bodhisatta*, Mahāsammata, Manu, and Śakra
Burma
  monastic lineage in and from, 26
  Mädavela Buddha image from, 128 n. 19, 129 n. 28
Butsāraṇa (13th-c. Sinhala Buddhist text), 56

Clifford, Regina, 121 n. 11
Cone, Margaret, 74, 81
Coomaraswamy, Ananda
  description of Kīrti Śrī, 17
  understanding of Kandyan art, 43–48, 108, 125–126 nn. 6 and 7

Daḷadā Māligāva (*see* map; Temple of the Tooth-Relic), 30, 36, 49
  destruction by Dutch, 13, 117 n. 10, 119 n. 6
Dam̆bulla (*see* map), 50, 54, 64–71, 129 n. 34
Danakirigala (*see* map)
Degaldoruva (*see* map), 38–39, 50–52, 66–69, 72, 74, 76–81
  painters at, 127 n. 15, 129 n. 34
de Silva, K. M., 17, 115 n. 1, 132 nn. 2 and 5
Devānampiya Tissa (first Anurādhapura and Buddhist king, 3rd-c. B.C.E.), 58, 61, 70
Devas (gods), 20, 39
  Baṇḍāra class in Kandy, 55, 121 n. 12
Dewaraja, Lorna, 16, 23, 27–28, 30, 124–25 n. 25
Dhamma (Sanskrit *dharma*, "teaching, truth"), 21, 22, 26, 65–67, 76, 77–78
  healing power of, 79
  Lanka as the pure abode of, 56
Dhammacakkappavattana ("Turning of the Wheel of Law," first sermon of the Buddha), 58
Dharmadasa, K. N. O., 16
Dīgha Nikāya (Pali Buddhist canonical text), 53, 75, 123 n. 22
Dīghavāpi (*see* map; one of the 16 sacred places), 60, 61
Disāva (Kandyan regional governor), 55–56
Divyāguhā (*see* map; one of the 16 sacred places), 61
Dodaṇtale (*see* map; Kandyan Buddhist temple), 54
Duncan, James, 18–20
Dutch
  attempts to proselytize Protestantism, 6–8, 116 n.7
  discomfort with Kīrti Śrī's revival of Buddhism, 27, 116 n. 7
  governers
    on the nature of Dutch power in Lanka, 4–5
    Loten's desire to supplant Nāyakkars, 11–12
    Schreuder's disdain for Nāyakkars, 6
    Schreuder's view of church and state, 116 n. 4
    Sinhala perceptions of van Eck, 117 n. 10
    van Eck's sacking of Kandy, 12–13, 117 n. 10
  ousting the Portuguese, 4
  Reformed Church's legacy, 116 n. 5

sacking of Kandy, 9, 109
strategy in relation to Kandyan kingdom, 5
Dutthagāmaṇī (2nd-c. B.C.E. Sinhala king), 49, 58, 61–62, 70, 112

Eḷāra (Tamil king in 2nd-c. B.C.E.), 61, 70
Ethnic identity and alienation, 97–108

Four Noble Truths, 63, 65, 123 n. 22

Gal Vihāra (sculptural venue at Poḷonnaruva), 64
Gangārāma (*see* map), 50–52, 56, 64, 66–69, 109–111
Gaṇinnānses (unordained Buddhist "holy men"), 23–24, 25
Gatellier, Marie, 53, 126, nn. 8 and 13
Gombrich, Richard, 74, 81, 87–88
Gopala Mudali (Muslim loyal to Kīrti Śrī), 29
Gunasinghe, Siri, 43–44

Jaffna (*see* map), 23
Jainism
ascetics, 62
tirthāṅkaras, 129, n. 31
Janata Vimukti Peramuna (JVP), 102–103, 107
Jātakas. *See also Khāntivāda, Sutasoma, Uraga*, and *Vessantara*
as subjects of temple wall paintings, 47–49, 65–66, 71–75
Jayasinghe, Gamini, 47–48, 50–51, 55
Jayewardene, J. R., 106–107
Jetavana (*see* map; one of 16 sacred places), 60–61
Jones, John G., 78–79, 87, 131–132 n. 4

Kākavaṇṇatissa (2nd-c. B.C.E. king who built the Tissamahārāma *stūpa*, which became one of the 16 sacred places), 62
Kälaṇiya (*see* map; one of the 16 sacred places), 27, 60–61, 116 n. 7
Kandy (*see* map), 9, 12–13, 20, 30–32, 109, 117 n. 10
Kandyan school of painting, 43–55
Kapilavatthu (the Buddha's home city in N.E. India), 69
Karmic retribution, 73–75, 78–79
Katikāvata (royally instituted program of monastic reform), 25
Kāvyadīpani (poem based on *Sutasoma Jātaka*), 123 n. 22
Kemper, Steven, 118 n. 4
Khāntivāda Jātaka, 79–81; plate 49
Kiri Vehera (*see* map; the *stūpa* at Kataragama, one of the 16 sacred places), 61–62
Kīrti Śrī Rājasinha
as an "alien king" amidst his Sinhalese subjects, 10
and the Aśokan model of Buddhist kingship, 18–19
attempted assassination of, 12, 27–29
British overtures to by John Pybus and Hugh Boyd, 9
Dutch threats to his reign, 3–13
and the ethic of giving in the *Jātakas*, 89–90
his inclusivity, 29
issuing of *sannasas*, 34–39
and the Kandyan school of art, 43–53
policy toward Roman Catholics fleeing Protestant Dutch oppressions, 7, 117 n. 8
regarded as a "heretic," 29–30
remembered as one of the greatest Buddhist kings, 16–18
reorganization of the *äsaḷa perahära*, 31–32
ritual circumambulation of Kandy, 30–32
sculpted and painted portrayals of, 54; see plates 1–2
treaty with the Dutch, 117 n. 11
Kuddhaka Nikāya (Pali canonical text), 53
Kusada Kāva, (18th-c. Sinhala poem) 129 n. 1

Lankatilaka (*vihāraya* located 8 miles S.W. of Kandy), 69
Liberation Tigers of Tamil Eelam (LTTE), 102–103
Lokapala deities (directional gods), 49, 65

Mädavela, (*see* map; Great Royal Monastery), 34, 37–38, 50–52, 54–57, 61–63, 65–66, 68, 72, 74–76, 86–87, 129 n. 29
Mahābodhivaṃsa, 69
Mahājanaka Jātaka Kāvyaya, 130 n. 1
Mahāsammata (primordial and model human king), 21, 36–39, 121–122 n. 17
Mahāvihāra (orthodox Theravada monastic fraternity in Anurādhapura, 70
Mahāvaṃsa/Cūlavaṃsa, 15–16, 17, 19, 30–34, 49, 53, 58–62, 69–70, 93–94, 109–114, 188 n. 2, 121 n. 10, 122 nn. 17 and 21, 123 n. 22; plates 20–22
Mahāyāna, 67, 79, 88
Mahinda (son of Aśoka who purportedly brings Buddhism to Lanka and converts King Devānaṃpiya Tissa in 3rd-c. B.C.E.), 61, 62, 70
Mahīyangana (*see* map; one of the 16 sacred places), 33, 36, 57–58, 61, 112; plates 3, 36
Majjhima Nikāya (Pali canonical text), 76
Makara toraṇa, 39, 55, 56
  defined, 128 n. 19
Makuṭa (stylized hair in the shape of a crown), 5
Malalgoda, Kitsiri, 15, 24, 28–29, 95
Malvatta Vihāra (*see* map; one of the two major Buddhist monasteries in Kandy and venue of the attempted assassination of Kīrti Śrī), 27–28, 30, 110
Mandaram Puvata, 15, 118 nn. 1 and 2
Manu (Brahmanic royal progenitor and model of kingship, 21, 36–39
Māra ("Lord of Death") and his three daughters, 64, 68, 71, 112; plates 40, 47
Māra yuddhaya ("defeat of Māra" often depicted in Kandyan cave and temple wall paintings), 64, 68, 129 n. 34; plates 40, 47
Meddagama, Udaya, 121 n. 8
Meegaskumbura, P. B., x, 118 n. 1, 125 n. 28
Metteyya (the future Buddha; Sanskrit "Maitreya," Sinhala "Maitri"), 35, 39, 112, 113, 120 n. 8, 129 n. 29
Milindapraśnaya (important Pali Buddhist text) 123 n. 22
Mirisaväti (*see* map; one of the 16 sacred places), 61, 62
Moggallāna (one of the early and most important disciples of the Buddha), 69
Moggalīputta, 121 n. 10
Moladaṇḍe Nilame (aristocratic conspirator against Kīrti Śrī), 29
Mount Meru (mythic mountain at the center of the cosmos), 20, 124 n. 27
Muchalinda (serpent king), 64–65
Mulgirigala, 49, 116 n.7, 123 n. 22
Mutīyangana (*see* map; one of 16 sacred places), 61

*Nāga*s (mythic prehistoric people of Lanka), 60, 68
Nāgadipa (*see* map; one of the 16 sacred places), 60–61
Narenappa Nāyakkar (regent father of Kīrti Śrī), 11, 23
Narendra Sinha (king of Kandy, 1707–1739 C.E.), 10–11, 27, 49, 118 n. 12, 119–120 n. 6, 122 n. 20
Nātha (Avalokiteśvara; one of the four national guardian deities of Lanka in Kandyan Sinhala cosmology), 112, 119 n. 6, 128 n. 21
Nāyakkars
  conversion to Buddhism, 15–18
  entrepreneurs in Kandy, 23
Nibbāṇa (Sanskrit *nirvāṇa*), 42, 65, 67, 73, 89. *See also Parinibbāṇa*
Nidāna Kātha, 63
Noble Eightfold Path, 65

Obeyesekere, Gananath, 55, 95

Padamanavaka Jātaka Kāvyaya (18th-c. Sinhala poem), 130 n. 1
Pagan (Burma), 26, 49
Parinibbāṇa, 49, 69; plate 16

Pattini (goddess, one of the four national guardian deities of Lanka in Kandyan Sinhala cosmology), 21, 119 n. 6, 128 n. 21
Paṭṭiye Baṇḍāra. *See* Thailand
Peiris, Gerald, 101
Pentacostals, 116 n. 5
Petikaḍa (cloth paintings), 126 n. 11
Petavatthu (Pali canonical text, "Stories of the Departed"), 70
Pilgrimage, 32–34, 125 n. 1. *See also Soḷosmasthāna*
Pitiye (Kandyan deity), 118 n. 12, 119 n. 6
Piṭṭināyakkar, 118 n. 12
Poḷonnaruva (*see* map), 22, 49, 64
Portuguese, 116 nn. 6 and 7
  confrontation with and defeat by Dutch, 4
  confrontation with the Sinhalese at Köṭṭe, 12
  establishment of Roman Catholicism, 4
Pradakṣinā (circumambulation rite), 30–32
Premadasa, Ranasinghe, 98
"Protestant" Buddhism, 95–96
Pūjāvaḷiya (13th-c. C.E. Sinhala text), 56, 67, 69

Rājādhi Rājasinha (brother to and successor of Kīrti Śrī), 17, 39, 50
Rājakariya ("service to the king"), 38, 125 n. 30
Rājasinha I (king of Sitāvaka, 1581–1593 C.E.), 33–34
Rājasundara, Suriyagoda (Saranaṃkara's teacher), 119–120 n. 6
Ratanaghara ("jewel throne"), 64
Ridī Vihāra (*see* map), 50–52, 58, 61, 64–66, 109, 112–114
Roman Catholicism, 116 n. 5, 117 n. 8, 122 n. 20
Ṛta ("order"), 20
Ruvanvälisäya (*see* map; one of the 16 sacred places), 49, 61–62

Saddharmaratnāvaḷiya (13th-c. Sinhala text), 128 n. 23
Śakra (Indra)
  model of Buddhist kingship, 20–21, 30–32, 35–36, 38, 124 n. 27
  in *Uraga Jātaka*, 75
  in *Vessantara Jātaka*, 86
Samādhi ("deep meditational consciousness"), 63–64
Saman (one of the four guardian deities of Lankan in Kandyan Sinhala cosmology), 55, 61
Samanakkoḍi (2nd prime minister to Kīrti Śrī), 27, 122 n. 20
Sāmaṇeras (monastic novices), 24, 27, 30, 36, 112 1. 20
Samantapāsādikā (5th-c. C.E. Pali Buddhist text), 61
Sambulada Kāva (18th-c. Sinhala text), 121 n. 1
Samsāra ("conditioned realm of rebirth"), 46, 64, 73, 90
Saṃyutta Nikāya (part of the *Suttapiṭaka*), 123 n. 22, 130 n. 5
Sandakinduruda Kāva (18th-c. Sinhala text), 129 n. 1
Sannasas (official royal land and service grants carved in stone or engraved on copper plates), 34–39
  described in general by H.C.P. Bell, 124–25 n. 28
  from Bambaragala, 39
  from Degaldoruva, 38–39
  from Mädapiṭiye, 35–36
  from Mädavela, 37–38
  from Suriyagoda, 36
  from Urulewatte, 36
  which help date cave and temple wall paintings, 50
Sānchī (important Buddhist archaeological site in Madhya Pradesh, India), 49, 74
Sangha (Buddhist monastic community)
  attempts at reform by Kīrti Śrī, 23–27
  role in attempt to assassinate Kīrti Śrī, 26–30
Sangharāja ("king of the sangha"; ecclesiastical head of Sinhala Buddhist monasticism): Kīrti Śrī's appointment of Saranaṃkara as, 27, 28

Saranaṃkara (important monastic reformer and conspirator against Kīrti Śrī), 16, 23–30, 94, 119–20 n. 6, 122 n. 20, 123 n. 22, 124 n. 25
Sāriputta (one of the early and important disciples of the Buddha), 58, 113
Śasanā Varṇanāva (19th-c. Sinhala Buddhist text), 28
Śasanāvatīrna (19th-c. Sinhala Buddhist text), 124 n. 26
Sat Sati (seven weeks of meditative reflection following the Buddha's enlightenment), 49, 58, 63–66, 68, 71; plates 4–7, 39–42
Seneviratna, Anuradha, 51
Seneviratne, H. L., 17, 23
Seneviratne, N. B. M., 43–46, 54, 127 n. 13
Skanda ("Kataragama Deviyo," one of the four national guardian deities of Kandyan Sinhala cosmology, 21, 61, 62, 119 n. 6
Silācetiya (*see* map; one of the 16 sacred places), 60–61
Silvattänas (orthodox reform-minded, monastic novices), 24–26
Sīmās (sacralized boundaries of monasteries), 25, 27, 70–71
Sinhala
  aristocratic mistrust of Kīrti Śrī, 12–13, 22–24
  attitudes toward the Dutch, 9–10
  fears of Tamil invasions from South India, 12
  and Tamil ethnic relations, 98–109
Sittaras (painters), 51
Soḷosmasthāna (16 sacred places), 34, 56–63, 71, 112–113, 128 n. 22; plates 3, 35–38
Southwold, Martin, 130–131 n. 2
Śrī Mahābodhi (*see* map; one of the 16 sacred places), 33, 49. 60–62, 70–71
Śrī Pāda (*see* map; Sumanakūṭa or Adam's Peak; one of the 16 sacred places), 33–34, 36, 60–62
Śrī Vijaya Rājasinha (first Nāyakkar king of Kandy, 1739–1747), 11, 16, 26, 117 n. 8, 122 n. 26
Śrī Vikrama Rājasinha (last Nāyakkar king of Kandy, 1798–1815), 50
Strong, John S., 121 n. 9, 121–122 n. 17
Stūpa (reliquary symbolizing presence of the Buddha), 31, 62, 65. *See* also *Śoḷosmasthāna*
  eight erected by the republican clans of North India, 70; plate 48
  as symbol of the Buddha, 70–71; plate 3
Suriyagoda (*see* map; monastery 7 miles W. of Kandy)
Sutasoma Jātaka, 52, 76–79, 123 n. 22; plates 28–29
  Sūvisi Vivaraṇa (the Buddha receiving the prophecy of his buddhahood from 24 previous buddhas), 58, 66–69, 71, 113 n. 23; plate 10

Tambiah, S. J., 133 n. 3
Tamils
  defeated by Vaṭṭagāmaṇi, 37
  ethnic conflict with Sinhalese, 97–108
Tapussa and Bhallika (two merchants who become first lay followers of the Buddha during the fifth week of *sat sati*), 65, 71; plates 6, 42
Thailand
  attempts to bring Theravāda Buddhist monks from, in order to reestablish monastic lineage, 26–27, 36
  role of prince (Paṭṭiye Baṇḍāra) in attempt to assassinate Kīrti Śrī, 27–30
Theoretical and methodological implications, 91–96
Thousand Buddhas, 67–68, 71; plates 11, 44
Thūpārāma (*see* map; one of the 16 sacred places), 60–61, 70
Thūpavaṃsa (13th-c. Pali Buddhist text), 69
Tibboṭuväve (chief prelate of the Malvatta Vihāra in Kandy) 27, 109, 123 n. 22

Tissamahārāma (*see* map; one of the 16 sacred places), 61–62

Upasaṃpadā (higher monastic ordination)
  eclipse during the reign of Narendra Sinha, 11, 19
  reintroduction from Thailand under Kīrti Śrī, 25–27, 30
Uraga Jātaka, 66, 75–76; plates 23–26
Urulewatte (village 25 miles north of Kandy), 36

Vaṭṭagāmaṇi (Sinhala Wälagam̃ba; Anurādhapura king 103–102 and 89–77 B.C.E.), 37–38
Vessantara Jātaka, 49, 54, 74, 76, 81–89, 93; plates 30–34, 50
Vessantara Jātaka Kāvyaya, 130 n. 1
Vibhīṣana (often among the four national guardian deities of Kandyan Sinhala cosmology), 55
Vidhura Jānaka Kāvyaya (18th-c. Sinhala poem), 130 n. 1
Vijaya (mythic first king of Sinhalese who migrates from North India to Lanka), 76
Vimaladharmasuriya I (king of Kandy, late 16th c.), 26
Vimaladharmasuriya II (king of Kandy, late 17th c.), 26
Vimānavatthu (Pali Buddhist canonical text, "Stories of the Heavenly Mansions), 123 n. 22
Vinayapiṭaka (Pali canonical text, "Basket of Discipline" containing the rules of monastic law), 25, 26, 53, 63, 65
Vipāssana (meditation), 68
Viṣṇu (Hindu deity who becomes one of the four national guardian deities of Kandyan Sinhala cosmology), 21, 55, 112, 113, 119 n. 6
Visual liturgy, 39, 42, 52–72
Vitarka mudrā (gestures of explanation), 63
von Schroeder, Ulrich, 126 n. 10. 127–128 n. 17

Walters, Jonathan, 123 n. 24
Wayman, Alex, 129 n. 33
Weber, Max, 96

*Yakkha*s (demons)
  in Māra's army, 68
  pacified and expelled from Lanka by the Buddha, 59
  as Sinhala symbols of the Tamils and Dutch, 62, 117 n. 10
  in *Sutasoma Jātaka*, 77

Printed in the United States
54204LVS00002B/313-327

9 780195 10757